ONE HALAL OF A STORY

SAM DASTYARI

ONE HALAL OF A STORY

MELBOURNE UNIVERSITY PRESS
An imprint of Melbourne University Publishing Limited
Level 1, 715 Swanston Street, Carlton, Victoria 3053, Australia
mup-info@unimelb.edu.au
www.mup.com.au

First published 2017
Text © Sam Dastyari, 2017
Design and typography © Melbourne University Publishing Limited, 2017

This book is copyright. Apart from any use permitted under the *Copyright Act 1968* and subsequent amendments, no part may be reproduced, stored in a retrieval system or transmitted by any means or process whatsoever without the prior written permission of the publishers.

Every attempt has been made to locate the copyright holders for material quoted in this book. Any person or organisation that may have been overlooked or misattributed may contact the publisher.

Typeset in 12/15pt Bembo by Cannon Typesetting
Cover design by Philip Campbell Design
Printed in Australia by McPherson's Printing Group

National Library of Australia Cataloguing-in-Publication entry

Dastyari, Sam, author.

One halal of a story/Sam Dastyari.

9780522872088 (paperback)
9780522872095 (ebook)

Includes index.

Dastyari, Sam.
Dastyari, Sam—Family.
Australian Labor Party.
Politicians—Australia—Biography.

To Naser and Ella,
for sacrificing everything to bring us to Australia.

CONTENTS

I THE BOX
The raw ingredients   3

II THE BASE
1 The day my mother lived   9
2 Refugees   19
3 Missing letters   32
4 Growing up Dastyari   42
5 Persians in the burbs   52
6 Layla   65
7 A name for a place   74

III THE CHEESE
8 Middle class on dodgy wheels   85
9 Everyone loves a wedding   94
10 Profile in the US   105
11 Inside the machine   112
12 Connections   120
13 Halal Elvis   126
14 Go ahead and hate me   135
15 How to conduct yourself around children   144

IV THE MEAT

16	Ideas in straitjackets	159
17	One Nation	169
18	The gateway and the victims	176
19	Banking on controversy	184
20	Twenty-six men	196
21	From away	204
22	Of houses and dogs	213
23	Drugs and the law	221
24	My friend Steve	228

V THE SAUCES

25	Bill Crews: the one I admire	241
26	Richo: the one for lunch	249
27	Rudd: the one who was king	257
28	Kaila: the one to watch	266
29	Bill Shorten: the one who will be king	273

Index	281

1
THE BOX

THE RAW INGREDIENTS

I could tell from the expression on her face that this wasn't what she was expecting. When I told the editor of the *Macquarie Dictionary*, Sue Butler, that I would take her out for lunch to sample one of the best halal snack packs (HSPs) in Australia, I think she was imagining a more refined establishment. Not that she said so. She was far too polite—very much part of Australia's literary establishment—to make a ruckus. But I could see from her slightly frozen face that I had caught her off guard.

Metro One Kebabs on Liverpool Road in Ashfield, Sydney, is a traditional kebab shop. We have all been to one—usually in the early hours of the morning; often after a big night out. 'The golden hour,' one owner tells me, is 2 a.m. 'That magic hour is what makes the economics of a kebab store work,' he effuses. Metro is run by Oktay Sahin and his Turkish family. It is one of 900 kebab joints dotted throughout Sydney. And, in the wake of the creation of the halal snack pack, and the attendant media coverage in 2016 and beyond, those joints have experienced a mini-boom.

'So are you ready to make one?' I ask her.

'A kebab?' she quizzes me.

'No. A halal snack pack.'

For someone who had requested that we meet in order to hand me the Macquarie Dictionary People's Choice Award for helping to nudge 'halal snack pack' over the line as the word of the year, Sue knew worryingly little about the product. The name had overwhelmingly won Macquarie's annual people's poll, and the judges had put it forward for inclusion in the next edition of the dictionary.

'Have you ever eaten one before?' I ask.

'Kind of,' she replies. Which, frankly, I take to mean 'no'.

'OK. We start with the container, because there'll be so much going on; things will need to be kept under control. Then there's the base—that is, the chips—the foundation from which we build our delicacy. Next comes the cheese, a layer of salty smoothness. On top of that we pile up the meat.'

Hitting a semi-reverential tone, I conjure the snack pack's summit. 'Lastly, and most importantly, the holy trinity of sauces—garlic, BBQ and chilli.'

My layered monologue was greeted by a long silent look from Sue.

'Is that it?' Sue asks.

On reflection, this was a much more poignant question than she had intended. Sure, on the face of it, a halal snack pack is just a creative and gut-busting marriage of the English chippy and the Middle Eastern kebab. But it is so much more than that.

I could have told Sue that this assemblage of ingredients amounts to a social statement, a uniquely Aussie expression of multiculturalism. For in a multicultural setting, food has always been a critical tool for breaking down barriers between people. The embracing of this 'halal' food, then, is a tongue-in-cheek way of rejecting reactionary politics and divisive ignorance. I say this because while it might specifically refer to food prepared in keeping with Islamic traditions, the word 'halal' has come to mean much more than that. In the language of far-right politicians and social-media trolls, 'halal' is code for 'Muslim'. So just as rejecting halal has become a way for bigots to nudge nudge wink wink their values to each other, tucking into a halal snack pack speaks to the embrace of a more open and pluralistic Australia. That, and a raging hangover.

I could have told Sue about the way my Twitter feed exploded on election night 2016, when I invited Pauline Hanson to share a halal snack pack with me on live television. Nearing midnight, as the counting confirmed that Pauline was soon to join me in the Senate, she responded with a firm 'Not happening; not interested in halal'. With one sentence she set the tone for everything that was to come for One Nation's next moment in the political spotlight: the barely veiled dislike of Muslims, the offhand dismissal of anything that didn't fit within their narrow Anglo worldview.

I could even have told Sue that, after inadvertently sparking a social-media storm with a half-joking speech to the Senate extolling the virtues of the halal snack pack, I thought a bit more about the humble HSP and happened upon some literary inspiration. The snack pack provided the prompt for a very unconventional book on politics: the one you're holding now.

While most political tomes are designed to lionise the subject, mine has all the layers, juiciness and spices of the snack pack. Barely contained, founded on a solid base, smooth in parts, occasionally breaking out—my book will trek some unusual paths. The snack pack provides me with a frame within which I can write about my shortcomings, my failures, my anxiety, my ability to ride a career on an upward trajectory and my misfortune in experiencing the humiliation of having to resign from the Labor front bench. My book is also about learning and pushing on. But I didn't say any of these things to Sue. They would have sounded too far-fetched— pontifications of a foodie overheating himself at the altar of cultural symbolism; more fantastical than reasonable. I didn't want Sue to think that I was reading way too much into the chips, cheese and meat that so splendidly jostled in the HSP.

So I just say, 'Yes. That's it. What do you think?' after she takes her first bite.

'Oh, it's very different.'

'Do you like it?'

'It's kebab and chips. What's not to like?' she smiles.

'You don't know the half of it,' I answer her.

We kept on eating while a queue of people lined up to order their own HSPs.

It's the evening of 3 June 2017 and I am in London for the UK elections, and explaining over dinner to three of my closest friends—Richard Angell, Andy Bagnall and Jo Milligan—about how I have structured this book like a snack pack.

'A snack pack?' Richard asks. 'What on earth is a snack pack?' I am about to explain when the conversation is interrupted by screaming in the street outside our restaurant in Borough Market. As we turn to look, a woman runs past the window clutching her neck, which is covered in blood. There is panic in the room and we all dive to hide under the tables. Some take command, directing people in whispers. Some get hysterical: 'It's another attack!'. I feel a great longing for my family. I want to be with my wife and my kids. I want to be back in control, and in the warmth of my parents' house. I stay calm by starting at the beginning, and asking myself: 'How did I get here?'.

11
THE BASE

1

THE DAY MY MOTHER LIVED

My mother, whose name is Ella, likes to tell me about the exact moment that she decided she would have me. It was 26 September 1981, and it was the day that she was not executed.

'Oh you can't start a book with that,' my mother says over wine in her inner-western Sydney home. 'It's all so glum. How about you start your book with the story of how we came to Australia? Start on the 12th of January 1988. Write about how hot it was. How shocked we were about the temperature—coming from the snow fields in Iran.'

Naser, my father, offers an alternative. 'Or,' he suggests, 'why not start with the 28th of July 1983, the date of your birth? During the Iran–Iraq War, and how we had to bring you straight home from the hospital because they were out of water and out of medicine. That the doctor told me to bring you home because you would get an infection if you stayed and they had nothing to treat it with. Start with that.'

'No,' I tell them. 'I don't think I can really tell the story without starting in 1981. How can I tell the story about living and coming to Australia if I don't include a story about dying?'

9

'Does that mean you are going to write about Hassan?' my mother asks—this being the elephant in the room.

'Yes,' I answer.

My mother hesitantly agrees; but my father is less sure. I suspect that he would rather I not write about any of it, but he won't tell me not to. He's polite like that.

Dad finally registers his blessing with an 'OK.' And he assuages his reluctance with a request. 'Just be kind to the dead.'

That day—26 September 1981—was not only the day on which my mother was not executed. It was also the day on which my father's best friend was.

'

The first time Hassan nearly killed my father was in 1977. Back then, Hassan and Naser were just twenty-one years old.

My father and his three closest school friends had arranged a reunion. Two of them, Faramarz and Abbass, had moved to London to pursue university studies and were back home for the break. Hassan and my father had stayed in Iran.

The four friends had been inseparable during their schooling years. The photographs of them, those that weren't hastily destroyed after the executions, show them laughing, playing and trying not to look like the awkward gawky teenagers that they were.

'Hassan was very good looking,' my father tells me. I've seen the photos, and he is right. Tall, with curly hair, Hassan was a leather-jacket wearing and poetry-quoting revolutionary.

For this reunion they were joined by one other person, my mother. My parents had married the year before.

My father had arranged for the group to hike to the Immortal Castle in the Clouds. This is the ancient Babah Citadel crowning the mountains in the Arasbaran forests, situated in the province of East Azarbaijan (north-western Iran). Built of sandstone and rock, the citadel looks as though it has burst through the top of the mountain, and could well belong in a *Lord of the Rings* movie.

It provides unparalleled views of the ancient structures that were built to resist invading armies. Over a thousand years old, it was deemed 'immortal' by virtue of its apparent impregnability in the face of the expanding Abbasid caliphate.

There are several routes spanning out from the foot of the mountain, but only one of them will take you to the citadel. The paths are misleading, and intentionally so. There are no signs or marked steps; there are only the same weathered paths that were used thousands of years ago. As you rise, the right-hand side forms an edge, giving way to a steep drop of 400 to 600 hundred metres. On the left side of the path, you are led back into the forest.

'We were lost. I assumed I knew the way. I had been there before but when we were presented with three different options, I took the wrong one.' This was my father's nonchalant recounting of what to me looked like a near-critical mishap. But then he offered a more sombre observation. 'These were not safe places to be lost. Especially as it became dark.'

'Politically unsafe?' I ask, assuming that he was treating us to one of his revolutionary stories.

'No, no … bears. Bears are worse.' Not the response I was expecting, but I resolve to take him at his word.

'When it became dark we stayed on the cliff face. We could hear bears in the forest and we knew they wouldn't come too close to the cliff. So we decided we would wait there until morning light.'

The plan was to stay awake all night and, at the break of light, find a way back to the town below. Hassan, though, unexpectedly fell asleep on the precarious edge; he lost his balance and started sliding down the cliff face. My father was able to chase Hassan down before he went over the edge into the gorge—Dad grabbed him and pulled him back to safety. Both young men struggled at the cusp of disaster.

Soon after, Faramarz pronounced solemnly on what had—or hadn't—happened. He turned to my father and said, 'It wasn't his time to go and it wasn't yours. You were protected.' Hassan, always the cynic and now wide awake, turned and dismissed this as ridiculous. Surely, as clear-sighted intellectuals, they could put these old Persian superstitions behind them. Eventually, dawn broke over the ancient citadel and they made their way home.

'The problem,' my father tells me, 'is that you have a very Australian view of death.' He has said this to me before, and every time he says it my ears are pummelled by its peculiarity.

My father doesn't like to talk about any of this. He's dealt with this particular period of his life mostly by pushing it away. Not until I was well out of school did my father ever speak to me about Hassan. Not to protect me, but I suspect to protect himself.

He goes quiet when the conversation ever turns to the period between the Iranian Revolution in 1979 and my birth in 1983. This four-year period matches the gap between the birth of my sister, Azadeh, and my own birth.

'Survivor's guilt,' my sister tells me. Neither of us is a physician, but we have done what every child does—try to diagnose their parents.

My mother talks through her stories as though they belong to someone else. She's as detached as he is but in a very different way. My father deals with his past by relying on denial, summed up in the question, 'Why does any of this matter?'; and yet—despite his predictable turning away—it is quite clear that all of it matters, certainly to him. My mother talks of the past as if she were reading it from a novel. Her memories exist only as stories, full of emotion but devoid of attachment. It's as if she, at some point, has memorised a series of short stories and can talk about them at will.

My father is seated on a deck chair on his balcony, holding a glass of New Zealand sauvignon blanc. Wearing dark brown Chino pants and a cream shirt, he looks every part the inner-city champagne socialist. Except, unlike most of them, the experiences with which he wrestles are real. Named Naser after the Egyptian leader, Abdul Nasser, he is 6 foot tall and striking. But he has absented himself from our discussion and broods, silently.

At 5 foot, my mother is dwarfed by her husband. But she's the more trendy of the two, and she, elegantly, sits back on her seat and only occasionally takes a sip of her wine. Both of my parents are funny and gregarious, and, though different in many ways, they are bound together by their lifetime of shared experiences, and by a genuine, deep and lasting affection for each other.

'What is so "Australian" about my view of death?' I ask, dragging my father out of his silence and back into the conversation.

'Perhaps not "Australian," but certainly very western. You keep trying to find a point to death. That people have to be killed or die for a reason. When the waves of terror came, each individual death didn't make sense—they didn't have to.'

He is right. The indiscriminate nature of individual deaths is something I have never been able to comprehend. It's not that I don't understand murder as a political tool; while morally repugnant and reprehensible, it is hardly uncommon. But the death of an activist, to my way of thinking, always had to have a point. 'Was so-and-so's death to stop X or Y?' I will ask my parents and they will always say 'no'. 'They were killed because they were there.' That was enough.

'The deaths were about stopping an idea. Dissent. That was it. Once you view it from that framework all of them make sense even though every individual one doesn't.'

It's not that Hassan's execution came as a real surprise. While the Iranian Revolution took place in 1979, the real battle for control, the bloodbath, occurred in the years immediately after that. Many of the student activists, Hassan being one, had taken an aggressive stance in striving for the removal of the Islamic regime and pushing for a democratic alternative.

These were dangerous times. The stench of death was everywhere. The war between Iran and Iraq had begun. Thousands were being slaughtered on the battlefield daily. At the same time, there was the battle for control between different Islamist groups, the removal of the king denying them their one unifying enemy. And then there were the student activists, the least prepared, least organised, most easily liquidated.

When, during a random car stop, a semi-automatic magazine case was found in Hassan's car, the young man's fate was sealed. He would be summarily executed.

Of course, there was nothing random in this at all. A tip-off had led the Revolutionary Guard, those entrusted with protecting the revolution, to him. The case was perhaps planted; it didn't matter. The decision to kill him had already been made before the arrest. They seized him and dragged him to the courtyard of the Revolutionary Guard outpost, where they would line up those who would be killed. There would have been an immediate trial of sorts, but that was just a formality, a grotesque prelude to a horrible taking of life. Dad goes quiet.

My phone beeps with a text message and I look away to check the screen. The message is from my wife, Helen, telling me 'kids down fine'—meaning that our two daughters, 5-year-old Hannah and 3-year-old Eloise, have fallen asleep. It is 7:45 p.m.

'It was from the paper that we found out he was dead,' my mother goes on to say. The paper published a daily list of the names of those who had been executed.

'We would buy the paper to see who had died. It was part of the terror, printing the names in the paper. Making you wait every day when someone had vanished. If you called the Revolutionary Guards you were just told to buy the paper the next day.'

It was Hassan's family that pieced together what had happened. He had been picked up in his car, then taken to the Revolutionary Guard outpost.

'They didn't believe it at first,' my father tells me. 'His parents weren't political. They were older. His brothers were, but for his parents it was too much to comprehend. They needed to be sure. So they went to his body.'

The bodies were buried in a mass grave not far from the Revolutionary Guard outpost. At night it was only chained but not guarded. So they went to find his body.

I can picture Hassan's brother-in-law, then twenty-five years old, climbing a wire fence and searching through the bodies of the recently executed to find the remains of his brother. But it is all surreal. I picture them as I picture how my friends, at twenty-five, would have jumped a fence. But we would have done it for a laugh or part of a pub crawl.

'He knew it was him from his shirt.'

'What would have happened if they caught him breaking in?' I ask.

'At that time the threat of being killed hung over us so heavily, we didn't think about these things.'

By the next evening my grandmother had burnt any photograph of Hassan that was in my father's house. These were not safe things to have in your possession. Hassan was dad's best man, meaning that only one photo from my parent's wedding now exists. Precaution trumped sentiment.

A breeze blows on the balcony, making the silence less oppressive. Perhaps my sister is right; perhaps there is guilt in surviving. Here we sit in peace, tranquillity and middle-class opportunity. On the wall, just behind my father's head, hang the pictures of his daughter getting her PhD and sitting at her desk at Harvard and of his son being sworn into the Senate. There is guilt in knowing that had the circumstances of a life been arrayed differently—perhaps had a different conversation been entered into at a particular juncture, or had study been undertaken at some other university, or had any of innumerable other details been different in some way—my father's place, and fate, might have been swapped with Hassan's.

My father's stories are not uniquely his. They are shared by his circle of friends. When moving house he organises a painter friend of his to paint our house. A few hours into painting on a hot summer day, the man removes his shirt, something he would not normally do in front of a customer. The markings of torture on his body are clear to see. The cigarette burns, the lashings, the cuts—these have left lasting impressions on his flesh. 'He was lucky,' my father tells me. 'He was put in prison for eleven years early on—he would have been killed when the terror came if they didn't already have him facing a sentence.' It's a very different interpretation of 'lucky'.

Perhaps it was while my mother was being arrested that Hassan was being executed. Perhaps it was later that afternoon, when she was dragged into the courtyard of the number three Revolutionary Guard outpost in Tehran for processing. Perhaps it was that evening. We can't be sure. All we know is that he was killed that day. The details, the timing, the nature of the charges remain a mystery. All these things, my father would say, are insignificant. And he is right in a way. Once you know that Hassan was killed that day and that my mother wasn't—what else matters? If I could give you the reason, or the exact time, nothing would be different. Hassan's body would still have been found a few days later in a mass grave, and my mother would still have made her way to Australia.

In life, you are defined by moments. Increments of time add depth to your being; your experience is layered by the accumulation of years of pain, or love or suffering. But there are brief moments in time that stand still in your memory, perfectly formed. Moments that change everything. This is the part that my father doesn't get. The details of Hassan's death, according to him, are now insignificant. What matters is that my father, once Hassan died, was never the same again.

For my mother, it was possession of a political pamphlet that brought trouble her way. She read propaganda in the form of a newspaper. This might seem innocent enough when others are killing each other with bullets and bombs, but the regime understood that ideas mattered. What might start as a routine arrest could escalate to death in hours, depending on what the material contained.

My sister was with my mother that day. Azadeh was just two-and-a-half years old—rounded up in the street and taken with our mother when she was arrested. 'Surely I can leave my daughter with my family,' the desperate mother pleaded, but they wouldn't hear any of this.

The Revolutionary Guard outpost was full and doubled as a holding space for those who would be kept at the outpost and those who would soon be executed. There was a calmness to the murder that went on. A bureaucracy had been built around it, exemplifying what philosopher Hannah Arendt once called 'the banality of evil'. Death was normalised. The screams were no longer heard.

My mother was blindfolded and had her hands tied behind her back. My sister was free to roam.

'They took me to the courtyard and held me there. Your sister was treated well. They were angry with me, but they weren't angry with the children. They saw them as the future guardians of the revolution. Souls to be saved.'

My sister thinks that she can remember the courtyard. But memories of a toddler are notoriously unreliable. Later she was told what danger they were in, but at the time it was another day playing in a courtyard. She will tell you she remembers the faint smell of urine. The gritty, grey concrete walls leading to the cells, a contrast with the colours of autumn outside. The flower bed in the corner—now just a handful of weeds. She will articulate her memories as though she is describing a photograph.

She was only a child and was given sweets if she agreed to tell the authorities if any of those arrested were moving or talking while they waited for processing. And so she went from being the sweet child playing in the flower bed to unknowingly being an agent of a system that was possibly going to execute her mother that day. All within minutes.

'Tonight you will be executed, you son-of-a-bitch.' My mother could hear the guard yelling at someone who had been thrown into the courtyard. Her blindfold had risen enough that she caught a glimpse of a skinny 17-year-old boy wearing a bandanna of the rival Islamic faction to the regime.

'There had been a rally that day in a different part of town. Those wearing the bandannas were the organisers; they would be killed immediately.' So my mother tells me. 'The regime wasn't after information, they didn't need to interrogate. They knew what they wanted to know and just wanted to remove them. That was all.'

A lot of questions clamour in my mind. I want to know how my father found out that the Revolutionary Guard had my mother. I want to know how deeply the news of both Hassan's death and my mother's arrest shocked him. I want to know why my mother was let go while the others in the courtyard were, most likely, all killed. And why, after my mother's release, did they go into the relative obscurity of her home town? How had this move led to my being born? I want to understand the random nature of life and death.

Questions spawn further questions, but I notice that my father isn't talking anymore. He is sitting back in his chair, quietly. I know what he is thinking: what does it matter—Hassan was killed and your mother wasn't.

There are a few more minutes of silence. It is 8:05. 'I think your father has had enough,' Mum whispers to me. I leave.

2

REFUGEES

For as long as I can remember, I've been telling people that 'I came to Australia as a 5-year-old child with nothing more than $10000 and a suitcase full of dreams'.

And, for as long as I can remember, my sister, Azadeh, has been telling me that my story is complete bullshit.

'You know,' Azadeh tells me, 'someone will fact check that one day and you'll be sorry.'

'It'll be fine,' I respond, 'everyone loves a migrant story.'

But, as with most things, my elder sister is right. Technically, I was four when we came to Australia. Actually, four-and-a-half; certainly not five.

But what my sister really has issue with is the '$10000 and a suitcase full of dreams' part.

'When did our parents ever have $10000 when we were kids?' she reminds me. And as for the 'suitcase full of dreams': that part undersells the practical reality of migration. Yes, I came with a suitcase, but it was crammed with the best rip-off western brands we could get—important paraphernalia that would help us to start our new life. Not only the best 'AT-I-DAS' and 'Rea-Book' clothing, but shirts emblazoned with western brands like McDonalds and KFC. Because that is what an Iranian in the late 1980s thought children in Australia were wearing. In the Iranian's imagination, Aussie kids were proudly sporting shirts plastered with the letters 'KFC'.

I'm often asked, once I've delivered my line, if I am a refugee. It's always asked as if refugee status is some type of agency that operates upon a person, an exotic moulder of the dimensions of personality—as if, being a stranger, your strangeness is determined by the refugeeism that counts as an explanation of what you are. The word works the alchemy of making you a being whose value hangs upon the answer to a particular question. 'Are YOU a refugee?' The emphasis falls on *you*. It's often well meaning enough—but completely fails to recognise that there is nothing glamorous or romantic about seeking refuge in another country. Nor, as a rule, does it succeed in prompting an appreciation of the traumas that the 'you' of the question—or the family that nurtures the 'you'— has endured. No one claims asylum for any reason other than desperation. The decision to leave your entire life, your family and everyone you know is not one that is taken lightly.

Everyone is shaped by their experiences. We like to think that we are masters of our own destiny, that we have some kind of control. But layers of circumstantial occurrence have their way with us. Some things, over which we have no mastery whatsoever, pull and push us here and there. Who are our parents and what have they done? And what happened to them? It may be that the lottery of birth has the largest impact on our identities and our opportunities.

For me, the single biggest event was coming to Australia, as a young child, from a small town in Northern Iran. Nothing I ever say or ever do will have a larger impact on my life than that one simple fact. This was a decision that shaped who I am but was made, fortunately, on my behalf.

And when I'm asked if I am a refugee, I always answer 'no'— which is partly true.

My Facebook refugee relationship status is—'It's complicated'.

My parents met as young student activists, studying civil engineering during the 1970s. But they never completed university in Iran at the time. They were expelled for joining the revolutionary movement, along with many of their friends. Some of those friends were imprisoned and tortured, and some were even killed. Young, pro-democracy student activist: this, as my parents can testify, was a dangerous job description in the Iran of the latter 1970s.

Sadly, photographs from that time of my parents and their friends—young, enthusiastic, energetic, hopeful—are rare. My grandmother started destroying them when the arrests and killings began. Possession of a photo, then, was enough to land you in jail.

The Shah of Iran fell in 1979. But when Ayatollah Khomeini returned from exile, my parents found themselves confronted by an equally repressive regime. A secular political tyranny had been replaced by a religious one.

In the wake of the revolution and their expulsion from university, my parents moved to the small town of Sari in Northern Iran. That is where I was born. It was a smart move to keep a low profile. We lived in Sari, in relative peace, until the eruption of the Iran–Iraq War and, with it, an intensification of fear that government oppression would be ramped up. This, for my parents, signalled that it was time to move. They knew the horrors of which the strong political hand was capable, and they must have lived in dread of what could happen to themselves and their children.

I came to Australia with my sister and parents in January 1988, days before Australia's bicentenary celebrations. We came under a family migration visa.

We fled the tyranny of Iran, but we did it without applying for refugee status. We did so because desperate people will use whatever means are available. For us, the family migration program represented the easiest path.

The refugee debate in Australia is nothing if not horrendous. Everything is placed within a binary frame: either you support an open-door migration policy (and, by implication, the death of thousands of people at sea) or you support a punitive treatment of people so inhumane as to suffocate the desire to come to Australia.

It's as if there is no space for a third option—that you can't support a restrictive policy that can, at the same time, treat people with humanity and dignity.

It's a debate that has been going on since 2001, and the nation has become divided by the hate that it stirs.

It's the punitive calculation that has always galled me. What does it say about our society if we turn a blind eye to abuse and mistreatment at detention centres on islands like Nauru and Manus? And what does it say about us as a people? There is no point pussyfooting around this. What we have been saying as a society is that we will treat one group of people so terribly that it will send a signal to others. Is that a morally justifiable act? Is there a better way?

Surely there is a more fair and just way, one in which we can have offshore processing but not destroy the hopes and aspirations of the people seeking to escape persecution.

So there I was at age four (not five), boarding the train to Tehran from our small town and turning to my 8-year-old sister to ask if she thought we were still going to come back to see my grandparents on weekends. 'I mean, how far can Sydney really be?'

The Australia of January in 1988 was a place of hope. The multicultural project was viewed, mostly, as a startling success, and when Australians gathered to celebrate 200 years of colonial history, there was a lot to be proud of. While the almost 40 000 years of Indigenous history had been largely airbrushed out, we were celebrating a remarkable two centuries. As far as migration was concerned, there was a consensus that had held since the end of White Australia. And there was no reason, back then, to think that this would change.

'So are you a refugee?' The question is often asked.

'Well, there is a difference between being a refugee and seeking refugee status.' I go on to explain. It might be a technical difference, but it is actually a very significant one.

'We never sought refugee status and never made a claim. So you be the judge,' I say to them, and we often go back to drinking our expensive beverages and the conversation turns to important topics, like mobile-phone battery status.

Occasionally, I'll sink back in my seat and ponder. Does it matter? Does it make a difference if I came here as a refugee?

And the short answer is that it would. Not if I had applied for refugee status in 1988, but certainly if I had applied for it more recently. Attitudes have changed.

And I go on to pose a question to myself. Given the circumstances that confronted my parents in Iran, would they have been any less caring people if, in their desperation, they had paid a people smuggler to get them to Australia?

The trade in people is deplorable. It is sickening. But are the desperate people who turn to the smugglers lesser people as a result? Were I to find myself facing the same challenges faced by my parents—and if being smuggled was the only way available to get my two daughters out of Iran—what choice would I make? Wouldn't I use any means available?

Even in the midst of the federal-election campaign in 2016, I knew that I had to show up. In the middle of a long period of no sleep and endless travel, I knew that I had to be at my sister's book launch. The subject of this, her second book, was the immigration detention centre at Guantanamo Bay. For an hour, I am to be with my parents and be a son, not a politician. For an hour, I will be someone's little brother.

Twenty years ago, Azadeh broke my parents' hearts by telling them that instead of intending to live the life of an impoverished musician (Dad's dream) or a misunderstood writer of unintelligible literature (Mum's dream), she was going to rebel and, to their horror, become their worst nightmare—a lawyer. It doesn't really matter that she isn't your typical lawyer. My sister has a PhD in international refugee law and has devoted her life to the plight of asylum seekers. I don't think she's worn a suit in her life or given legal advice to anyone that has ever had any money to pay her, but the betrayal is still raw for my parents. 'She was so talented,' they like to say, with a sadness that is palpable. 'She really could have made it if she hadn't sold out.' 'I always thought that selling out meant actually making money,' my sister likes to retort. Mum and Dad may be the only Middle Eastern parents in the world mourning the fact that their successful child chose a respected field over the difficulty and uncertainty of an artistic life.

Azadeh speaks passionately about her hopes for some of the world's most vulnerable people. She tells us how, as a law student, she would visit detention centres and step out of her law classes to take phone calls from distraught people broken by their years in immigration detention. She won't say this in her speech later that night, but all of this nearly broke her.

She was, in those student days, too young to be taking on the responsibilities of this sort of work, and she was too emotionally involved. But the challenges that she faced didn't stop her, and decades on she continues to campaign for more compassion. There is no oddity in Azadeh's becoming a 'refugee academic'. It's not that other options weren't available to her, but shaping influences—the tugging of familial experience, ideas absorbed, attitudes acquired and cultivated—were at work. The corporate-law scene never interested Azadeh, and, as she always put it, 'how much good can be done when you are charging at six-minute increments?'

'You know,' Azadeh goes on to tell me, 'Humphrey Bogart in *Casablanca* was actually a people smuggler.' She is full of such observations and doles them out regularly.

'So why have you come here?' asks Kilian Kleinschmidt, fix-it man for the United Nations High Commissioner for Refugees (UNHCR). He is responsible for Zaatari, the largest refugee camp in Jordan.

'I just wanted to see the camp for myself,' I answer.

It is August 2014, in the height of the Jordanian summer, and the temperature is searing, above 40 degrees.

In this weather, the best answers are quick ones, but Kilian will be doing most of the talking. I suspect that he's given this spiel a few times.

He reels off a list of politicians, journalists, celebrities and UN officials who've made the one-hour drive across the lunar landscape from Amman to Zaatari. Harvey Weinstein had recently skipped the Cannes premiere of one of his movies to visit with cartoonist Neil Gaiman.

I realise that shepherding an Australian politician around for an hour is just another meeting that he has to undertake. Glad-handling is part of Kilian's job. In the months after our visit, Bono, Angelina Jolie, Ban Ki-Moon and Peter Dutton will hear the same story.

A few steps away our Jordanian security detail are waiting, clearly bored with their assignment.

'It's more for show than real security,' Kilian tells me. 'If they were worried about your safety they wouldn't have organised a five-car motorcade—they would have brought you here in secret.'

The motorcade is a sign of respect. I remind him that, being Iranian, I'm well aware of the importance of show.

I'd been convinced to visit at the urging of my sister and friends from across the world, who thought that the Australian obsession with people arriving by boat was hiding the enormity of what was going on in the world. It helped that my friend and parliamentary advisor, Cameron Sinclair, was up for the trip.

'They will take us up to the border if we want. But I've said no,' Cameron tells me.

'No?'

'I'm not sure that crossing into Syria is exactly what you want to be doing. The border is obviously safe, the conflict is internal. But you do realise how bad an idea it is for us to enter Syria?'

'Bloody hell,' I whisper under my breath, frustrated that Cameron is right.

A former New Zealand foreign affairs official, Cameron has one job, as he tells my friends over a beer. That job 'is to try to stop Sam being Sam'. They tell him that he's landed himself mission impossible. Cameron is tireless, thorough, unrelenting and very pleasant when he isn't talking about CrossFit.

A year earlier, on 21 August 2013, I had been appointed to the Senate. A few hours later, in a different time zone, Syrian government forces launched surface-to-surface missiles containing Sarin gas into two neighbourhoods in eastern Damascus. Footage was uploaded to YouTube and began playing on television over the next few days, and I watched hundreds of civilians—including large numbers of children—writhing on the floor of makeshift hospitals, limbs trembling and twitching in involuntary spasms, froth building up on their lips.

Some of the kids caught up in that attack, a year earlier, were now here. They were in this camp.

By Kilian's own admission, the Zaatari assignment should have been relatively easy. Compared to refugee camps in other parts of the world, Zaatari does have some advantages. 'We have electricity and water. The camp is near town. The capital city, Amman, with a population exceeding four million, is just an hour away, and the roads are sealed. But nothing is easy.'

Many westerners imagine that a refugee camp consists of crowds of desperately poor people lugging sacks of flour or bottles of cooking oil. They imagine that social order has collapsed, and that a camp will be devoid of culture, of humour, of wealth. But Zaatari is as diverse as any bustling town, and people's faces catch your eye because their personalities shine through, resistant to the difficulties of the situation in which they find themselves. Kids chase each other around buildings and run alongside our government car, about the only thing that makes our security detail uncomfortable. They have ice-cream stains on their shirts, and they play football on makeshift dirt patches. The neatly dressed woman standing next to us at the supermarket may have been a dentist, or perhaps a school teacher or a small-business owner.

'How do they survive?' Cameron asks, thinking out loud.

'What do you mean?'

'How do they get by, month after month?'

I don't know either, so I ask Kilian.

'Oh, they find a way.'

He tells us about the UN-funded cashless-card scheme, which allows refugees to buy staples from stores throughout the camp, and from some national chain stores.

'These people are very enterprising and great traders. But the tank is starting to run dry,' Kilian sighs, noting the inevitability of 'donor fatigue'. He looks me in the eye and tells me that it makes no sense for Australia to be spending billions locking up boat arrivals when the need is here. I wonder, now, what Peter Dutton thought when this point was made to him.

As we are getting ready to leave, we hear that a new family is arriving at the camp from the Syrian border. The son is shoeless. The father has thick stubble that has been growing for at least a week. He is sunburnt and the wind has taken its toll. They tell us through a translator that they have been walking for five days. They are not sad. They are not upset. They are just exhausted. And they are more interested in eating a hot meal than recounting their ordeal to a bug-eyed politician.

Cameron and I return to our motorcade and leave in a contemplative silence. A week later we will be back in Australia and it will all seem quite unreal.

It's interesting what you remember. For me, it's our street in Iran—that thin dirt road in the town of Sari. Dirt roads in Iran are not like the roads here. The red dirt of Australia signifies an untouched area. The dirt roads of Iran resemble construction sites. And these are old roads, scratched into the earth in a place where to be 'old' is to have existed for centuries, not decades.

Our street ran off a main boulevard, and every house was enclosed by high walls. There wouldn't have been more than a dozen houses, but, to a child's way of thinking, the dwellings articulated along the lane seemed to stretch into an ungraspable distance. The hidden courtyards were situated in the front. You would walk through a courtyard and into the house. The idea of a 'back yard' was unthinkable.

We would play football with a plastic ball, trying to make sure that it was never kicked into the courtyard of the old lady who constantly complained about us to our parents.

I remember my dirty shoes. I recall my unshod neighbours—shoeless, they said, because feet were toughened by the playing of barefoot football. The reality was that each of the boys in question possessed one pair of shoes and that, for them, shoes were reserved for wearing at school. They couldn't risk having their shoes ruined by football.

I remember the tale of the trunk of gold that an ancestor had apparently buried, generations before, in our street, right beside our house. The old shoveller had wanted to keep his bounty well hidden. We dug to unearth the treasure, not realising that the family myth had prompted others, before us, also to dig. My grandfather was one of the empty-handed diggers—he had spent his childhood searching for that elusive trunk.

And I can still see my mother saying goodbye to her family, crying uncontrollably as she loaded us into her car, heading for Tehran and then to Sydney. The likelihood was that she would never return, and would never see them again.

I remember the cold snow of January in Iran falling on the car as we drove away, my mother sobbing and my father trying to maintain a faltering composure.

I don't remember how it made me feel. Perhaps I was too young to comprehend, perhaps I was too caught up in other people's emotions that swirled around me and couldn't find a way to process whatever it was that I was feeling. So maybe those feelings just washed over me, coming and going quickly, overtaken by events. It seems that, at the time, I didn't analyse or interrogate what I felt. The affections, as it were, seemed not to affect me. But sometimes you don't recognise the most significant moments of your life until well after they have passed.

It took two days of continuous travel to get from Tehran to Sydney. But that was nothing compared to the cultural shock we experienced when we arrived in Australia.

The Australian summer, the funny language, the unusual customs. All of this was part of a strange new land. The drive through the streets where children were playing on lawns with sprinklers, the open houses, the relaxed atmosphere—all of this was different. We had much to learn.

Time, we are told by scientists, is not linear, but relative.

It is amazing how different paths to the same destination can result in dramatically different outcomes.

Reza Berati was born in Ilam Province, half a day's drive from my place of birth. Bordering Iraq, the region was devastated by the Iran–Iraq War of the 1980s. Reza had studied to become an architect and had graduated, but his political activity in Iran left him with the view that he had no safe option but to leave. The journey to Australia was hazardous, and I wonder if he had any understanding of the risks that he was facing.

Twenty-five years separated our common journey from Iran to Australia. We, who shared so much, were living in very different circumstances in 2013. That was when Reza Berati was adrift in the world, stuck somewhere between the danger of Iran and the relative safety of Australia.

I try to imagine Reza's predicament in August 2013. Most likely, he was in Java, deeply anxious about his circumstances and prospects, and waiting for a boat ride to Australia. At that time, I was helping to run the campaign operation for Kevin Rudd, then in his second term as prime minister. Kevin called to tell me that he was flying out to Papua New Guinea and had a deal to establish a refugee camp there.

'Manus Island,' Kevin said on the phone. I was packing my bags to head down to campaign headquarters in Melbourne. 'The PM will be standing up with me, joint announcement.' 'Standing up' is political speak for holding a press conference, and the PM to whom he was referring was Peter O'Neill, the Prime Minister of Papua New Guinea.

'I've never heard of it,' I replied. But I didn't dissuade; in fact, if anything, I was supportive of the idea. It was weeks out from an election and the 'refugee' issue—made so tangible by boat arrivals, deaths at sea, tales of human trauma, disagreements about how to settle asylum seekers—had haunted Labor for over a decade.

Kevin went on to say that Manus 'will fix the problem'. I knew that Kevin had been working on a plan for a few months during his stint as a backbench MP. I didn't know the details but I appreciated its significance. He didn't need to explain what 'fix' meant. It meant *stop arrivals by boat*. It meant *make the problem go away*.

One journey, two people, twenty-five years of separation—and everything is different. The path that you take to come to Australia and the moment at which you embark on the journey will be of life-altering importance. The result will depend on prevailing circumstances, which are relative—shaped by other factors. The circumstances that carried me to Australia in 1988 differed utterly from those that prevailed upon Reza in 2013. Necessarily, the results differed.

'I am a refugee and I am seeking asylum,' Reza Berati claimed as he tried to come to Australia. He spoke these words after months of travelling from Iran, through dangerous lands, down to Java, and then surviving the treacherous passage on a leaky boat headed for the Australian coastline.

'I swear allegiance,' I said, in a small council chamber in Hornsby, Sydney, with my parents. I was becoming an Australian citizen, unaware of the significance of the protections and privileges that were about to be bestowed upon me.

Vehalman khom - nazan—I imagine Reza directing these Persian words to the Revolutionary Guard. The words can be translated as

'Leave me alone, stop'. Reza was being beaten on the mosquito-infested island known as 'Manus'. The final blow, a blow to the back of Reza's head, caused the haemorrhage that led to his death.

'I pledge allegiance.' These words I said in the red Senate chamber as I was sworn into the Australian Parliament. I was thirty years old, and my family sat safely and comfortably in the gallery above. Soon after, we headed off for cocktails and dinner.

Prosperity, security, aspiration—these artefacts of time's relativity were for me, not for Reza.

Silence. A body is dragged out of the compound with everyone told to keep their mouths shut or else the same fate will befall them.

And I can sit here, in our house in Sydney's inner west, and watch my 5-year-old daughter run around in the same tattered shirt I brought with me from Iran, pleading with my wife not to throw it out—because in this life, you have to hold on to something.

3

MISSING LETTERS

My abiding, and perhaps first, memory of my grandfather is that he was particularly fat. Which is a very unkind way of remembering anyone, let alone a blood relative. He was big—of that, there is no doubt. I left Iran as a child, and there in heavy repose in my child's mind was the image of that chubby old man. Children hold on to memories such as that.

I remember that his face was red, and that his breath had the stench of alcohol. Not the processed liquor to which we have become accustomed. It didn't smell like beer, or rum or vodka. It was medicinal alcohol. Following the Islamic Revolution in 1979, alcohol was banned and quickly became a scarce commodity. What my grandfather drank was pure, medical grade alcohol. It was mixed to break down its devastating qualities and could be procured by his medical friends. It was dangerous. Not only could it get you arrested, it could rupture your liver or cause blindness.

'What did you expect?' my mother asks me. 'He needed something to calm his nerves.'

I have a tendency to discount the excuses that members of a family make—I might, in more cynical moments, say 'concoct'—

for one another. Everyone has a reason when it comes to drinking or taking drugs. But my mother has a point. If I had lived half the life that my grandfather had, I'd need something too. In the small town of Sari in Northern Iran, the men dealt with their demons alone.

My mother and I spoke on Australia Day in 2017. It was one of those hot Canberra nights, too hot to sit inside. We relocated to the balcony. I had brought Mum to Canberra so that she could spend some time with her grandchildren, and the conversation invariably turned to her family in Iran. I had been drinking wine and my mother drinking tea. My two daughters had been asleep for an hour and I realised that it had been years since my mother and I had been alone together—it certainly hadn't happened since her father, Ahmad, died.

'You know my father had a lot of untold stories. A handful he told me on his deathbed. Others he took with him to the grave, those that would get the living killed.'

The stories of my grandfather were always shrouded in mystery. When I knew him he was already an old man. I knew that his marriage to my grandmother was scandalous in its time, but I didn't know why. I knew that he was politically radical, and therefore out of sorts with the mindset of the small-town Iranian establishment in which he operated. In Ahmad's world, the rumours that circulated were viscous and the memories that retained them were imperishable.

I remember him happy and jolly. He was always making a joke, endlessly playful—until the darker moments would set in and subdue him. He would go quiet and become sullen. He was back in Iran, back in the small town, facing his past.

My family history is littered with cases of outsiders, those in exile and those escaping harm. This is particularly in evidence on my mother's side. Our tendency to estrangement—to the state of being non-native, to the act of going elsewhere—is best embodied by my grandfather's mother, Naneh.

Everyone always said that there was something different about her. Some knew of my great-grandmother's hardships. She was married at nine years of age to a man thirty years her senior, and was widowed at eighteen with two children. Naneh was a foreigner in Sari, but it was not of her foreignness that people remarked when they spoke of her as being different. For one thing, many did not know the extent to which she was foreign. They did not know of the persecution, the migration, the desperate need for safety. Many did not know that her people were not from Iran at all. A handful would whisper that her family emanated from an unnameable place on the other side of Russia, which explained their fair skin and the startling sapphire blue eyes of some of their babies. Some knew that her parents had come from Babol, a town near Sari with a large Jewish community. But no one talked about the forced conversions of the Jewish people in Babol in 1866, the year her family migrated. No one mentioned the day on which eighteen Jewish men were killed—several burnt alive. There was no talk of the hasty exits, the families that relocated for protection and adopted new lives. No one discussed the interference from the British and French ambassadors that led the then King of Iran to cease the persecution and forced conversion of the Jewish community. No one asked why so few Jewish families went back to Babol, or why so few trusted the change or felt safe. No one asked what our great-grandmother was doing in Sari.

Some would have felt no compulsion to ask because they already knew the answers.

When they said that my great-grandmother, Naneh, was different, they often referred to her strange views. She was a feminist before the word had any meaning in her town and exhibited an acceptance of people's lives and sexualities that is rare even today. Her father, a doctor and a merchant, had amassed great wealth in Sari, but you would not know it from the way that our great-grandmother carried herself. She was humble, generous, unassuming.

I never met Naneh. I don't walk the streets that she walked. I'm not reminded of her by passing that grand home painted aqua and deep blue that would explode with the heady scent of orange blossoms in spring. I never collected the flowers or helped make the perfumed jam that added customary zest to breakfasts served in her home. I do not get to think of her by seeing older women wrapped in the floral chador that used to engulf her small frame in a cascade of daisies, and I am not reminded of her by the sound of the call for prayer.

Others remembered more. My grandmother, Minou, for example, recalled that it was Naneh who stood by her when she, poor and desperate, came to Naneh's house as a bride to her promising son. It was intended that the son, a medical student, would marry someone of wealth and status. But Naneh was prepared to disregard the conventional view. Naneh told the women from the good homes and the respected families that humble Minou, the butt of their jokes and gossip, would not only be welcomed into her home but that she, Minou, would have two rooms and a private courtyard. Everyone was warned that anything said against Minou would be treated as a personal insult to Naneh. The gossiping and jeering ceased. And so it was that Minou, our grandmother, who had been orphaned as a child and raised by an impoverished brother, became a lady.

Minou, too, was escaping something. She was escaping hunger. She told me once that the thing she is happiest about is that her grandchildren have enough food. She did not want us to face the indignity of being hungry.

It was from his mother that my grandfather, Ahmad, got his politics. In the aftermath of the revolution, no one was safe. In that context, politics mattered.

However, there was only so much reach available to the Islamic regime. Power is decentralised and dissipated through distance, and while the regime had its networks of mosques, radicals and believers, it still had to contend with the fibrous residue of thousands of years of culture and identity that defiantly endured in Iran. In the regions outside the cities, the communities maintained traditions resolute enough to have snubbed the invasions of Greeks, Abyssinians, Moguls and Persians. Viewed in this light, no recent revolution was going to drain life out of the ways of things that had always been. The towns, for example, were encrusted in custom. A town's old wise men, its leaders, had to be afforded respect. This was an important tradition, a way in which social relations were conducted and lines of authority acknowledged. My grandfather was a local wise man.

On that stifling Canberra evening, my mum continues her story. 'They were suspicious of my father, but were never really able to prove anything,' she tells me. 'It's hard to work out how many lives he saved; there was obviously never a list. But it gave him comfort when he was dying.'

They would have fired my grandfather if they could have found an excuse. He wasn't one of them, and he held far too senior a position for someone whose faith, and whose political convictions, were suspected by the new authorities. As a bureaucratic leader in the Department of Education, he had access to the most valuable commodity for the future of the regime—namely, the next generation.

But he was also old. Had he lived in Tehran, they would have borne the community backlash and got rid of him. Not in the northern towns, separated from the heart of the regime by distance, enveloped by mountains—townsmen of the north were more able to proceed on their own terms. Besides, Iran was at war with Iraq, and the regime was distracted by internal Islamic opposition. The regime might keep watch on people like my grandfather, but its focus was directed at multiple points, which were elsewhere than Sari.

'The people of the north were never the more religious ones,' my mother reminds me. There is history behind this statement.

The north was conquered later. As the agricultural food bowl, it was self-sufficient in a way that a lot of the more barren parts of Iran, reliant on the state to sustain themselves, could not be. It was wealthy and had been for generations.

It was while he was dying that many of the stories about my grandfather came to light. A man whom my mother did not know appeared at my grandfather's deathbed. This was strange. The town of Sari had grown exponentially in recent decades. But my grandfather's world hadn't. His web of sociability did not enlarge with the passage of years. When my mother returned to Iran to bid him farewell, she saw that the stream of people coming to see him consisted of the same old men of the community whom she had known when she was a small child. If one of his friends or comrades was not alive to visit him, a child or relative would come in their place.

'I could have told you twenty years earlier exactly who would be present as my father was dying,' my mother tells me. 'The town was like that. As progressive as they were, they were still just old men in a village and they had their rules.'

The unknown man was around fifty years old, wearing jeans and a collared shirt. He didn't have a beard, and he smelled of cologne. These were small signs, very evident to someone trained to notice, that the man was no regime sympathiser. He never told anyone his name and my grandfather didn't ask.

'Did your father know him?' I ask my mother.

'If he did, he certainly didn't give any indication of that. But he was good at hiding things. Compartmentalising. Breaking up his life into different sections,' Mum explains.

My grandfather had been taken home from hospital. He didn't want to go home when he knew he was dying. At eighty-six, it was his time.

'It has been years that I have been looking to find you. I'm happy that I found you,' the man told my grandfather. 'I heard you went to Australia. Years and years I looked for you. I just want to tell you one thing … I want to say thank you for keeping me alive.

During those years I couldn't understand. I hated you. I was angry at you. You kept moving me from one town to the next. Every six months I would be moved. I thought you were punishing me for my politics. Now I realise you were protecting me from death.'

There is always this talk of death; death has a way of infiltrating Iranian conversations. 'Of course,' my mother says. 'What else is there to discuss?'

'It took me years to notice,' the man continued, still addressing my grandfather. 'Thank you.' And with that, he left.

My grandfather never explained the details to my mother; he didn't need to. Responsible for teacher placement, he would move teachers around the small towns as he saw fit. When he got anonymous tip-offs from the Islamic department that a teacher was being investigated on suspicion of disloyalty to the regime, he would move them to another town. My grandfather was actively disrupting the regime's capacity to assemble incriminating evidence against persons of interest. The persons concerned, like the man who visited my grandfather, might resent the 'punishment' that he was administering, but his were kindly ministrations. He was a guardian to the endangered, and few of the endangered knew it.

It's not just elephants that travel to die. People do it too. In the early 2000s my grandfather travelled to Australia to live, and then travelled back to Iran so he could die.

The irony isn't lost on me that my grandparents were granted asylum at a time when John Howard and Philip Ruddock were in power. When I tell people that I wasn't a refugee, I never tell them that my grandparents were. They sought and received asylum fifteen years after my arrival in Australia. The case was open and shut and went through without a hiccup. But let me say this: the term 'queue jumper' is a frightful insult to people who have faced a lifetime of persecution.

By the time that I knew my grandfather, his once athletic body, sturdy and strong from years of weightlifting and wrestling, had become pudgy—a sign, he joked, of a life well lived. He would point to his large belly and laugh that his stomach was his biggest investment. Portliness was not cheap. His whole being would bob up and down as joy bubbled through him. He could laugh with street cleaners and professors, with the rich and the poor. He laughed with everyone because he understood what united them all. He understood the absurdity of life and laughed at it.

He never had much stamina for sitting and concentrating, but by the time that I knew him he didn't have to. He would tell me delightful stories about the trouble he used to get into as a child in class, causing havoc and distracting his peers. But he wouldn't tell me the stories about being expelled from the medical school of the prestigious University of Mashhad, during the 1950s, when he had to flee back to his home town. Nor did he tell me of events that followed the revolution. He told me nothing of why, as an old man in the early 2000s, he packed his belongings and took my grandmother on a plane to Australia. This was done at short notice, when the darkness of his past re-emerged and threatened to engulf him. The years during which he should have been in peace were the years in which he felt the greatest fear. He had become a strange man in a strange land.

I picture him as an old man walking the streets of suburban Sydney. Old, sad and tired; stripped of his identity. In his small town he was a person of respect. Here, he was politely treated as an oddity.

It seems hackneyed to speak of the Iran–Iraq War (1980–88) as a horrific event. But it was. The horror crushes you when you think about how the children suffered—children were killed in appalling numbers during this conflict. Teenagers and pre-teenagers went to war; children were used to clear minefields. Children were fed a diet of propaganda and were promised the rewards of martyrdom.

Many hastened to participate. The paramilitary wing of the Iranian Revolutionary Guard, the Basij, assembled the teams of child soldiers.

It was the missing letters that almost got my grandfather into real trouble after the revolution. These were letters from Iranian children asking to go to the frontlines during the Iran–Iraq War.

'It just doesn't make sense,' said the cleric to the management group of senior bureaucrats at the Department of Education office for the town of Sari as the war was underway. 'While the other regions are producing so many volunteers, the north has consistently failed to meet its targets.'

While, officially, one had to be eighteen years old to join the war effort, children as young as twelve were joining the militias. The only authority to check was the regime, and they were desperate for recruits. They would recruit straight out of the schools, sending speakers to urge the children to become martyrs for the cause.

My mother claims that her father told her, 'I actually supported the war. But I just couldn't play a part in the deaths of these kids. I just couldn't be responsible for them going to their deaths'.

It was after the first batch of children did not return that my grandfather knew that he had to do something. He would often be the first to see the mail and remove the envelopes that looked as though they were either letters from children or reports from teachers. He would pass an unopened pile to his secretary, a regime sympathiser who was there to keep an eye on him.

'Isn't it too hot to have the fire running?' the secretary would ask my grandfather, wondering why the old man couldn't handle a little cold weather. He never realised that the old man was burning the letters and the reports.

Then in November 1981 he almost got caught. There was an inquiry. 'No, no … we just get very few letters from volunteers up here. The people of the north are not as reliable as those from the south.' This is what the inquiring cleric heard from my grandfather's secretary, the one approved by the authorities, the one oblivious to what was really going on.

'Did they ever find out?' I ask my mother.

'They suspected. But they could never prove anything.'

'How many?' I ask. As if it would have been less brave of him to have saved five lives rather than fifty.

'I never thought to ask.'

It would have been the first thing that I would have asked had I been her.

Of course there were a few complaints. Rumours of missing letters circulated. But when a country is at war and is in the process of bedding down a revolution, the loss of mail is a small issue.

'How come he never spoke to my sister and me about any of this?' I ask my mother. 'It's not as if he didn't have the opportunity. He lived with us for so many years.'

'He didn't want to burden you with the past.'

'But it's *our* past,' I protest.

'No. It's *his* past. As far as he was concerned, you came to Australia. You didn't have that past anymore.'

And so we sit on the balcony in Canberra, the air finally starting to cool as the breeze picks up. And my mother thinks of her father.

After a long pause my mother turns to me and says, 'He wasn't fat when he died'. As if it mattered.

4

GROWING UP DASTYARI

My paternal grandmother was sixteen when she married my grandfather, who was already twice her age. When introduced to her husband for the first time at her wedding, she turned to her mother and said, 'Oh phew, I was thinking you were going to marry me to the bald one'. This was 1930s Iran and despite all the genetic defects that inflict the Dastyari family, absence of hair is not one of them.

We are at uncle Kamal's place, enjoying drinks on his balcony, and the host is regaling my fiancée (now wife), Helen, with this and other family stories.

Kamal was the patriarch of the family. He raised his brother—my father—when their father died. My dad, Naser, was then still a teenager, and Kamal was in his thirties. I've been told that I look like Kamal, though his looks tend towards Omar Sharif whereas mine gravitate to Rowan Atkinson. Much like the singer of the same name, Kamal always spoke with a deep baritone voice, and tonight he was in fine form.

'Then there was the matter of your father,' Kamal said. 'You know the story about your father—right?'

I thought he was going to tell the story of my father's wedding. He was a student activist who married my mother against the wishes of his family. They viewed my mother with suspicion; she was a radical and, even worse, came not from the city but from a rural province. The family had almost collectively boycotted the wedding.

'Because we did everything we could to help our mother abort him,' he went on to say.

'I'm sorry,' I interject. 'To abort him?'

'Oh yes. I was fifteen when our mother became pregnant with your father. Dad was living in Tehran and we were in Tabriz, half-way across the country. As your grandmother was illiterate I wrote the letter to our dad saying she was pregnant.'

My aunty jumps in, 'You never thought it was weird that your father's four siblings are all in succession and there is a ten-year gap before your father?'

I hadn't. My uncle then proceeded to go on and disgorge upon Helen the past thirty years of inter-family feuds, which meant that we didn't leave until the early hours of the morning. He pulled it off with a story-telling flair that would swell the chest of the bard himself.

Earlier in the day, I had given Helen a crash course on my family. I had started with a flow chart that ended up resembling a mathematical proof for a hypothesis in quantum physics. Or something like that.

My father came from a family of five children. By the early 1990s the whole family had migrated to Australia. There were three boys—Kamal, Jalal and my father, Naser—along with two girls, Mahin and Shahin. Between them, they in turn produced eleven children and, at any time, up to half a dozen factions.

It wasn't until 1990, at my grandmother's funeral, that my father believed we finally belonged in Australia. He quoted Gabriel García Márquez's *One Hundred Years of Solitude*: 'A person does not belong to a place until there is someone dead under the ground'. This was deep and meaningful, but I was interested in the other family drama taking place.

For the past twenty-five years, we had been living in our own private family reality-TV show. Any mug can create drama at a wedding. The skill lies in doing the same thing at a funeral. This, when you think about it, is a decidedly hard thing to do. Navigating the many family alignments and realignments, where one wrong step results in the miscreant's being cast for a decade into the wilderness, makes the internal operations of a political party seem like a cakewalk. The gravesite is where the true politicking gets done.

'Are we spending Christmas morning at the gravesite again?' Helen would ask me, every Christmas.

'Yes. Yes we are. And Dad wants me to bring his guitar for him. His boot is full of food.'

This was our family tradition. On Christmas morning, while others were opening presents, we would go—about thirty of us with instruments—and get ourselves judged badly. When I was growing up we used to celebrate my grandmother's birthday on Christmas Day. Not because that was actually her birthday, but simply because it was convenient for everyone else.

The concept of a 'birthday' is actually a very western one. In Iran in the 1920s, no one would keep track of the day of the month on which someone was born. Frankly, that was an irrelevant detail. What year you were born mattered, but the day itself meant nothing. So when filling out the paperwork that enabled my grandmother to come to Australia, the family needed to invent a date of birth. They went with Christmas Day.

With the passing of my grandmother, the tradition of the family get-together on Christmas Day continued for a while, but at the gravesite. You might think that this would result in a calm and solemn occasion whereby the family comes together to ponder the meaning of life, but anyone who entertains expectations like that doesn't know my family.

As far as we are concerned there are only two appropriate noises at a gravesite: wailing and sing-alongs. There is no third option. This has led to the complicated and confusing situation in which the two forms of noise are unleashed in cacophonous coincidence. For outsiders, it isn't pretty on the ears.

Then there's all the eating at the gravesite. And I'm not talking a few slices of cheese with crackers, or a picnic basket. What eventuates is a full-blown competition to determine who can roll up with the most elaborate array of food. It has taken all of our strength of purpose to stop the cooking of kebabs at the gravesite with a home-made fire. 'They say no fire, but why? There is nothing to burn down. It's ridiculous.' The Persian complaints about the nanny state revolve around not being able to light a fire at a cemetery.

The old songs at the gravesite misled me for years. 'In the mountains, his heart is alive, he is bringing the gun, the flower and the wheat ear.' We would all sing, together. For years I thought that this was a cute song about nature, not realising that these were lyrics sung by communist guerrillas during protracted periods of hiding out. Which would misleadingly leave the impression that my grandmother died in armed conflict, a rather dramatic interpretation of Sydney's outer suburbs even in the 1990s.

I like to think that we provide relief for the many grieving families, perhaps the only good that can come from our antics. Other families gather and realise that despite their loss, things could be worse. We—the weirdos who are wailing and singing pop songs and trying to light a fire—are offering bemused onlookers the service of showing them that while they are not in great shape, we scarcely have any shape at all.

It was at my grandmother's funeral that I realised we were onto our fourth generation of Dastyaris living in Australia. Sure, three of those generations migrated together, but the fourth (my daughters included) were born here.

My grandmother, despite being an Australian citizen, was never really an 'Aussie' in the cultural sense. Since my childhood, she was an older Iranian woman who happened to be living in Australia. She loved this country, and the people, but fitting in when you start in your sixties is just too difficult. She was happy that her children had chosen this country, that they got out of Iran. Frankly, her happiness was for her children, not for herself.

Her entertainment was watching daytime soap operas, in particular *The Bold and the Beautiful*. The tales of the Forrester and Logan families were complicated by interweaving marriages and relationships. My grandmother could tell you that Taylor was brought back from the dead on three separate occasions, which is necessary when your relationship profile attains the complexity that Taylor's had; that Brooke had married Ridge and proceeded to remarry him five times; and that thirty-eight characters had managed to kick the bucket, which perhaps consorts well with the funereal interests of my family. Bearing in mind that she didn't speak a word of English, it staggers me that my grandmother was able to keep on top of the intricate plotlines that the likes of *The Bold and the Beautiful* served up.

It was no doubt through the prism of these television dramas that she watched her grandchildren parade the series of boyfriends and girlfriends who trooped in for inspection. She might not have had fluent English, but she kept abreast of the family feuds, notwithstanding her children's best efforts to keep any bad news from her. But she was a grandmother, and was therefore in full command of mystical ways of knowing the things that her nearest and dearest believed would never be known by anyone.

As Australian Iranians, our cultural offerings were not limited to the celebration of pyrotechnically inflected feasts at cemeteries. We wanted to bring our festival *Nowruz* (meaning 'new year') to Australia. Largely, this wasn't an issue. It occurs around late March every year, and celebrates the official coming of spring (that is, the northern-hemisphere spring). For the most part, the celebratory

GROWING UP DASTYARI   47

components of the festival take place in the privacy of one's own home. But *Nowruz* also includes a raft of outdoor activities, which became challenging to complete. Unsurprisingly, my family decided to embrace the fire celebrations.

You can't really understand the Australian tolerance for multiculturalism until you have to explain to a council officer why they should let you light fires in the local park. There is a tipping point at which the theory of cultural tolerance and the reality of obtaining council permits conflict with one another. We all can be supportive of a tradition like Chinese New Year when it involves private family dinners, but when firecrackers are being let off in the middle of Sussex Street, Sydney, and dancing dragons are stopping traffic, the depth of the community's empathy is put to a tougher test. The Indians have their *Holi* festival, where coloured paints are thrown on dancers; the German's have Oktoberfest; the Irish have St Patrick's Day; and the Mexicans have their own excuse for a party, *Cinco de Mayo*.

The Iranian tradition of *Chaharshanbe Suri* is the 'Festival of Fire'. Held on the last Wednesday before Persian New Year, it is an ancient Zoroastrian cleansing festival. So far, so good. But here's the challenging bit: formally, one participates in the festival by jumping over a row of fires. In reality, it is a chance to burn anything. For one day each year, everything goes. Picture Fourth of July celebrations in the United States without boundaries. This idea is inspirited into the mind of every Iranian child.

'Sam, what are you doing setting fire to those plants in the yard?' my dad would scream at me and my childhood friends. But we were simply engaging in the pyromania that engulfs all 10-year-old boys.

'*Chaharshanbe Suri* is coming, just burn them then.'

The fires, usually between five and seven, are lit in a row, and participants line up and jump across them. It's actually safer than it sounds. Local government officials weren't so sure.

'So you want to create a series of fires and have children jump over them?' the council official would ask.

'It's like Carols by Candlelight,' my sister would explain. Her English was always the strongest, even when we were children.

'Except you jump over the fire.'

'Yes.'

'And the children.'

'They jump over the fire too.'

'Right. So you want a permit to light a series of fires in a park.'

'They are small fires.'

'Yes. That's also how big fires start. Small. And children will be jumping over these fires?'

'Everyone. Well, obviously the babies won't. That would be crazy. They are tossed.'

'Right. Can you put all this on the form and we will get back to you.'

We never got a permit for the year we hosted it. In Iran, the festival has become quite political, a symbolic act of defiance against an intolerant regime. In Australia, it has become a snubbing of the nose at local council fire restrictions.

While we were happy to partake in this celebration, the black-faced Persian New Year clown routine was a bridge too far. We, the younger generation of Iranian Australians, felt compelled to stage our own intervention, of sorts.

The Iranian Father Christmas is a guy named 'Uncle Nowruz'. He is bearded and hands out presents, not unlike Santa. It's his side-kick, called 'Haji Firuz', who causes the pain. Dressed as a clown in red satin and wearing a Turkish *fez* (a cap or peakless hat), he attends the Persian New Year celebrations covered in black soot.

Modern Iranians still trying to hold on to the tradition claim that he isn't black, but simply 'dirty'. The reality is that he is meant to resemble a black slave—a throwback to the Indian Ocean slave trade. Kids will dress up like him on the streets of Iran and go door to door with the goal of earning money—imagine Halloween but with everyone in black.

'Oh God! They're doing it again!' my cousin would moan as family friends—faces blackened with cheap paint—arrived at their home in Western Sydney. They'd do the Haji Firuz dance. 'If anyone saw this … we'd be dead!' Our families, blissfully unaware of the mortal insult in which they were partaking, insisted on group photos with the costumed men.

Progressives in Iran will now only go half black-face—as if that is somehow better. 'Oh it's not racist. He is now both a black and a white slave,' they argue. 'And look at his character, he's always so happy.'

Ah, the 'happy slave'—that old chestnut. Yes, the person who wants to be in chains, walking the streets, playing the fool. Since the 1970s, African diplomats in Tehran have been quietly objecting to this tradition through official channels. Here in Australia, the children have been screaming about it.

'They're all going to be surfers.' Azadeh, my sister, makes this announcement to all of our cousins on a balcony. It makes no sense to anyone.

'Serfs?' I ask my sister.

'Surfers! They will be surfers,' she insists. 'You know the saying. The first generation sacrifices, the second generation studies and the third generation surfs. Our kids are all going to be surfers.'

'Iranian kids don't surf,' my cousin corrects her.

Azadeh hits the nub. 'That's the point. They aren't Iranian like we were.'

She was right. Not about the surfing, that's stupid. But about the family: every single one of my cousins was born in Iran. But all of their children were born either here or in another western nation.

We are gathered at another cousin's house to see her brother and his family who have flown in from San Francisco for the summer holidays. It's a nice suburban home in inner-western Sydney. They're living the type of middle-class lifestyle to which we aspired as migrants and yet never appreciated once we achieved it.

Our children are playing, the first time that all of our internationally dispersed offspring have been together, and the conversation turns to the subject that always needs to be anatomised when our Persian families converge. The talk pours out of a question: how many times were we sacked by our parents?

My father, Naser, owned cake stores with Shahin and Mahin; one of my uncles owned bookstores; and uncle Jalal has a Persian restaurant. The network of small businesses created a sort of employment round robin for my generation. As you were fired by your parents, you went to work for an uncle or aunty somewhere else.

'I was never fired!' declares my cousin from San Francisco. 'Perhaps because I was the only person to do work.'

This was probably true. I was never an especially productive employee when I worked in my parents' small business. My time was consumed by two activities: fighting with my parents, and trying to chat up the staff of the adjacent Muffin Break chain.

My sister was fired countless times; it became a weekly occurrence. Family disputes, arguments between cousins, regular rivalries among teenagers all played their part. My cousin once splashed a glass of water in my face while we argued about the merits of the Michael Jackson trial. We were both fired for that.

All of this occurred on weekends, across a series of small businesses, in front of unsuspecting customers. In the current era, this would have made fantastic reality television.

'Do you think our kids will ever be fired?' I ask my cousin.

Before she can answer, Azadeh jumps in and drops an abrupt question. 'How can you be fired from surfing?'

Picture this rowdy tableau in about 1997. Position the protagonists not in a nice suburban home, but in the back office of one of the small family businesses. There'd be an eruption; mutual recrimination would explode; objects would be thrown, or water splashed; some sort of clamorous confrontation would carry the scene to its oft-repeated conclusion. The noise would assault the twitching ears of customers, and the boss—a parent, an uncle or an aunt—would swoop to effectuate the sackings.

We're older now, and we've mellowed. The strings of mutual forbearance have stretched; we can happily wink at the small offences that we enact against each other. And we have children; we're responsible. So I just glare, imagining a glass of water pouring over her head.

5

PERSIANS IN THE BURBS

There is a Chinese kid right now screaming at his mother. 'Why do I have to go to Chinese class on the weekend when everyone else plays soccer?' Elsewhere, a Greek kid lays down the reality to her father. 'It's just weird to have Christmas on a different day to everyone else.'

Talk to any plumber, taxi driver or tradesman; or to any kitchen hand, cleaner or manual labourer. If they are above a certain age, there is a good chance that they are migrants. Pull them aside for a few minutes, and in an exhausted tone they will tell you a variation of the same story.

'I sacrificed everything. My own dreams, my own opportunities so that I could come to this country to give my children a better future.'

And you will nod. Because you are polite. But really, you will be thinking this is boring. 'This,' you will tell yourself, 'is the same story I have heard a thousand times before.' And you have.

If you talk to their adult children, they will tell you how proud and appreciative they are of their parents' efforts. They will tell you that they have *always* felt this way. And they will be lying through their teeth.

There isn't a migrant child who, at one point, hasn't resented their parents for being the agents of *difference*. The different food that has to be eaten, the different cultural norms that have to be observed, the different identity that casts an uncomfortable spotlight—for these things, the parents are to blame.

I am reliably assured by wise souls of my parents' generation that a time awaits when my daughters will resent me. I will embarrass them, they won't want to hang out with me on Saturday night and they certainly won't want me to talk to their friends.

Being embarrassed by your parents is certainly not unique to migrant kids. But there is something about the migrant experience that makes you more susceptible to feeling isolated. And as I struggled to understand a strange culture and to find my place in the community, I blamed my parents for bringing me somewhere where I was the one who was different.

The reality is that one generation sacrifices everything and the next, sheltered by the relative safety and ease of Australian society, spends at least a part of their youth being embarrassed by their parents. For my sister and me it boiled down to a cup of coffee. Turkish coffee, to be precise.

Fortune telling using Turkish coffee: in Iran, this is a playful game; the extraction of life guidance from the muddy coffee residue is considered an amusing parlour trick. In South Penrith, around 50 kilometres west of Sydney, the interpretation inclines more to the gnomic—the coffee residue occasions mystical insights from the local gypsy. She speaks in broken English and is accoutred by odd furniture; her animated face adds a tangible atmospheric to the drama. This woman was Ella, my mother.

When Shelly from two doors down came to ask Ella which of her boyfriends was the father of her soon-to-be child, the mystic peered into her coffee cup and told her it was Dylan. This came as a shock to Chad, who had parked a motor home in our street in a bid to win her back. Chad was engaging in one so-called romantic gesture after another. And while some would think the way to win back a lover was with flowers, love letters or poetry, Chad's strategy was to blare New Kids on the Block's 'Step by Step', which, one can only assume, was 'their song'—and, for him, an anthem to be summoned whenever he was confessing his love for her. 'Dylan is better than Chad,' my mother told Shelly, this apparently obvious from the black smudge of thick coffee at the bottom of her cup. That, and the fact that everyone wanted to be rid of the motor home in the street.

Margaret was urged to leave her abusive husband, while her daughter was admonished to 'stay in school' instead of running off with her 15-year-old boyfriend. Everyone was told to stop drinking so much and, importantly, to stop sleeping with each other. All of this advice, my mother would tell them, was guided.

'How can you tell all of this from the coffee cups?' Azadeh would ask our far-seeing mother. My sister has a fine nose for smelling out a scam.

'Mostly I just let them talk for an hour while we drink coffee. Then I just advise to do what their heart wants to do anyway. They don't come here for advice. They come here to have someone to talk to.' And my mother was getting free English practice to boot.

The irony, of course, is that this wasn't my mother at all. This was a role that my mother had decided to play. To fit in, she had chosen to be different. Expecting difference, the locals found satisfaction with the exotica that Ella gave them. They would have shown little interest in a middle-class woman from Iran. They didn't care that she was one of a limited number of women who had studied engineering in Iran. Of no concern to them was her political activism—if anything, this made her sound suspicious. She was from a far-away land and they expected her to play a role. And so she did.

When they came around for coffee, she wore the outfits that one keeps for traditional events but would never wear day to day. She read them poetry in the western Iranian language of Farsi— the far-outness of which was given aromatic scaffolding by the incense that she burnt.

While our mother's difference made her a popular street identity, this did nothing to make my sister and me any more accepted. The very qualities that made the women in our street gravitate to my mother drove the other children away from us. Children aren't looking for 'different', they are looking for conformity. We were friendless while Mum became a local celebrity.

So she, realising that her children were struggling to be accepted, resolved to insert herself into the equation. Everyone loves a good story, and when you've had people try to kill you, you end up with some great ones. Hers were icebreakers that she would share with our childhood friends—regardless of how inappropriate the stories were.

When Michael from across the street came to show me his replica gun that his father had acquired (and Michael had snuck out), my mother's reaction was not to be scared or shocked, or even to wonder why anyone needed a replica pistol. Rather, she reacted by furnishing an analysis of the replica's bona fides.

'It should be cold. The barrel of the gun. Doesn't matter how hot a day it is. Unless it has been fired recently, when they put a gun to your head you just realise how cold it is. This is a bad replica. This is too warm.' It was delivered deadpan, with furrowed brow and piercing eyes. Michael stopped coming over.

Our next-door neighbour's daughter, who would visit every second Saturday, boasted that she had an uncle in jail. Mum wanted to know what his conditions were like and explained that it is rare to find someone who can withstand more than two hours of torture. She illustrated the lesson by telling the poor girl that in Iran during the revolution, when someone got picked up and put in prison you had two hours to flee. This was the kind of information that children in Western Sydney needed to know.

Then we would proceed to fry them sheep's tongue or liver or kidney, exotic foods that kept the children awake at night in fear. And, of course, other children would hear about it. The 'weirdos' with their 'weird food'; the woman who would break out into an unintelligible language and whose advice 'was responsible for

Mum kicking Dad out'. So the kids avoided us. We would go to school and come straight home. And we resented our parents for this.

'If only Mum didn't have this gift. This ability to read fortunes. Then we wouldn't have these problems,' I would tell my sister. I was too young to realise that it was all smoke and mirrors. My sister, older and worldlier, skipped the mystical middle man and just blamed our parents.

Our parents had fled a war and travelled across the world. They gave up their own careers and sacrificed everything. But because we were children—and lucky, and privileged—we didn't see that it was our culture and identity that made us who we were. We saw the taunts. We were hypersensitive to one word. *Different*—how much cultural resonance did that word contain and discharge? And we resented it.

My parents had taught themselves English before coming to Australia. They had listened to audio tapes, taken lessons and written down words on small index cards. All of which was totally useless for the day-to-day life that we were living in South Penrith. It turned out that people, in everyday conversation, don't talk about the items found in a classroom. Phrases like 'this is a blackboard' don't help when you're trying to obtain residency documents. Regardless of how clearly it's enunciated, 'Please pass the salt' won't cut the mustard with the locals when you're trying to enrol your kids in a school. And 'I like you' can be downright creepy if said in the wrong context or, as in our case, said too often.

'We are moving to South Penrith,' my father excitedly announced to my sister and me. 'We have bought a house.' At this point, the four of us were living in a single-storey apartment overlooking the railway tracks in Blacktown, around 35 kilometres west of Sydney. 'South Penrith?' I thought. I had never heard of Penrith, let alone South Penrith. 'Is that near Tehran?' I asked. It wasn't.

PERSIANS IN THE BURBS

South Penrith in the early 1990s was hardly the multicultural melting pot that it is today. This was before the influx of migrants out west, the Sydney property boom and the growth of McMansions. My parents bought in this far outer suburb of Sydney because houses there and then went cheap. Our street hosted seven houses, and all but one were single storey.

Having forgone his engineering degree in Iran, my father began doing what many migrants do when they are desperate to start making a living in a new land. He drove a taxi. And every taxi ride was an opportunity to practise English.

'Did you say you were from Iraq?' they would ask.

'No—I am from Iran,' my father would correct them. As if this made any difference to the passengers he was picking up. When you are travelling from Penrith station to Penrith Plaza, the geographical breakdown of the Middle East and the Sunni/Shia split in Islam is hardly a pressing reality. But my father felt he had given up enough of his identity by this point, and he wasn't going to let that one slide.

A successful career, a life, an identity given up so that his children could be safe. All the while my sister and I would laugh that he didn't know anything about the latest television show or the latest movie. We would whine when he'd want to listen to Persian music on the radio. And we'd beg him to stop our mother telling everyone's fortune.

When you have no money, friends or language skills you make do with what you have. And what we had was, as far as we were concerned, better than those things. We had a 1983, 13-inch Magnavox colour television. It had two separate knobs, one for changing the channels and the other for manipulating the sound.

Today, such an item would be dubbed 'retro'; back then, in 1990, our 1983 Magnavox was 'old'. But we didn't care. This was our guide to understanding the ways of the strange new land. Having come from Iran, where broadcasting is heavily censored, I was astonished by the breathlessly open quality of Australian television. It was through a daily regime of five solid hours of television that my sister and I learnt English. Sure, she went on to get a degree in English literature, study at Harvard and write a thesis on refugee law, but I'm most proud that she can still rap the entire intro to *The Fresh Prince of Bel Air*, *Degrassi Junior High* and *Heartbreak High*. Get a few drinks into her and she can perform a mashup that would make *Glee* proud.

Before *Sunrise* and *Today*, before the realisation that there was a market for morning advertising, breakfast television was the domain of children's shows. I suspect not much care or attention was placed on what was actually being broadcast in the early-morning hours. *Agro's Cartoon Connection* dominated breakfast television for much of the 1990s. Agro was a passive-aggressive puppet who, before a live audience, tormented his fellow host Ann-Maree Biggar. In today's world, he'd have gone down for workplace harassment. To amuse himself, Agro would engage in inappropriate commentary that clearly was not intended for the children.

But the kids thought it was sensational. And while many of the jokes would be lost on us, we knew that there was something naughty, something devious, about this puppet in need of a wash.

Recently, the puppeteer who played Agro, Jamie Dunn, explained, 'Everyone used to think I was touching her [Ann-Maree Biggar] up under the desk'. That he felt the need to explain this, perhaps, says more than enough. In recent years, Agro and his puppeteer have been going around the country doing their own 'adults-only show'. You could say that they've finally found an appropriate audience.

The afternoon's television regimen was more free flowing. We would watch anything that was on television from our arrival home at 3:15 until sleep time. And we watched with a passion and focus that we would never apply to our schooling, so desperate were we to learn and to emulate.

'The TV used to get so hot,' Azadeh reminds me, 'that we had to put ice packs on it to stop it short circuiting.'

From the American sitcoms we learnt about western culture. *Cheers, Family Ties, Fresh Prince, I Dream of Jeannie* and *M*A*S*H*: these shows had done the prime-time rounds and were now played in the afternoons. From the game shows like *Vidiot, A*mazing* and *Sale of the Century* we learnt Australian trivia. Spelling and fashion was assisted by *Wheel of Fortune*. We were inducted into Australian identity through *Heartbreak High, Around the Twist* and a steady supply of ABC Australian children's programming. But all of these were interchangeable. *Degrassi Junior High* was not.

I learnt more from watching five seasons of a dysfunctional Canadian school than I ever learnt from my own primary- and lower-high-school experiences.

The greatness of this 1980s television masterpiece was evident from the very first episode. This was the election episode. I didn't know what 'all the way with Stephanie Kaye' actually meant in 1990. But that was the campaign slogan an election candidate was prepared to endorse when she ran on a platform of kissing boys for votes. A lesser show would have wheeled out moral platitudes and made sure that the naughty girl got her just desserts. But this was Degrassi, and in Degrassi she wins the election—for the sole reason that she went dirty.

The Australian classics *Home and Away* and *Neighbours* were the shows that we really wanted to watch. Here was heaven on earth—beautiful bodies abounded, everyone was accepted, no one 'spoke funny' and problems would be resolved. You could watch the episodes and be taken in your fond imaginings to a place where 'difference' didn't get in the way of living.

'My biggest gripe with our parents,' my sister growls, 'is that they would come home before *Home and Away* finished and wanted to watch the ABC news.'

I agreed. 'As if you can learn anything from that.'

Within our street, people were having affairs and going through divorces; were inflicting and suffering family violence; and were getting pregnant, even as teenagers. But we were excluded from all that. So we would stay in our television world, where we were accepted. We could then leave the real-life dramas to our mother and her Turkish coffee smudges.

'They said he was gifted. He's very gifted, you know.' That was how my mother explained to my father that I had been asked to repeat the fourth grade. I know this because, in what could be described as a bid to totally humiliate me, I was asked to be there at the meeting with the principal.

It was strange, taking the note home with the request that my mother come to the school. I spent days wondering what I had done. I wasn't an *anything* kid—no labels on me. I was certainly not a troublemaker; that would come later. We had moved from South Penrith to Castle Hill, a suburb in north-western Sydney. My parents had purchased a small business in the local shopping centre.

That was the second time my mother had been asked to meet with a school principal. The first was in my first year of school.

'Mrs Dastyari, we are worried about your son. He comes to class and just sleeps on the floor all day,' she is told.

'Yes,' my mother responds. 'He doesn't speak a word of English. What do you expect him to do? I'd be sleeping too.'

On the second occasion, the opening line to her is more ominous; its tone is premonitory, soaked in intent. 'Your son, Mrs Dastyari, is very gifted. He just seems unable to apply himself. He's not very well adjusted. We think it would be best if you considered that he repeat the year. He's quite young. It would do him a world of good.'

The principal turned to me and said, as slowly as he could and in a tone that summarised what he thought of my intellectual abilities, 'DO YOU UNDERSTAND WHAT THAT MEANS?' I knew exactly what it meant: total and absolute humiliation.

'Don't you have to be functionally illiterate to repeat the fourth grade?' Azadeh helpfully chimed in at home that night. 'It's the fourth grade. Don't you pass just by knowing your colours?' She then proceeded to hold up pencils. 'This is yellow. This is red.' She was in the seventh grade by then and on scholarship at the Conservatorium High School, training to be a professional classical guitarist. By this stage our lives had decoupled. My sister was going from strength to strength, and I was going back to the fourth grade.

To add insult to injury, I was moved into the same class as some of the students who had progressed to the fifth grade—it was a composite class—so that all of my old friends could see that I was now no longer in their year. The brutality.

'You know, you are not very good at this whole "school" business, are you?' asks my high-school principal, Tony Fugaccia, rhetorically. It is three weeks before my final school exams and he is addressing the pesky problem of my close-to-100 unexplained school absences. 'I'm coming under a fair bit of heat from the regional office of the Department of Education about your attendance. You have the single worst attendance record of anyone, ever, trying to graduate from Baulkham Hills High School.'

The problem is my marks—not that they are bad, but that they are good. If my marks were bad, I would simply have been expelled. He now has a different problem.

'And why exactly,' he asks, 'can't your parents be at this meeting?' Which is a fair question. We are working out a strategy to keep me from getting kicked out of school.

'They are travelling in Cuba,' I respond. I want to tell him the whole truth, that they are in Cuba to learn about the pure form of socialism. But that would have been self-indulgent and he wouldn't have understood that it is a joke.

'And when will they be back?'

'After the Year 12 exams are over.' Sensing his horror, I work in a mitigating addendum. 'I get more study done when they aren't around.'

'Any siblings?'

'One. She's in Amsterdam.' I want to tell him the whole truth, that she is in Amsterdam to learn about the pure form of marijuana, but again, the joke would have been lost on him.

'Right, so you are living by yourself?'

'Well not really, all my friends are pretty much there all of the time. Look, Tony …'

'Please call me Mr Fugaccia.'

'Mr Fugaccia, I can't see the problem. I come to school most days. I just don't go to class. I'm here pretty much every lunchtime. I just teach myself. I don't fit in a classroom environment.'

'Yes, I can see that. I just worry that you don't quite "fit" anywhere.'

Recently, I spoke with Tony Fugaccia, and he said to me, 'You frustrated the hell out of me when you were at school, with your lack of focus and attendance'. To his credit, he did talk the regional office of the Department of Education into letting me graduate.

But he never did accept the Cuban cigar I gave him after the completion of my Year 12 exams. Nevertheless, he was interested to know what my future might hold.

'So what are you going to do?'

'Politics.'

'Yes. Well, your desire to do that is pretty clear. You spend more time at the Labor Party offices at Sussex Street than you do at school. But what are you going to study at university?'

'I've been accepted into medicine and law. I think I'll do law.'

'You know you'll have to show up?'

'I'll be fine,' I tell him.

'One day you won't,' he admonishes.

Sixteen years later, at Senate estimates, I ask the former dean of the Sydney University Law School, Gillian Triggs, then the human rights commissioner, why she had kicked me out of Sydney University Law School for the sole transgression of not showing up for a decade. She laughed and said she would take it on notice.

'Hang on, your parents just moved to Cuba during your last year of school?' My friends now ask this, trying to make some sense out of what, to them, seems completely bizarre behaviour.

The truth is that my parents didn't just move to Cuba. Cuba was the start. They backpacked through all of Asia, travelled the Silk Road and have been to pretty much every country in the world that doesn't have functioning five-star hotels.

And while this never made sense outside our family, to us it was rational. For a huge chunk of their lives, they played a role. They became people they never intended to be. They travelled across the world to Australia; lived a suburban existence; ran a small business; protected my sister and me. They did all these things to get us up and running. And when they realised that we were fine on our own two feet, they let us go.

Now, as a more secure (and some would say overly confident) adult, I can very honestly say that I am so proud of my parents and appreciate their sacrifices to give me the life that I have. Not just because I know I should say that, but because it is true. I regret how I felt about them, at times, while growing up. I regret being embarrassed by being different, and I now know how much that must have hurt them. It took me a long time to be proud of my Iranian heritage. I proudly send Hannah to school with posters about Persian New Year and take people to my uncle Jalal's Persian restaurant. From time to time after family dinner, I will even request that my mother make Turkish coffee.

In his speech at our wedding in 2010, my father-in-law, Peter Barron—who is well known in political circles for his ability to craft a world-class line—said this, to raucous cheering from the

Dastyari contingent: 'Who would have thought that at age sixty I'd be lucky enough to become just a little bit Persian?' The truth is, I haven't always been 'Snack Pack Sam'. It took me a long time to admit that, despite very much growing up as an Australian, I'm just a little bit Persian too.

6
LAYLA

He sits behind his computer in London. It could be an iPad, or a laptop or a phone. But I decide to picture him sitting behind a desktop computer. He is in his early thirties and from the same part of Iran as me. I have never met him. I doubt I will. But since we left Iran at around the same age, London being his destination and Sydney mine, I imagine that our experiences are not too dissimilar. But that is just guesswork.

Having befriended on Facebook some lost friends of his mother, he finds a post praising his deceased mum. It's been three years since she died, and while the occasional post still pops up on her birthday or to mark her passing, this post doesn't fit that pattern. So he reads it.

At first there is nothing too alarming. The post outlines what a great woman she was, how kind and caring. But then it goes on to explain the murders for which her mother-in-law (his grandmother) was responsible during the aftermath of the Iranian Revolution. He starts reading that his own relatives who passed away, spoken of glowingly in family circles, were killed because his grandmother had reported them to the Revolutionary Guard, and that his mother was the one who stepped in to put a stop to the killing. All of this is new to him—family secrets that had been left behind in Iran. Buried a lifetime ago. He tracks down the number of one of those who posted, picks up the phone and calls Australia.

'You should go and see your mother,' my father calls to tell me in 2016. 'She has been crying all week.'

'Crying all week? What about?' My head raced through the many things I had done that would warrant that response from my mother. Frankly, the list is long. My initial assumption whenever Mum is upset is that it is my fault. Azadeh often reminds me that it usually is.

'Facebook,' Dad responds.

I've had my frustrations with Facebook—I'm not alone there. But crying? Geez. Surely that's a bit overblown.

'Facebook?' I ask my sister.

'Yeah, she hasn't slept in a week.'

'Facebook? I barely knew Mum was on it. Did some troll come after her or something?'

'No. Layla died. She's distraught.'

Who, I wonder, is Layla? Because, except for the Eric Clapton smash hit, that name leaves a blank. Before I can ask, Azadeh jumps in. 'Her best friend from school.'

I consider myself pretty close to my mother and I have never heard of Layla before. I find out that neither had my sister.

'She died in 2013,' my sister adds. 'Mum just found out.'

'Have we met her?'

'No. Mum apparently last saw her in 1981.'

Now I'm a bit shitty because I decide that all of this is getting ridiculous. Mum has been crying all week over the death of someone three years ago with whom she lost contact in 1981. If this is someone you care about and are close to, why, in over thirty years, haven't we had anything to do with them? And if you don't know that someone has been dead for three years, why would you spend a week crying over it?

The answer, I find out, is because life is complicated. We all have people who have shaped us and left: friends, ex-lovers, estranged family, perhaps even a former spouse. And while these people are no longer in our lives, that doesn't change the impact they have had on us. It takes a very human occurrence, like a death, to stir up those emotions. That, and Facebook.

I arrive at my parents' place to find Mum in her bed. Her hair is blonde again. It's gone through the cycles. I've seen it red, black, brown and even with a purple fringe. She's tired. She looks like she hasn't slept. Bringing my two daughters to see her was probably a mistake. No one sleeps while they are around.

For those who were political activists in revolutionary Iran, everything has a tinge of the dramatic. My friends and I fall out because of invitations to parties, drunken slurs and perceived slights. My mother and Layla fell out because, as my mother puts it, 'We were in different factions and when the executions started it wasn't safe to stay friends'.

I realise that there is more to this story than I had bargained for, so I ask my mother to start at the beginning.

Layla was born in the small town of Gorgan in northern Iran, near the Caspian Sea. Gorgan is an ancient town, a place where history stopped in the thirteenth century when the great Persian kings succumbed to the Mongol invaders. Her town and the town of my mother were about 130 kilometres apart. Layla and Ella knew each other a lifetime ago, in a different Iran, before a generation of Iranians became political activists choosing sides between the king and others, and then later between the Islamists and the lefties. This place no longer exists.

In the Iran of the 1970s, if you wanted a decent education you left your town and went to Tehran, the capital, for your final few years of schooling—only, of course, if you could afford it. This opportunity was restricted to the privileged few. The education available in the small towns left a lot to be desired, particularly for women. The rights of women in that Iran were as progressive as anywhere in the Middle East, though, I stress, this could only be said of urbanised Iran. So if you lived in the rural areas and you had the means to learn, you moved. My mother went to Tehran for her final three years, Layla for her final six. Tehran was around 240 kilometres away from Gorgan, and the mighty Alborz Mountains made the route between the capital and the north both difficult and dangerous.

Layla had big eyes. She had an athletic build, and her long black hair was tied, conservatively, behind her head. She possessed the height of the star volleyball player—which is what she was—but without the lanky awkwardness that often goes with it. By Persian standards, her skin was light, a giveaway that she came from the north of Iran.

The Tehran of the early 1970s was a cosmopolitan metropolis, more like Istanbul than the city it has since become. The 'school of fire', as it was known, was situated in the middle of Tehran. This concrete monolith housed girls uniformed in dreary grey. The headmistress was constantly measuring the lengths of the uniforms, lest the good pious girls of the school try to modify their garments to impress the boys. Not that any of the latter attended this prestigious all-girls school.

They met on my mother's first day of school. 'She only sat with me on that first day because she had fallen out with her friends. They had rejected her. So she sat with me, the very new girl. The girl from the village who was still an outsider in Tehran.'

Layla's family wasn't religious back then. And neither was she. Her six brothers and sisters had moved to Tehran in order to get the education that their family wanted for them. Their mother moved with them, while their father, the town doctor in Gorgan, stayed home.

Ella spent every day with Layla. Every afternoon after school, along with every holiday and weekend—the two were just about inseparable. They talked of what girls that age talk about: clothes, people and, above all, boys. And Ella knew the secret that no others did. The maths tutor her mother had organised for Layla—the nice, quiet, religious boy, the older one from the university—was secretly her boyfriend.

'You have to understand how sheltered we all were. A young man, a university student too … coming to her house every day … that was a huge event.'

'Did people have sex with their partners in Iran back then? I assume they did, but is that what happened?' I ask my mother, forgetting whom I'm speaking to.

'There are things you don't ask your mother.' Apparently it's OK to ask about executions, but sex before marriage remains taboo.

Layla was in love in the way that only teenagers can be. Such was the innocence of her love that it could erase the real—ignore the fact that the boy came from an extremely religious fundamentalist family. They were supporters of Ayatollah Khomeini, the then exiled cleric with a long beard and a big future. Layla loved with such need that she could change who she was. She adopted his faith, his religious fervour, his devotion.

And so their paths began to diverge. My mother went to university to become a radical, an activist. Layla went to university to pursue her love, and was drawn deeper and deeper into religion. With the coming of revolution in 1979, you were on a side. You were either on the side of the king or on the side of the revolutionaries. But that was not when the real blood was shed; the removal of the king was the relatively painless part. It was the fight for control, between the Islamist factions and the student radicals, that spawned the real horror.

Teams of rival militias sprouted, killing on a whim. A Revolutionary Guard emerged. My mother will list the names of her friends who were executed. She will tell me stories about each of them, and this will go on well into the night. In her words, I can hear the flowing tide of the dead.

Layla was not on the side of my mother, or so my mother believed, and this made such friendships dangerous—dangerous for all involved. 'She came to my wedding,' Mum tells me, 'she was my only friend from school who did.' But this was still before 1979, before the Ayatollah's consolidation of power and the massive bloodletting.

It was in May 1981 that they last saw each other, in Tehran after the revolution. Layla, holding her daughter's hand, showed up at Ella's door. Layla's daughter was two years old and named Azadeh; with my sister she shared both name and age. Both were named after the Farsi word for 'freedom' to mark the revolution; my sister was given this name in the hope that the revolution would bring democracy and peace, Layla's daughter in the hope that it would restore Iran to Islamic roots. In her left hand, Layla held the veil that covered her face. Not the simple scarf that my mother would wear now that the law dictated it, not the Arabic hijab, but the Persian-style sheet, long and black, that is held around the face under the neck and has to be constantly adjusted.

My mother noticed that she looked much older than the twenty-four years of age that she would have been then. She was panting.

Mum spoke animatedly of Layla's physical state. 'I remember the panting. Out of breath. Exhausted. Her once excited eyes, soggy. Dreary with pain. With nights crying. She was searching and she breathed easier when she saw me. After so many years of searching.'

'For what?' I ask.

'For peace. For closure. For hope. For those things we all searched for when we were surrounded by death.'

In a low voice, Layla said to my mother, 'Help me … I can't sleep at nights, I have to do something. You have to do something.'

My mother didn't respond. Layla asked again for help. A dilemma had been posed that required judicious consideration. Mum's friends had been killed. The Laylas of the world shouldn't be trusted. They were lures, and the regime used them to catch you.

But Mum could see the pain in her eyes. This wasn't just any religious activist; this was her friend. And she trusted her.

'Without giving me time to ask any questions she took me to the closest pay phone and started dialling a number.' Her daughter all the while retained the look of calm of a child who is used to being dragged around.

'I need you to tell this man what I tell you,' she said, as the dial spun around the way they did on old phones. 'I need you to do it in the Turkish dialect of the far north. The one you learnt at university. It *cannot* have come from me, nor be traced to me. If you do it in Turkish, he will not think it came from me.'

And so my mother complies. She holds the phone and a man answers. She just starts repeating what Layla tells her to say, translating it into Turkish.

'They are coming for your third son. They know where he is. They will kill him tonight. Get him out of Iran. The same woman who reported your other two sons knows where this one is. He will be killed like they were.'

The man goes quiet on the phone and simply asks one question. 'Who is the woman? Who reported my sons?' And my mother responds with a name she is given by Layla, a name she knows. Layla's mother-in-law.

'But it cannot be her. She is my family,' he responds.

My mother gave the same name and hung up. The call had already gone for too long. They were in public. Who knows who was listening. It was too dangerous.

Layla was shaking. She could barely hold herself up. And my mother was angry, for there had been no call when they came for her friends. She was angry at that, and at all the bloodshed and the pain and the memories she knew would haunt her for the rest of her days.

Layla turned around and walked away. They didn't speak. Layla didn't give an explanation. She didn't need to. The last image my mother has of her is her walking away, holding her daughter's hand in one hand and fixing her veil with the other.

And so for thirty years they parted ways. Both would leave Iran, Mum for Australia and Layla for London. Contact was lost. Ella didn't know that Layla's daughter would grow up in the west, nor that Layla would have a son the same age as her son, nor that they would both contract breast cancer in the same year, nor that the cancer would kill Layla.

And, for years, she wouldn't know. Also unknown to Mum is that Layla had left a message for her on her Facebook page. A message from the past, a second cry for help. The post remains, sitting there, in a sea of messages. 'I wish to hear your voice,' Layla writes. 'Unfortunately I stopped working last year as I became sick, and I am under heavy treatment. God knows what will happen to me, please pray for me. I think it is enough for now … Please answer quickly.'

But this was no longer 1981. And this wasn't Iran. The message went unanswered. Unread.

It was Mum who discovered that Layla had died. Tracking down her Facebook page through friends, Ella found the message that had been left for her. She contacted the dead woman's son, and he told her of the cancer.

And so my mother writes a post, setting down the story of Layla she had held for all these years. She writes about the friend whom she has lost. Hers is the voice of one mourning over priceless losses. The revolution took so much that was unspeakably dear, so that even in the living there is a part of them that will always be dead.

The son contacts her. He has never heard the story of his grandmother, nor understood why his mother was so keen to get out of Iran. He knew that secrets had been kept, histories put aside. And he says to my mother, 'The same blood, the blood of the person who killed her own family, my grandmother. That blood runs through me'. And my mother responds, 'There was a lot of killing then. There was a lot of pain. That wasn't remarkable. What was remarkable was what your mother did. That is the blood that runs through you'.

And with that, Ella pictures Layla again, not as the desperate fugitive adjusting her veil, but as the young girl at the table with the fair skin. The tall volleyball player. The outsider, like my mother, from the small town.

7

A NAME FOR A PLACE

'You don't seriously still want to name our daughter Trudy or Martha, *do* you?' Helen is playfully laying down the law of baby nomenclature as we drive to the hospital to give birth. 'This is not the 1930s and you are terrible at names. We have decided on Hannah and we are sticking with it.'

When Helen was pregnant with Hannah, I wanted a good, solid, old-fashioned name likely to come back into style in the future. My friends laughed at me for my ridiculous taste and at the distinct possibility that I would name my child after a cartoon duck (this was before 'Donald' was the name of a US president). As for a 'Persian name', well, there was too much baggage for me to go with one of them.

I've always had a funny relationship with names. Names, at core, are fictive things. Someone, at some point, engages the imagination, picks out a name and pins it on you, and perhaps your ancestral kindred have been passing it on, in generational succession, for hundreds of years. Not so in my case—at least, not the 'hundreds of years' bit.

I was born Sahand Dastyari and only officially changed it to 'Sam' long after we came to Australia. My grandfather invented the surname 'Dastyari', so really the whole thing is made up.

'Dastyari? You want to be called "Dastyari"—isn't that a little bit weird?' So asks the public official, who is quizzing my grandfather, in the family story that has been passed down to all of us.

'It means "a helping hand".' My grandfather had his reasons.

'I know what it means. It's just a very odd name.'

In the first decades of the twentieth century, Iran introduced ID cards. Rather than adopting the traditional method of naming people by patronym or by place name, the country gave its men the opportunity to pick their own surnames. Here was a rarely made journey into mass invention—millions of fictive acts, officially endorsed, on a national scale—and, what is more, undertaken for the sake of no trifling matter. Names are powerful things in Iranian culture. A name defines you. And for a people enchanted by words and poetry, this opportunity to define their legacy and shape their people was met with enthusiasm.

My grandfather walked to the ID office with a clear idea of what he wanted from himself and his yet unborn offspring. The names that his friends bestowed upon themselves were redolent of prosperity and affluence, but my grandfather picked something very different for us. *Dastyari*—'a helping hand'. Tasked with defining his hopes, aspirations and desires for himself and everyone who would follow him, my grandfather picked generosity and giving. He wanted his people to be the helpers and the carers.

My parents named me 'Sahand' after the mountain in Iran. This was a name, I thought, that reflected my parents' desire for me to be strong and steadfast.

At ten, however, I was told by Azadeh that she had heard from our cousins that I was named 'Sahand' because that was where I was conceived.

'On a mountain?' I demanded to know from my elder sister. My understanding of child-making was sketchy at best.

'They were hippies, you know. Everyone was doing it on mountains back then.' This is how my older, wiser, 14-year-old sister supplied the context of my conception.

And while I've subsequently become aware of the faultiness of my sister's contextual backfill, she left me with an image, and a set of associations, that I can't shake. To this day I still won't climb a mountain.

Azadeh is the Persian word for 'freedom'. My sister was born in the year of the Iranian Revolution (1979), and every girl born in that year in Iran seems to bear that name. You are, however, unlikely to find too many Azadehs before or after the revolution. The word is potently reflective of a national tragedy.

It turned out that it was my sister who was conceived on a mountain. This was a collective discovery—beans spilt by my father in the speech that he gave at her wedding. 'The blue of Azadeh's eyes are the blue of the river below the mountain she was conceived on,' my father intoned, poetically. This was a worrying story—not only because it was more information than anyone required, but also because her eyes are in fact brown.

I became 'Sam' so that I could fit in and belong. It's the same reason why so many migrants change their names. Azadeh became 'Az', my uncle Jalal became 'Jim', Behrooz became 'Barry' and Khosrow became 'Bill' (no one can explain that one).

'Oh but Sahand is such a beautiful name. It's so different, why would you change it?' It is the question that I have been asked for years. Always from someone of Anglo or European heritage who considers the whole thing 'exotic'. I don't begrudge them the question, but the fact that the name is *different* is precisely why I was so desperate for it to change. The same person invariably points to Barack Obama, saying 'well he had a funny name', and I point out that he grew up calling himself 'Barry'.

This tendency holds fast, even in a context in which a quarter of Australians are not born in this country. Don't we all know a Chinese Australian called 'Michael', 'Winston', 'Kendrick' or 'Pinky'?

Does any of this actually make a difference? Do I belong more because I have a name that you can pronounce? Does that change who I am?

My sister believes that Sahand and Sam are completely different people. Sahand was her younger brother, the kid of the family who used to joke around, play with her toys and cry uncontrollably at the sight of a spider. Sam is the politician, at times obsessive and, as she puts it, 'a bit of an arsehole'.

'I think I liked Sahand as a person more than Sam,' she tells me. Which is a pretty fucked thing to say when you think about it. And so I told her.

'That's a pretty fucked thing to say,' I tell her.

'Yeah. That's the kind of response Sam would give; Sahand would have found it funny.' That is what passes in my family as checkmate.

And so, while I have anglicised my name for the sake of a misguided view of fitting in, I've gone way too far in the other direction when naming my pets.

We are 'those' people. The strange neighbours with far too many pets. I'm making a special effort to befriend a new neighbour down the street—firstly because she is really nice and secondly because she is dating a veterinarian, and that's a connection I'm going to need.

I was out of phone reception for a total of three hours before Helen used the opportunity to buy a bunny and a guinea pig for our daughters. Hannah (my five year old) and Eloise (who is three) had both expressed their desire for new pets for only about a week. Helen and I had agreed that it would be crazy to add yet more animals to our present menagerie, comprising two dogs, two cats and a hermit crab. We agreed to stay strong. We were on the same page, completely united. Until Eloise, pausing momentarily at the pet-shop window on the way to buy shoes, declared, 'That's Peter Rabbit and I love him, mummy, and you shouldn't leave anyone you love behind'. Helen caved.

I had no part in this decision. I was out of range, caught behind a bushfire driving up the Pacific Highway and uncontactable. This does nothing for my paranoia regarding what happens when I don't have my mobile phone with me.

'But I tried to call you,' Helen insists.

'I should have been consulted,' I reply.

'Like when you got Sasha?' Helen replies. 'When was I consulted about that?'

Helen had a point. On the night before we moved in together, in August 2008, I surprised her by bringing home a Siberian Husky I purchased from the *Trading Post* that afternoon. The owner claimed that it was a purebred and promised to mail the papers. The papers still haven't arrived and his number has now changed.

That Helen didn't leave me then and there was a pretty telling sign that there was something special in this relationship. I'm told that I've now tested that threshold countless times.

'And the girls are naming them!' Helen got this in quickly; she had learnt from experience. That's why our bunny is called 'Peter Rabbit Vanessa' and the guinea pig is 'Fluffy Rosie'. I would have called them 'Nixon' and 'Reagan'.

I had never wanted to name my Siberian Husky 'Sasha'. Frankly, it is not a Siberian Husky name—I had wanted to name her 'Gorbachev'.

'What kind of a name is that?' Helen demands. 'I'm not going to let you name our dog after a Soviet leader. I can't very well yell for "Gorbachev" at the park, can I?'

'It's a Siberian name,' I persist—'a "HUSKY" name.'

I lost the argument not because I conceded, but because I was too disorganised to complete the registration papers and Helen is a paperwork savant.

It is hardly surprising that Helen and I keep accumulating animals. Our courtship involved 'rescuing' stray cats behind a take-away Thai restaurant in the Sydney suburb of Concord. After dinner one night we spotted a large group of stray kittens, with no sign of the mother cat, in a back alley. I vowed to Helen that I would save them all. But first the little creatures needed to be taken into domestic captivity.

At first, we attempted the task without wearing gloves and simply used cat food and kind words. On the first night, Helen was able to coax a kitten to come to her, but it proceeded to attack her and got away. While she bandaged her hand that night, I named the lost kitten 'Putin', mostly as payback for being denied the name 'Gorbachev'; and sticking with my theme, I decided that I would go back alone and catch it for her. I failed miserably. It seems that my pacing up and down loudly making phone calls was not appealing to kittens.

A week later we successfully rescued our first kitten, which I named 'Lenin'. Helen never agreed to this name, but I was persistent and planned to wear her down with wit and charm. When that failed I used my next strategy and was belligerent about the whole thing.

This poor tiny kitten was so traumatised by the whole experience that we decided to get him an already 'rescued' friend from the RSPCA. I named him 'Trotsky'.

'Lenin' and 'Trotsky' played together, shared their food and were the best of friends. It was a socialist utopia. Naturally, I had to ruin it by surprising Helen with a third kitten. When 'Chairman Mao' arrived, all hell broke loose. While I have no proof, I stand by the supposition that 'Chairman Mao' orchestrated the sudden unexplained deaths of both our other beloved furry comrades.

'Oh you can't blame Mao,' Helen retorted. 'She's just a cute kitten. She couldn't have caused Trotsky's heart attack, and the vet said Lenin had problems from being a street cat.'

As far as I was concerned, Helen was just making excuses. I knew we had a feline serial killer in our midst and I resolved never to get another cat to add to Mao's kill count. This was a firm, principled position. I was able to sustain it for a week.

'I rescued another cat,' Helen called from the car. 'The vet down the road had a sign. So I had to stop. You can name her—but stop naming our cats after communist leaders. It's weird.'

That's how we got 'Margaret Thatcher' (or 'Maggie').

Maggie and Mao are not on speaking terms. Maggie has decided (perhaps wisely) that she wants nothing to do with Mao, which I feel is best.

'You are turning into Dad,' my sister winces, after I explain the complicated communist naming system I have for our cats. 'Remember how he used to insist on naming our pets, and messed it up every time?

Once we'd settled in Penrith, my father decided that we should get a dog, mainly because everyone else in our street had one.

Ethnic parents have no business raising pets, let alone naming them. In the town in Iran from which we came, stray cats litter the streets and dogs are either chased out of town or killed. Our father, to this point, had never actually patted, let alone owned, a dog. It showed.

'I'll get us a dog,' my dad announced to the family over dinner one night. My sister and I could not have been more excited. I was expecting a small, fluffy dog, perhaps a terrier or even a rough collie like Lassie. Dog ownership was going to be our ticket into this new society.

But we were new to this country and had no money, so when there was an offer for a free puppy from a neighbour, it was too good to refuse. And even though that same neighbour was rumoured to be awaiting trial, a free puppy is a free puppy.

We shared our back corner fence with Theo, whose pit bull had been impregnated by a stray. He claimed that the pups from the litter were destroying his property, though there was no evidence that the dogs had done any damage to the pile of rocks that constituted his yard. That his dog's claim to fame was being 'undefeated' in an underground dog-fighting ring should have sounded alarm bells. All I knew was that we were getting the pup of a 'champion' dog.

While the pup's father was unknown, I suspect that he was a hyena. This was not the first dog anyone should have. It probably wasn't a dog *anyone* should have at all. The only thing more inappropriate than the dog was my father's choice of name. He called our puppy 'Mishy'. Mishy is the Persian name for something that is rust coloured. This was the dog's natural coat colour, and it was visible only in the thin moments that fleeted between our washing him daily and his rolling around in his own faeces. I considered the name 'cute' until, in my twenties, I learnt that 'Mishy' is urban slang for something that is both 'Mushy' (as in caring) and 'Horny' (as in horny).

My goal was to use Mishy to facilitate my own acceptance by the kids in the street. I would use my puppy as a conversation starter. I would say things like, 'Oh, how about Mishy comes over for a play date'. Alas.

While Mishy was readily accepted by the kids (and dogs) in our street, I still was not. Mishy, it turned out, fitted right in, probably because he was a blood relative of many of the other pets in the street. Theo, we discovered, had been giving everyone free puppies for years. As Mishy morphed from puppy into dog, he began to realise that our poor social skills were cramping his opportunities, and he set himself the goal of escaping our family. And at that, he succeeded.

After the failure of the dog-ownership experiment, the fading of the posters and the non-finding of our 'lost dog' that never wanted to be found, Dad decided that we weren't 'dog people'. So we got a cat, which Dad named 'Pissy'.

'Pissy' is the sound that Iranian migrants apparently think a cat makes when it hisses, but unfortunately it was also the action that our new cat kept performing on our beds, couches or wherever he felt like it. While it would have been hard enough to explain to my friends, if I had any, that my cat was called 'Pissy', the urine stench in and of itself would have caused the unfriending of any such hypothetical friends.

'You know, if you put pinecones on your couch the cat will stop peeing on it,' was the advice that a neighbour gave us. And that is how my sister and I secured our unasked-for commission to source pinecones, which one can safely assume are not native to Penrith. The pinecone-spreading plan had the added disadvantage of not actually working.

'I'm nothing like Dad,' I finally correct my sister. I resort to this insipidity after she accurately lists around a dozen characteristics that make me exactly like him.

'If you name your cat after communist dictators, why would you be surprised when they turn on each other and create their own fight club?' Azadeh asks, accusingly.

Was she right? Was Chairman Mao conducting her own cultural revolution in our house? And did Putin attack Helen because we named it 'Putin', or were these just badass cats and the others were destined to die anyway?

I still don't know the answers. But Helen has made me promise that I will never name one of our cats 'Stalin'. She fears for the children.

III
THE CHEESE

8

MIDDLE CLASS ON DODGY WHEELS

There are times when I truly embrace my Iranian heritage and fit the stereotypes of a Middle Eastern man. I love kebabs, I can eat buckets of fetta if given the chance and my favourite beverage is *doogh*—a yogurt drink with salt and water described by a friend as 'possessing a taste equivalent to that of the bubonic plague'.

Where I let down my heritage, however, is with cars. I know next to nothing about these machines that can make some grown men and women weep. I suspect that I'm impressed by the wrong things. I will, for example, get very enthusiastic about your novelty dice car hanger, but tune out when you describe the engine. This is not my fault. Like most things in life, I am the product of my upbringing.

My parents know a lot about many things. They will never let you down if you have a question about avant-garde Italian film directors of the 1960s or need to answer a trivia question about the writings of Gabriel García Márquez. What they don't know about is *cars*. I suspect that they too are impressed by the wrong things.

It was during our second year in Australia that my father bought the family our first car. It was during the fifteenth year in Australia that he bought our second. During those thirteen years we lived the ultimate Australian car dream, if by dream you mean getting into heavy debt to buy an American-designed motor vehicle.

There was perhaps no greater sign of our acceptance into this country than that—though we had little to no income, and though interest rates were elbowing 30 per cent—the fine financial institutions of this great southern land were prepared to give my father $30 000 to buy a brand-new silver 1990 EA-series Ford Falcon GL, with air conditioning and luxury tape deck.

'Can you feel that?' my dad would enthuse, with the air conditioning at full blast.

'What?'

'CAN YOU FEEL THAT—THE AIR?'

'OH YEAH!' my sister and I would screech, struggling to be heard over the bloody racket being made by the air conditioning.

Yes, we could feel it—the glorious feeling of middle-class debt, and, having crossed the seas to be here, we were hell bent on embracing every moment and every manifestation of it. To us, the Falcon was the epitome of class, every bit as smooth and sexy as the Bentleys, BMWs and Cadillacs driven by the cast of our beloved *Beverly Hills 90210*.

Our car was silver and therefore—to us—fancy. It goes without saying that a gold car would have been an even bigger indicator of our rising status, not unlike gold teeth grills. Maybe silver was even better. All our life we had been warned about making people jealous—warned to beware the evil eye. Surely a gold car would have tempted fate.

The car was treated like the high-performance off-terrain vehicle that it wasn't. Creek up ahead? Sure, the Falcon can do that. Sand dunes? Send in the Falcon. Why waste money hiring a car for the school formal? We wanted our Falcon.

While the Falcon was known to others for its bad suspension and a dodgy paint job, we would hear none of it.

Over the years, that car saw it all. It was reliably there for the 5:00 a.m. starts at the small business, easing the passage while Mum, half-asleep, applied her make-up—a high-stakes daily thrill, as any small bump in the road could have led the mascara to cause permanent eye damage. The Falcon, in short, heralded our entry into middle-class Australia. Even when he could afford it, my father refused to replace it. And we didn't want him to.

During its last days, the car's bumper was held together by rope. There is no question that it wanted to die. It had had enough. We, however, loved it too much to let it pass gracefully into vehicular paradise; like families who can't bear to euthanise their obviously pained animals, we could not say goodbye. Sometimes in nature, other animals will attack an animal that is suffering, thereby putting it out of its misery—I'm sure David Attenborough explained that somewhere. Perhaps a similar force was operative when our car, stationary and lacking means to defend itself, was hit by another vehicle. So it took the trauma of a collision to convince us to let the decrepit Falcon rest, at last, in peace. The car's final retirement for $300 at a scrap yard led to a period of mourning and a longer—unfinished—period of remembering.

After the Falcon, the car in which I spent the most amount of time in my youth belonged to my close friend Prue Car—until I was accused of burning it down.

In a bid to become independent, Prue had purchased a late '90s model red Saab, which was exactly the kind of car you would not expect her to have. As far as status symbols went, this was it, something to which Prue was completely oblivious. The leather seats were more akin to those you'd see in a car doing laps around the Parramatta city square, with on-board teenagers discharging crude remarks through a window in a misguided view that this is how one woos the opposite sex. My life experiences can attest to the fact that this is an ineffective strategy.

Prue had chosen the car for its safety profile, but when you max out at 40 kilometres per hour a high-speed collision is the last of your concerns. The bigger worry for Prue was always that a passenger would do their nut during the course of one of her four-hour daily commutes and strangle her at that point at which frustration, having devolved into and beyond annoyance, surrenders to delirium and hysteria. I know, I've been there.

Prue was (and remains) the second worst driver I have ever known. Her only redeeming driving feature was that, unlike me, she was aware of her own driving limitations. Well past her thirtieth birthday she would drive the entire way from the Penrith satellite suburbs of Western Sydney to the CBD without changing lanes. So if she found herself behind a truck, you could add another half-hour to the trip. 'Why don't you just change lanes?' we would plead with her, but to no avail. She had her system and it wasn't going to change.

'Are you praying?' I would ask before she started the car. The anxious, terrified look overtaking her face lives on in my memory vault.

But Prue was the first of us to have her own car. Not her parents' car that she could borrow, but her own one. And the wild, big-drinking party Prue of our youth had turned into the most responsible of all drivers. Her new-found sobriety was fodder for our mockery until the penny dropped and we realised that in Prue we had a permanent, fool-proof designated driver. Even if, given her driving, it was often faster to walk.

The situation around the burning down of Prue's car remains vague and, even ten years later, there is a caginess to the accusations. A part of her, I'm convinced, still thinks I'm responsible.

'My car got torched last night,' Prue laments. 'But you know that already,' she adds, darkly, over the phone.

'Why would I know that?' I ask.

'Oh just come clean with it. It was torched a few blocks away from your house.'

'I'm sorry—am I getting accused of burning down your car?'

Prue had a prang while on the phone with me on speaker, turning onto Parramatta Road. It happened in one of the rare moments she wasn't just going straight. I arrived at the scene and, with Prue still shaken, helped her park the car a few streets away, near where I lived. That was where it was found, burnt to a crisp.

'But why would I torch your car?' I still ask all these years later, both of us now in parliament.

'Oh you know. You kept saying things like … "If you don't change lanes and drive faster I swear to god I'll burn this car". So when the car was actually burnt down, I went with the guy who kept threatening to do it.'

Fair point. I never had the heart to tell Prue that we loved the car; it was her driving that we couldn't stand.

After Prue had lost her car, it became clear that I actually needed to drive. I never had the privilege of learning how to drive in the family Falcon because it was an automatic and my misplaced pride dictated that I should learn to drive a manual. The mysterious torching of Prue's car also took it out of the equation.

This was when Bob Nanva came to the rescue. Bob was the only person I knew with a suitable vehicle for learning. I use the term 'suitable' loosely.

Bob had a 1992 Daihatsu Charade. In politics, we put a lot of work into picking a slogan, and pretty often they are dull—there have been several incarnations of 'Working Nation' and far too many 'Stronger Togethers'; and when all else fails you go with something like 'A Fresh Start'. I've sat through endless focus groups and meetings working on trying to get the right name for a policy, initiative or campaign. There is a view that this is done better by the corporate world, that the slick marketing types are experts in naming products and initiatives. That would, however, naturally preclude whoever named the Daihatsu Charade.

I imagine the meeting that was held in the Daihatsu think tank back then—when would it have been, maybe 1976? Names are being proposed and discussed; finally, a decision of destiny is made. The executives resolve to go with 'Charade'. I can picture the alarmed junior staff exchanging glances with each other and timidly suppressing the urge to suggest to senior management that further rumination might be prudent. Surely someone knew that the name means an 'act of dishonesty' or 'pretence', a 'travesty' or 'farce' or 'sham' or 'pantomime'—which perhaps, ironically, brings a level of unsuspecting honesty to the process. Perhaps it was a translation issue, but somehow this exquisitely anomalous name was able to pass all the relevant checks and balances and arrive on the international market.

The same level of care and dedication to the naming process was seen throughout the development of the car. This was a car so bad that its lasting impact on the Australian market is its legendary poor quality. I'm reliably told that it was a piece of shit in 1992 and, unlike a fine wine, ten years of ageing had done nothing to improve the value or performance of Bob's vehicle in 2002, when I started to learn how to drive. It was off-white, which means that it was once white but the paint job was, like every other feature of that car, done on the cheap—so now it was permanently stained dirty.

This car was, to put it mildly, a disaster. To drive it, you had to keep accelerating at all times. So both feet were always needed. Even while braking you needed to accelerate, or the car would stall. Which is both counterintuitive and highly dangerous.

I picture the old ladies of Burwood sitting on their porches, their serenity hobbled by the Daihatsu Charade's ghetto blaster—Bob's only gift to this indigent car—hammering out the Prince classic 'Little Red Corvette', our song of choice. Turning the corner would be two ethnic men clattering down the road in a rhythmic stop–start lurch at 15 kilometres per hour, one barking essential orders at his uncoordinated companion. 'Don't take your foot off the accelerator you fool—it'll stall.' The song would reach its powerful chorus, and we would scream with Prince, 'Baby you're much too fast'—in the circumstances, a patently incongruous lyric. They would occasionally smile, the old ladies, no doubt persuaded that the prophecy of the end of times was a distinct possibility.

My own first car wasn't much better. Not blessed by a bountiful budget, I did what every sensible early-twenties urbanite would do. I decided to maximise such quality as my few dollars might purchase. This, naturally, led me to one of the fine second-hand-car establishments along Sydney's Parramatta Road.

When purchasing my first car, a second-hand white Subaru Liberty, I was not informed that the model was the vehicle of choice for the carrying out of high-speed robberies. The car was discreet enough to blend in, fast enough to use as a getaway and easy enough to steal. These were not characteristics that the trustworthy second-hand-car salesman felt I needed to know. Rather, he emphasised that it had only the one previous owner, who would drive it to church and to the local shops.

During the second month of its possession by me, when it was stolen for the third time, I realised that there was a problem. On the first two occasions it was taken simply for a joyride; on the third occasion it was used in a hold-up.

After successfully explaining to the police that I had not indeed used my car to rob a service station, we were able to get down to the business of working out who the culprits were.

The insurance company was less acquiescent. They weren't keen to pay for repairs and had sent an investigator to interview me and my housemates.

'So you can categorically state that you have no knowledge or awareness of the use of this car on the night in question?'

'Yes. I'm pretty sure if I had decided to procure a shotgun and rob a service station I would have remembered. And who breaks into their own car for a robbery?' Quite a few people, I later learn. Certainly enough to warrant the allocation of an investigator to the task.

'So you are saying no?'

'Yes.'

'Yes?'

'Yes, I'm saying no.'

The police had found the car a day after the robbery, abandoned in the western suburbs of Sydney.

A detective called to explain that the car had been left on the side of the road, unlocked and empty. Well, almost empty. There was a CD left—but everything else had been taken.

'Now what was in the car?' the detective asks.

I ran through a list including my sunglasses, a CD wallet full of CDs, books, clothing, a tent and an electric heater. Suddenly feeling self-conscious, I explained that I did not, in fact, live in my car.

'OK. What were the CDs in the CD wallet, in case they turn up?'

My heart started to palpitate. How honest did I need to be? I wasn't planning to lie, but certainly omission was OK. Did I tell them about the S-Club 7 back catalogue (no), the Backstreet Boys (no) and the best of Vengaboys (no)?

'Ah, well there was one CD that was left,' he goes on to tell me, 'Coldplay's *X&Y*'.

On finding out that the CD was not in the CD player prior to its theft, the detective deduced that someone had gone through the wallet, selected the CD, removed it and placed it on the seat. And, as there were no prints, the person achieved this either by subsequently wiping it or by wearing gloves.

'Do you have any idea how hard it is to take a CD out of a CD wallet while wearing gloves?' he asks me. While the CD had a tough time with critical audiences, it was, as far as I was concerned, not that bad.

I had seen a fair few seasons of both *Criminal Minds* and *Law and Order*, so I saw myself as a bit of an expert in these matters.

'Is that a clue?' I ask the detective. 'Is this a message being sent by the criminals?'

'Didn't I just explain that they robbed a convenience store without masks? I'm not sure they were criminal masterminds. And there was a fair bit of cocaine on the dashboard. It's pretty obvious who we're after.'

I eagerly awaited his insight. Perhaps their actions would lead to a profile that could be used to deduce the list of potential targets. I was ready to learn.

'We are after someone who really hates Coldplay,' he says laughing so heavily into the phone that his next line, 'Well, that narrows it', isn't even properly delivered.

I still picture them sometimes, the four who were eventually arrested. Driving on Sydney's roads with the windows down, cocaine on the dashboard, blaring out music en route to an armed robbery. One of them pulls out the Coldplay CD and their friends reject it, 'What are we—animals?' they would say while turning up the Backstreet Boys.

These days, I'm much more likely to have Disney blasting out of my car than 1990s boy bands, and my wife, who is more knowledgeable than I am in everything—including cars—has selected a sensible, suitable vehicle for our family. My parents, too, have moved on. They now drive a reliable car that happens to be bright yellow, a step closer in colour to the gold that would have filled us with no end of excitement in our childhood. I indulge myself with the thought, though, that they sometimes miss, just as I miss, the thrill of not knowing if your car will start or the surge of adrenalin that energises you when you're breaking down on a highway.

9

EVERYONE LOVES A WEDDING

'He's going to arrive on a horse,' the brother of my friend Daniel tells us at a wedding reception the night before the big day.

'Oh this is going to be good. Has Daniel ever been on a horse?' I ask. The consensus was that he hadn't. But if you live with the theory that you should learn something new every day, why would your wedding day be any different?

I'm not sure if there is such a thing as a 'horse person', but Nitin 'Daniel' Mookhey is certainly not one. Standing 5 foot 7 inches, and wearing glasses, he is a spectacular debater and dresses like the inner-city hipster that he is. Daniel and his fiancée, Tamsin, had decided that they would hold a traditional Indian wedding ceremony in the rural central New South Wales town of Armidale. And while Armidale is not usually known for its Indian community, for one night this was all going to change.

In northern India the groom traditionally arrives at the wedding in a procession that involves drums, music and, when an elephant is not available, the bride's horse. No elephant was available and the bride did not have a horse. While Tamsin's family was from Armidale, her current inner-western Sydney address in Newtown was not the place for large animals. So a polo horse had been procured for the occasion from the daughter of the wedding-venue owners. In India, the tradition of the entrance is known as *Baraat*.

While one doesn't want to be culturally insensitive, Daniel is actually from Parramatta, in Sydney's western suburbs, and while he has visited India on several occasions, a few liberties had been taken with his ancestral Punjabi tradition of wedding entrances.

The groom's procession had been arranged to rendezvous 300 metres away from the wedding venue, so that we could meet with Daniel and the horse and lead them to the ceremony. Drums had been distributed and I had been given the job of 'DJ-ing the event', which really just required the holding up of speakers in 1980s ghetto-blaster style while the three or four Indian songs that were known to us were put on endless repeat. We were all dressed in a mixture of traditional wedding outfits (suits for men, dresses for women) and anything that could plausibly be taken to 'look Indian'—which, in far too many cases, involved the conscription of a table cloth to be passed off as a sari. I can only hope that the custodians of an ancient tradition might lightly have indulged such cringeworthy deficits of the cultural imagination.

Not that the Punjabi tradition had been all that well explained to the 15-year-old girl who was lending her horse for this occasion. One can imagine the conversation with her parents. 'Oh look, darling, the young couple having their wedding this weekend need to borrow the horse for his arrival.' She was perhaps picturing a suited man, a modern knight, arriving to collect his wife on horseback. The reality was far from this.

The polo horse was not impressed by the arrangements. A beautiful and well-kept animal, this horse was used to running around a polo paddock and, as the horse approached our group, it took a good look and turned around. Perhaps it was the drumming; perhaps it was the ghetto blaster banging out Punjabi MC's 'Mundian To Bach Ke', which means 'beware of the boys'; perhaps it was the woeful dancing—who knows. I like to think that the horse realised we had been drinking in the Armidale heat from

11:00 a.m. and it had become wise to the deception about its going to a polo event. In an act of racial snobbery, the horse had decided against participating in the wedding.

Rest assured. As there was a group of us from Sydney who had also never ridden a horse, we were full of suggestions.

'Perhaps we can scare the horse while Daniel is on it, and it will get moving and run up the road,' Daniel's cousin proposed. Daniel was not sure that a rampaging frightened horse was what we needed, but we put his pessimism down to wedding-day jitters.

'It's just thirsty,' someone else assured us, pouring water on the horse's face, clearly having no understanding of how a horse would drink.

Another friend, who had been drinking longer than the others, decided to try to talk the horse into participating by explaining the Indian tradition, which would have been effective if we were dealing with Mr Ed.

Perhaps if Daniel just climbed on top, all would be OK. Daniel had, of course, never done this before, and his friends, in simply pushing him onto the horse, did nothing to make the discontented beast any more amenable. By this point the young girl, watching her horse, could not decide whether she wanted to cry or laugh. Either of which would have been entirely appropriate.

In the end, it was Daniel who walked the horse to the wedding, not the other way around. Which, frankly, as far as everyone bar a dozen family members at the large wedding knew, was what was supposed to happen.

'Do you think I can make it to Byron Bay in forty-five mins?' I ask at the desk of the hire-car company at Brisbane airport.

'Not unless you want to get killed. Byron Bay is a safe two hours from here.' Damn. The wedding was starting in thirty minutes. Assuming that proceedings would be running a little late, the best I could hope for was a 45-minute window. My close friend

Jim Chalmers was marrying his long-time girlfriend, Laura, and I didn't want to miss the ceremony.

'Want to take the reduced excess for a small fee?' I'm asked.

'Yeah—considering my driving, that would be best,' I reply. The two people behind the desk laugh before one of their faces drops.

'Did you … um …. write off one of our cars in Melbourne … this morning … three hours ago?'

I had. 'Yeah,' I respond. 'That's why I'm so late. Actually, I think it was their fault.' This was a view shared neither by any of the witnesses, nor by the other driver nor by the driving laws of the state of Victoria.

Helen would later ask questions to fig-leaf her mockery. 'Why did you go to the same car company if you had already written off one of their cars that day?' The truth is that they were the cheapest.

Phone calls were made to their head office.

'Um … I'm told to give you the car. But I have to warn you, please don't try to make it to Byron Bay in forty-five minutes.' All the jokiness in her voice had now left.

At first, the crying was cute. A few tears from the groom is a lovely gesture. It shows that he isn't caught up in that silly male bravado, that he has emotions. It can even demonstrate how much he is in love. I've seen a few of my friends tear up on their wedding day and it is always touching. It was when the service had to be stopped because Bob Nanva started sobbing that the masculine sentimentality really had gone too far.

Bob Nanva is the National Secretary of the Rail, Tram and Bus Union. He is a hard, tough negotiator who is personally responsible for creating train strikes across the nation. Six foot tall and with the best mullet in Australia, he is not the sweet, sensitive type. Or so we all thought.

But we should have seen it coming. At first, while his fiancé walked down the aisle, there were a few tears. I passed him a tissue, thinking that would do the trick. As the bride arrived, the tears gushed. Slightly odd but still manageable. When the priest started speaking and could not be heard because of the guttural noises emanating from Bob, we all started to worry. It was more of a howl than a whimper.

The priest paused the service and offered Bob some quiet words of comfort. 'Listen, mate, you are only getting married, it isn't that bad.' This broke the tension and gave Bob a chance to compose himself. But the moment of reflection that followed only compounded the problem.

'Is he OK?' I asked his brother, a one-time bodybuilder who was the best man. He looked like he could bench press the entire bridal party and, considering how desperately we were after a distraction, all options were on the table. By this time we had exhausted the reservoir of tissues, and another groomsman suggested that we probably needed a towel.

'Is he dying?' another groomsman asked.

'Considering it took him twelve years to propose, you would think he'd be better prepared,' his brother opined. This was a good point.

Bob and Sally had been dating since their Year 12 formal. They were co-school captains at their school and, as Bob tells it, he has never held the hand of another woman, let alone kissed one. It had always been a spectacularly cute love story. The story makes you believe in teenage love; its lesson is that there is 'the one out there for you'. Or as Bob's brother puts up, 'When Bob was seventeen he found someone who was finally prepared to date him, and the smartest thing he ever did was not let go'.

Everybody loved Sally, all of which made it strange why it had taken Bob so long to propose to her. It started off with subtle hints. On the eighth year, suggestions were being made. 'Geez Bob, it's been eight years, you've been together a long time, almost like you are married.' By year ten, the subtlety was being stripped back. 'Bob, you really should think about finally marrying Sally. It's been a decade.' Then, finally, everyone had had enough and the truth bombs started being lobbed. 'Listen Bob, you are punching well above your weight. If you don't settle down soon you run the risk she is going to come to her senses and then you are screwed.' When he finally proposed, it was more a sense of relief than excitement.

It was late 2008 and Bob had asked me to be a groomsman at his wedding. It was a decision he would soon regret. The bridal party had been made up mostly of family, with me and a friend of Sally's the add-ons. A limo had been organised and it came with champagne. Free champagne. The family had decided that it was best that they—the members of the family—not drink during the three hours of photos. I did not place any such restriction on myself.

'When we looked over the wedding photos it became apparent you had ditched Emma, the bridesmaid you were meant to enter the reception with,' Bob later complained to me. 'She couldn't get herself from the pier to the boat. There she was, trying to hold her dress up and climb onto a boat and you had pissed off.'

'That doesn't sound like me.'

'You ran in to "Eye of the Tiger" by yourself and started high-fiving random guests. It's in the photos.'

While I professed my innocence, this sounded—with or without photo evidence—exactly like me.

The groomsmen had worked together on Bob's wedding speech. It was a beautiful tribute to Sally. Their twelve years together, how much she meant to him, how he wanted to spend his life with her. It would have really moved the guests if he had been able to deliver any of it. Instead, he stood at the microphone and broke down. We learnt that the wedding ceremony had only been a warm-up. Now he had the chance to let go full-throttle. His brother and I started heckling him and reading out parts of his speech that he was unable to deliver.

In the car home that night, I told Helen everything that had happened—at least, the parts that I remembered. Helen and I had only just started dating and she wasn't in attendance at the wedding. 'It was fantastic,' I told her. 'I heckled the groom, but it was all in good fun.' Helen wasn't so sure, but this was during the early stages of our relationship, before she realised just how embarrassing I can be. I convinced her to stop at a service station for a street-side kebab that night. I kept thinking about how much I loved Bob and how happy I was for him. Perhaps it was the chilli sauce, but I got teary. There was, however, no wailing.

The pain was incredible. The stings were sharp—it was as though I'd been punctured by thousands of needles. And I ached with the deep ache that you feel when you've been kicked by a horse. I was also bleeding.

'Oh my god. WHAT HAVE YOU DONE?' my sister, Azadeh, demands.

I was in a small hotel room in New Delhi, India, and I was FaceTiming my sister. Having just waxed my chest, I was in unbearable pain, but Azadeh couldn't hide her mirth.

'Why?' she asks. 'Why would you do that?'

'I'm worried they will paint my chest for the dance,' I respond, annoyed that she is deriving so much pleasure from my distress. 'I thought I was too hairy.'

My sister says, 'If you think you will be dancing without a shirt, you have more problems than you realise.'

The image that Helen and Azadeh had of me sitting in the hotel room was grainy, but they could clearly see skin that had disappeared from the world's view around the time that I turned twelve years of age, just as Persian puberty was intervening to give me a solid covering.

To be honest, it was not a pretty sight.

I was in New Delhi for Aditya Berlia's wedding. It was to be a small and intimate affair—in attendance would be just his lovely fiancée, Priyanka, Aditya himself, me and their closest 3000 friends. The number of people at the wedding was to exceed the population of many Pacific Island nations.

Aditya had become one of my closest friends. We'd met several years previously when we were joint participants on a conference panel. His wedding was the most amazing event that I have ever attended in my life. It was the mother of all weddings, and it went on for four days.

Leading up to it, I had spent my spare time in my Senate office practising the dance moves, thanks to a video that had been prepared for me. (It didn't take me long to realise that dancing will not present itself as a career opportunity should politics fail.)

Later I found out that Aditya's other international friends were as uncoordinated as I was, and that our dance—choreographed by none other than a contestant on *So You Think You Can Dance India*—became, unintentionally, one of the wedding's more memorable comic interludes.

This was a different world for me—a world of spectacular colour, of gigantic families, of Indian culture and the expression of Indian identity.

The wedding was magnificent. Well, it would've been—if I hadn't been sitting in a hotel room laughing and trying to stop my chest from bleeding.

If he had shown up on time, that would at least have been a start. But when the MC misses the wedding service and arrives minutes before the reception itself is about to begin, you know you have a problem.

It's 30 January 2010, the date of my wedding to Helen.

For months, we had done what all couples organising a wedding do: stress and plan. Because I am an organisational mess, I was given only two jobs. I was to arrange the MC and hire the cars, both of which I blew spectacularly. Luckily, this was the wedding day, and we had hit the point of no return; Helen was unable to back out. The facade of organisational ability that I had confected for all of this time needed to hold only for one more night.

On the weekend before our wedding, Helen and I had moved in to the first house that we purchased together in Sydney. She had grown suspicious when, in an act of accidental genocide, I had killed all forty-five fish in the fish tank by turning up the water temperature. 'You cooked my fish,' Helen still reminds me, unable to let go. This act of barbarism had made her dubious, but it was merely the tip of a considerable iceberg. Helen had little inkling of what a disaster I could be.

I had hired only one car to make the journey from where we were staying to the wedding venue vineyard in Bowral, a pretty town south of Sydney. It had to keep doing trips to pick up the bridal party, which delayed the ceremony by thirty minutes. The driver was excited that he was doing a wedding, as 'usually I only do school formals'. I'm sure that when it was first designed, in the mid-1980s, this limousine was a beautiful car, but now it was too old to be 'modern' and too new to be 'classic'. It was, however, 'cheap'.

The second task with which I'd been entrusted was to organise the MC. The outcome of this responsibility was that at least it showed, relatively speaking, how good I was at organising transport. Yes, the MC missed the ceremony and arrived late. Yes, he opened with the unforgettable words, 'I'm only the MC because Sam didn't think we were close enough to have me as a groomsman'. And yes, he showed up dressed like he had walked out of the bar scene from *Star Wars*.

All of this was bearable, but then he delivered his *coup de grâce*: 'The Dastyari family must be so happy with Sam—he went and bagged himself a white one'. The room went completely silent. Then the silence gave way to the muttering of Persian family members. 'Did he say "white one" or "right one"?' 'White one,' he corrected the crowd, thinking this was why they hadn't laughed— that they hadn't heard the joke.

During a break, someone was sent to drag him outside to talk to him and beg him to tone it down. 'If they didn't want edgy, why did they ask me to MC?' he asked. 'Listen,' they went on to say, 'this is a wedding, not open mike night at the Apollo. So just pull it together.' It was with these failures that I erred on the side of caution and let Helen name her friends David Cubbin and Chloe Bennett as godparents to our children. It was the right move. Both can be trusted with a microphone, which is more than can be said for many of my friends.

There is a confidence in how to parent that can only be experienced by people who have never actually been a parent. They exhibit the false sense of security that stems from total ignorance.

'How hard can it be?' they think. 'Everyone does it.' The answer? Very. Just because so many people have children doesn't mean that parenting is easy. And it's by no means a given that if you find yourself parenting you're doing it well.

Hannah was six days old at the wedding of Sam Crosby and Rose Jackson. Not only that, but I was the best man and so we offered to bring the cake. Since the wedding was to take place in the Hunter Valley, a couple of hours north of Sydney, we decided to make a weekend of it.

We drove up with Helen sitting in the middle of the back seat, trying to work out what to do with a crying baby on her left and a disintegrating croquembouche on her right.

It was a wedding that perhaps was surprising to all of us, me in particular. If you had told me a decade earlier that Sam and Rose would end up together I'd have poured scorn. Student politics is the pettiest of all forms of politics, and the rivalry between Sam and Rose on the Sydney University campus was legendary. As his best friend, I was the captain of 'Team Crosby', and when he fell in love with Rose, I felt he had gone soft on the enemy.

'You know we left university years ago?' he mitigated. This was true, but it didn't make the betrayal any easier to bear.

'Whom is he "betraying"?' some would ask. 'Himself!' I would yell. 'She was his enemy for all those years.'

In the end, every single one of Sam Crosby's other friends came to realise that Rose is actually a really sweet and amazing person. So did I, but I held out the longest. 'So you were wrong about Rose for longer than anyone else?' Sam will ask me.

'That's one way of putting it.' I elaborate with, 'Another interpretation is that I was just loyal for the longest'. This would make sense if the definition of 'loyalty' was 'being a really difficult prick about a girl your best friend is in love with'.

Years earlier our friend Prue had held the theory that Sam and Rose would end up together. Her ex professo retrospect carried vague plausibility. 'You didn't think that was perhaps why he was so obsessed with her? That he didn't always hold a flame for her? Like the kid that pulls the hair of the girl he is in love with in primary school, Sam was always in love with Rose. Even if he didn't know it.'

I refused to accept this reasoning—why listen to the airy speculations of a vivisectionist of the emotions when reality can be teased out of a raw political analysis? I should know; I had runs on the board.

For years I had followed Sam in his fight against Rose. When she wrote articles in the student newspaper urging people not to vote for his student political run, I was there, downing drinks and vowing revenge. When the police were called over a stolen banner, I was there, downing drinks and vowing revenge. During the campus fights over offensive statements accusing us of all kinds of heinous crimes, I was there, downing drinks and vowing revenge.

And here I was, downing drinks and vowing to give a best-man's speech at the wedding.

10

PROFILE IN THE US

For most people, a trip from Sydney to Los Angeles takes sixteen hours, the length of the long-haul flight; for me, it takes closer to twenty-four.

While I'm never embarrassed of being an Australian of Iranian origin when I am in Australia, that changes once I am in the United States.

The customs official, a middle-aged lady of Hispanic heritage, sheepishly hands me a small piece of paper. On it are the words 'US Patriot Act', and the note outlines that they have the right to ask me questions. Moments earlier, the passport-scanning device had started flashing red and three large armed security guards approached me.

'The Patriot Act?' I ask. 'I'm getting picked up by the Patriot Act. What the …?'

My initial thought was that I'm not an American patriot, so how can this law be picking me up? On reflection, that was kind of the point.

On 26 October 2001, President George W. Bush signed into law an Act of Congress. This Act goes by various titles, some of which are called 'short'. One of these runs as follows: *Uniting and Strengthening America by Providing Appropriate Tools Required to Intercept and Obstruct Terrorism Act of 2001*. Don't ask for the 'long' version. The Act was about to catch up with me.

My friends have proceeded ahead and I'm facing the armed guards alone. It is November 2006, and I'm twenty-three years old. It had never occurred to me that I would make the grade for a terrorist profile.

Young male. Tick.

Single without children. Tick.

Born in the Middle East. Tick.

Travelling on a western passport with minimal security checks. Tick.

And to make matters worse, I had been on a delegation from the US State Department, meaning that I would also come up on that database too. The security officials seemed unsure if I was a potential terrorist or if—now that the State Department system had a record for me—I was a potential spy. Neither, I suspect, was going to be a good outcome.

Then there were the questions.

'Who packed your bags?'

'Why are you travelling to the United States?'

'When and why did you leave Iran?'

The Australian in me wanted to break the tension with jokes.

To the 'Who packed your bag?' I could reply, 'Oh well, officer, we all just gather together at the mosque so it's really hard to know what everyone's up to. It might have been Abdullah, or maybe Mustafa. Then again, Ahmed was around so it could have been him. It's hard to know with all the chanting of slogans at infidels who is really doing what.' But I rightly guessed that they weren't the joking type.

After countless hours of questioning, I was given a special serial number and told that from now on I would have to register in and out of the United States.

I fall into the pre-September 11 generation of migrants who left the Middle East for a better life in the west. This was the first time I personally experienced that there was a 'post' generation too.

Perhaps I was unique, but I never experienced racial profiling when growing up in Australia. Not that it didn't happen—I'm sure my experiences would have been a lot different if I was, say, Indigenous.

But being from the Middle East in Sydney before September 11 simply meant that I was treated the same as all young migrants, be they Greek, Italian or Latin American. After the twin towers collapsed, all of that changed. The fear and the labels have been normalised—another step in twenty-first-century humanity's denaturing of human nature.

I have no doubt that a generation of Middle Eastern migrants after me could ring their own changes on this theme.

Halloween in the United States is a truly surreal experience. It took the Americans to turn All Saints' Day into a consumer-marketing opportunity. There is, well, something so 'American' about the whole thing.

I am walking down Church Street in Orlando, Florida, on the same trip that I first experienced the 'differentness', if I can put it that way, of the United States. I'm carrying a small backpack when I'm stopped—randomly, I'm assured—by the police. They want to check my backpack.

People around me are dressed up as sexy nurses, sexy monsters or sexy vampires (the 'sexy' part being the guiding thread). I was dressed in a collared shirt and chinos.

'You had no costume. You stood out!' my friend set me wise on my return. But I refuse to believe that dressing up as a sexy pumpkin would make me less conspicuous in any environment.

The Americans are far more blatant about racial profiling than Australians are. The American idea of multiculturalism differs utterly from the Australian, which I'm sure accounts in part for the explanation. The Americans have the melting-pot theory. As Ronald Reagan once said, 'Anybody from any corner of the world can come to America to live and become an American'. But being American also involves an element of the relinquishing of national identity. The Australian multicultural experience draws breath from the governing notion of co-existence, the idea that values and identities be maintained for the sake of adding to, and enriching, the Australian identity.

All of this is now being tested in the new order of things, where sleights of mind are putting communities on edge. People are being viewed with well-tuned suspicions; it's becoming easier to perform conceptual mergers and categorical affiliations, to assimilate 'migrant background' with 'potential terrorist'.

I find the concept of 'home-grown terrorism' difficult to grasp. The idea that a young Muslim from the suburbs of Sydney would want to travel halfway around the world to fight a battle in which he has no role—this idea strikes me as insane. It pains me to say this, but before I travelled to the United States and felt the indignity of being dragged through the ringer on account of my Iranian ancestry, I was far more complacent about other people's loss of civil liberty than I have since become.

For years I took the view that racial profiling was one of those necessary evils with which we have to live. Sure, it is unpleasant; but a balance must be struck between the nurturing of liberties and the maintaining of security. So the imperatives of civilisation—in which opportunity engenders the prosperity that embellishes the liberties that need to be made secure—dictate that racial profiling anchors the common good. This is a view, it turns out, that is actually wrong.

'Firstly, "racial profiling" can mean different things in different contexts. But my problem with racial profiling isn't simply that it hurts those wrongly targeted—it does that, but, more simply, the data shows that it is not an effective tool.' Anne Aly knows this subject, and she speaks decisively. 'It doesn't work. It's looking for a shortcut where there isn't one.'

Anne Aly, aside from being a Member of Parliament, has a PhD from Edith Cowan University on counter-terrorism, media and culture (on which she has written a series of books) and has founded her own de-radicalisation programs.

As Anne tells me, part of the problem is that there are actually only a handful of terrorists to whom you can talk, and even if they are telling the truth, a majority can't necessarily articulate their own reasons. So people search for simplistic answers.

'You just have to look at the Silber and Bhatt model. Which all seems logical but actually misses empirical evidence,' says Anne, underscoring the point.

'Yeah—the Silber and Bhatt model. Where *is* the evidence for that!' I have no idea what Anne is talking about, but I counterfeit comprehension lest I appear unenlightened. I make a mental note to google this model as soon as I walk away, which I do.

Mitchell Silber and Arvind Bhatt were both members of the New York Police Department Intelligence Division and co-authored a hugely influential report entitled *Radicalization in the West: The Homegrown Threat*. Despite having been heavily criticised in recent years, this report is still one of the most influential documents of its kind, and to it may be traced the roots of many of the policies that we have adopted in recent years.

Radicalization in the West claims that a terrorist evolves through four stages. The first stage is 'pre-radicalisation'. This refers to life before the process really begins.

Stage two is 'self-identification'. Here, individuals begin to explore the more radical interpretation of Islam, the 'Salafi' model, and start associating with people who share the model's radical views. Normally, it takes some kind of 'personal crisis' to get this far.

Stage three is 'indoctrination'. And the final stage is 'Jihadisation'.

I can't see what is wrong with this predictive model, so I go back to Anne.

'The problem is that it's a really inefficient way of targeting. The model says that anyone who is a Muslim is somehow predisposed to terrorism, which isn't backed by the evidence and can do more harm than good,' Anne says.

It turns out that the data, what there is of it, shows that religion plays less of a role than does isolation. When radicalised British nationals go into Syria and Iraq, it's common for them to carry 'Islam for Dummies'. It stands to reason that if you intend to commit atrocities in the name of your religion you would, by that point, have progressed beyond the learner phase of your faith.

The argument that racial profiling saves law-enforcement time and resources is not backed up by the evidence. There are no easily identifiable, consistent physical or other characteristics that serve to trace out religious radicals or their neophyte proxies. The whole argument for 'racial profiling' is shot to bits by the poverty of the so-called 'evidence' on which it relies.

On leaving Los Angeles airport I dutifully reported to the designated nondescript room to which the officials directed me in order to register my departure from the United States. This was now part of my travelling routine. Waiting ahead of me in the queue was a Jordanian businessman in his early thirties. Clean-shaven, he was wearing a suit. He told me that he flies to and from the United States regularly and always goes through this process.

We struck up a brief conversation.

Ahead of us I could see a group of teenagers. I counted seven but, from what I could hear, they were waiting for two others who were on their way. I was perhaps being overly sensitive, but I did get the feel that they were receiving more attention than other folks in the vicinity. It wasn't apparent to me why.

They seemed normal enough. They were dressed as any upper-middle-class Middle Eastern migrant would be dressed in the main streets of Sydney or Melbourne. They wore baggy designer clothing, nothing out of the ordinary.

'All of them,' the businessman whispers to me, 'all of them have the surname Bin Laden.' Whether they did or didn't I wasn't able to verify. It wasn't exactly the kind of room in which you ask too many questions. Nor could I discover whether the 'Bin Laden', in this case, denoted relationship to he of international notoriety or whether it was just a surname coincidentally shared. None of it really mattered.

I didn't have the heart to point out to my new friend that if the Bin Ladens up ahead were indeed relatives of the renowned—and at that point, still hiding—terrorist leader, then we were victims of a sleight of mind that put us all aboard the same boat.

11

INSIDE THE MACHINE

The date is 23 December 2010, and I'm late to the NSW Labor Party Christmas lunch because I can't stop vomiting. It's causing some uproar.

'How long has he been throwing up?' The question is posed by Walt Secord, then chief of staff to the Premier of New South Wales, Kristina Keneally, and is directed to my offsider and campaign organiser, Brendan Cavanagh.

I can hear them through the thin walls of the bathrooms at the NSW Labor Party head office at 377 Sussex Street, Sydney. Brendan has called Walt in an effort to stage a mini-intervention and coax me out.

'Are you sure it's not food poisoning?' Walt asks him.

'No. He read the polling and then ran into the bathroom. They are waiting to order lunch for everyone at Circular Quay and we can't get him out.'

'Is he always this dramatic?' Walt asks Brendan. 'How long have you known him?'

'Almost a decade.'

Unfortunately, this was not my worst diva moment. Six months earlier I had taken over as the General Secretary of the NSW Labor

Party, putting me in charge of the party organisation when, at twenty-six, I was nowhere near emotionally ready to face the worst time the Labor Party had experienced in its 100 years of history. It took me a while to accept the fate that awaited the Labor Party in New South Wales after sixteen years of government. It was a fate that we'd entirely brought upon ourselves.

By this point, I was still working through the five stages of grief and had arrived at stage four, depression.

Stage 1: denial

Travel back some months—back to February 2010. Kevin Rudd was prime minister and Kristina Keneally had become state premier a few months earlier.

'Baby, I need to go for another run,' I tell Helen on our honeymoon on Kangaroo Island in South Australia. We were on the remote island where mobile-phone reception is intermittent, allowing us finally to get away from the hustle and bustle of the last few years.

'Again?' Helen responds. 'Isn't that your third run today? Are you taking your phone?' Helen was smart enough to know that I am far from a fitness freak and that I must be up to something.

'Oh yeah. Just, you know, in case I get lost. For safety,' I lie, putting the phone in my pocket so that Helen can't see that there are forty-seven missed calls registered on my handset.

I was then 'number 2' at the NSW Labor Party head office, and there were changes underway—changes that, unfortunately, were taking place while I was on my honeymoon.

The text message from my boss, Matt Thistlethwaite (then party secretary), read 'Running for Parliament. My job is yours if you want it'.

Two years earlier, my bid to become party secretary had been dramatically shot down when anyone with any influence in the Labor Party turned around and sneered, 'Isn't he just a kid?' A handful added the warning, 'You know he's a completely loose cannon'. At twenty-four, I was both. Two years later and with the implosion of the NSW Labor Party, such luxuries were no longer available to the naysayers. I'd love to convince myself that the Labor Party turned to me to run its organisational wing because of my acknowledged ability and potential. The reality is that the Labor Party anointed me out of desperation. There was really no one else left standing.

'Sure the NSW Labor Party is in some trouble,' I'd say. Perhaps this was after the twelfth or thirteenth minister had been forced to resign after some scandal. 'But we will pick up from here. A good campaign will fix all of this.'

My previous decade had been spent in the Labor Party, and I was young enough to believe in its infallibility. I had joined the Labor Party when I was sixteen years old. It was the defeat of the republican referendum that inspired me to join. I ran the Sydney University ALP club, was the president of Young Labor and did all those infuriating things that young political professionals do. The campaign rallies, the election campaigns, the fundraising chicken dinners: these were my bread and butter.

And here I was now, thinking of myself as the party's fixer of messes. It was the denial that comes from inexperience. I'd like to put it down to youthful exuberance, but that would be sugar-coating it. But I thought that I was bulletproof. I was unstoppable and could do no wrong. I inflated myself with these and other self-made conceits.

The ancient Greeks knew about haughtiness. They called it *hubris*, and *nemesis* was the payback. In Australia, we call it 'cocky', and 'chucking ya guts up into the dunny before lunch' was only part of the payback.

Stage 2: anger
'Kristina, they are dragging you into the mud.' A few weeks into the job and it was becoming clear that nothing was going to save the NSW Labor Government.

Initially, once Kristina took over the premiership, the party was scandal free. That was from December 2009 to May 2010. But, unfortunately, the salad days didn't last. Good fortune was not on our side. By the end of the campaign we could've turned out a cricket team, with twelfth and thirteenth men to boot, peopled by the ministerial victims—deadbeat dads, drunk drivers, the corruptible, the compromised.

The real icing on the cake, for me, was the former police minister who had to resign for dancing in his underwear on his chesterfield couch on budget night. While this had occurred before I became secretary, and before Kristina was premier, it really set the stage for what was to come. The allegation was that he was wearing a green g-string and jumping up and down on the furniture yelling obscenities to the daughter of another MP as he jokingly jumped atop her mother. In fairness, he always denied this part of the story, but the damage was done. He had to resign over the incident a few days later.

'You get what you get.' Kristina had consoled herself too. She was angry but maintained a calm air throughout that entire period. Hers was a calm not shared by anyone else while Rome burnt. It certainly wasn't shared by me; I was imploding, melting down, spilling over.

'I just expect when the lift opens at Governor Macquarie Tower [the ministerial offices]—I expect to find people eating grapes off naked bodies while others are in the corners burning documents,' I tell Kristina. 'I'm going to get my revenge on those who have torn the place down,' I would profess in fits of rage as the next daily scandal broke. But the public would do that for us as soon as the state election came around.

Stage 3: bargaining

Most campaigns start from the middle and work their way to what can be won. We started at the top and worked down. By this I mean that we worked out what seats we could possibly hold, and forgot about anything that would ordinarily be 'in play'.

That is how we ended up with the most depressing campaign message of all time: 'Don't give them too much power'.

Kristina and I worked on the strategy together. Kristina had to give people hope, stay positive and make sure we were able to get the campaigners out of bed in the morning. She tackled the job with a zeal that, considering the circumstances, was incredible.

But while Kristina maintained a positive tone, the campaign itself took a darker turn. What we were really relying on in the 2011 state campaign was something little short of a cap-in-hand plea for an unmerited redemption: 'Look, even we know we don't deserve to win this election and we are not going to ask you to vote for our record, just vote to keep the other mob in check'. It was a sad way to go out after sixteen years in power.

We clung to a strategy wholly designed to keep as many bits of the 'furniture'—the parliamentary seats—as we possibly could. We were copping it from every quarter. When people walk out of focus groups, and refuse to take their $80 participant's fee, because, to quote one of them, 'I could never stoop so low as to try to help this mob with my opinions,' you know that the vessel is just about sunk.

Even though they liked the premier, Kristina Keneally, they weren't prepared even to think about giving NSW Labor another go. Which, considering our track record in the foregoing few years, was hardly surprising.

'Oh but there must be a way we can win a handful more seats,' I would demand from the campaign team. 'There must be A PATH to a decent result. No matter how thin.' But there wasn't. There was just the bleak reality that while we did good things as a government, there were some really bad people occupying positions of responsibility, and *that* sad fact made observers think the whole show was atrocious. We were getting what we had coming to us.

The campaign team itself cultivated a levity that wore the stench of imminent death. The whole team pretty much knew that they would be unemployed once we lost government and so decided they might as well enjoy the last few weeks of the campaign. There was a lot of gallows humour, and even more tequila shots, as the campaign descended into Destination Wipeout.

Stage 4: depression

'It's over,' I keep declaring to people as I examine the polling results that show that Labor is unlikely to win enough seats to be able to maintain our major-party status.

'The polling isn't bad—it's disastrous,' Chris Minns, the party's assistant secretary and my great mate, starts ventilating to any journo who will listen. The goal isn't the lowering of expectations. The goal is the *destruction* of expectations.

In March 2011 Chris is out there spinning the results with my eventual successor, Jamie Clements. A week before the election I'm too depressed to operate and am barely leaving my office.

I had never experienced full-fledged depression before. It made its visitation as the campaign was coming to an end. I had been clinging to the fantasy that the campaign was, just possibly, going to pull out a good enough result to keep the party alive.

But the polling results progressively worsened, and I collapsed into a gloom.

'Oh it's all over,' I would say, pouring it all out to anyone who would listen, baiting them to tell me that it would still be OK.

By now, just days out from the one poll that matters, I'm convinced that the end of my own career looms. I would wear the blame—no doubt about it. Utterly, utterly self-indulgent, considering the mess that the party was in, but I was little more than a kid, and life was stomping on me before I'd had a chance to prove my worth.

It became apparent that Labor was going to struggle to hold any seats. We need to find people 'outside the matrix', Chris and I conclude. That meant that if you consumed English-language media, drove to work or had any real community engagement—chances were there was no way you were going to vote for the mess of a government that we had become.

So we targeted the outsiders, the migrants—people who, for one reason or another, had not really consumed the media that explained what a catastrophe we were. It's a pretty depressing state of affairs when, having governed the state since 1995, you're

searching for those who don't know who you are but who might—
just—be convinced into giving you a go.

Stage 5: acceptance

'Get off the phone,' Chris barks at me on election night, 26 March
2011. Kristina is about to make her speech.

'I'm on the phone to her,' I tell him.

'Is she quitting as leader?'

'Yep.'

'Fuck.'

'Are we a lock on Blacktown?' The state seat of Blacktown
was being contested by John Robertson. If we didn't win that we
would be stranded without a leader.

'Looking dicey, but OK.'

'YOU HAVE TO STAY.' I'm still on the phone and I'm
begging. 'You have to stay as leader.'

Kristina wasn't going to do that. Her reasoning was simple. The
Labor Party needed to move on. A new leader had to be chosen to
take the party into its future. And the party needed the opportunity
to repudiate positions that she had taken. She maintained that she
would have been a distraction, and would have compromised the
rebuild, had she stayed on as leader. I still believe that we would
have recovered more quickly under her leadership than anyone
else's. But I was always biased when it came to Kristina. Bob Carr
and Anthony Albanese, among a host of others, urged her to stay.
But she wasn't going to budge.

Kristina was better to the Labor Party than the party ever was
to her. She took over the party at the worst of times and held the
show together through sheer determination and grit. Of course,
she will never be thanked for that. This is, after all, the Labor Party.
The history books will treat her well, or at least they should if they
are fair.

In the end, just over a quarter of people in New South Wales
voted for us. Given the context, this was a huge endorsement.
Because, frankly, we were like a 1980s band that had put out an

experimental recording just to see who the real fans were. There was no reason why anyone should have been voting for us, let alone one person in four.

Having emerged from depression, I was consoled by the sweet and soothing balm of relief. I was still on a downer, just less down. Out of the toilet. We even celebrated, despite having won a meagre twenty seats out of ninety-three. But with the polling telling us to expect fewer than ten, we took what we could.

The community had more faith in the party than the party itself deserved. I went through my stages of grief, taking, along the way, a crash course in *nemesis* Australian style. I learnt that it wasn't all about me. We narrowly maintained party status. My vision and the party's infallibility had taken a beating. The experience left me no longer the kid, but not quite the man.

12

CONNECTIONS

I wake up suddenly on the overnight flight from Perth to Sydney. I'm disorientated, sweaty and verging on panic. I've been having the dream again, the same one. It's been haunting me, relentlessly, for years.

It's a snippet of life that, by rights, I should have completely forgotten. There's a girl from school, and she's telling me that she is in love with one of my friends.

We were in Year 10, and riding the afternoon bus home.

When the dream comes, I can smell that gross combination of Lynx deodorant and overripe bananas that penetrates the atmosphere inside every school bus. I can feel the worn shiny fabric seat with patterns lacing it, right there, under my fingers. I can glance outside and notice that the afternoon has become windy and that rain clouds are assembling.

I remember her necklace, and how nervous she was about sharing her secret; she was giggling and looking shyly sideways. Don't get me wrong, we weren't an item. If we had been, it might make more sense that I remember all of this so vividly. But we weren't even particularly close friends.

It's just a perfectly formed memory, one that plays over and over in my head while I sleep. I doubt that she remembers it.

The dream itself is innocuous enough. But I'm uneasy about its persistence. It's as though the recurrence, the endless playback, is itself at the disposal of something malevolent, and that my inability to understand what it means is *the very point* of its ceaseless ministration. It joins a long list of odd things that can, and do, make me anxious. But why?

I've stared down PMs, had epic fights with bank CEOs and negotiated more than one sleepless night of critical number-crunching. But, always, when I wake from this weird dream I'm clammy, wild-eyed and overwhelmed by dread.

'What's wrong with me?' I ask my friend Jen Rayner, for at least the eighty-eighth time.

'Should I start with the overbearing love of your mother, your migrant inferiority complex or your vigilante's preference for mob justice?' she deadpans, cracking open a bottle of white wine.

It's another of our sessions in my Parliament House office— the ones that usually start with Jen flinging open the door and shouting, 'So-and-so can go get fucked!'

Jen is a walking contradiction. She has a PhD in political science and a policy mind, yet also has the tattoos and vocabulary of a particularly uncouth sailor.

'I need to get Peter's opinion,' I tell Jen.

'Do you ever make a decision without getting his opinion?' she asks me.

'Only the bad ones I later regret.'

Peter Barron is Helen's father and, once upon a time, was Bob Hawke and Neville Wran's fixer. I know that all my friends think it odd that I talk to my father-in-law twice a day. Even I know that it is a bit much—who speaks to their father-in-law more than once a month? But, then again, my friends don't have one of Labor's legendary strategists on speed dial. The ancient Greeks had the oracle at Delphi. The Labor Party has Peter Barron. A lot of people in the party love Labor history. Peter has lived it.

He's shaped it. He was the wordsmith for Hawke, Wran and Keating. I lap up his advice; I listen carefully to what he says—I'd be nuts not to.

Peter once told me that 'politics is the only game where you make a living on your wits'. That's Peter. He's not a process man or a management-structures person. He's never going to put together a pie chart to win people over. He prefers, as he says, 'to sit and think and talk'. His advice is always bookended with a bit of self-deprecation. 'You might think I'm talking rubbish here.' 'You might think this is completely crazy.' And then he'll follow up with a set of clear, made-for-TV lines that demonstrate his innate wisdom and his mastery of the matter at hand. The lesson will end with a half-rhetorical question: 'Did that sound any good to you?'

The trick to deriving benefit from Peter's counsel is to write down what he's saying as he goes. Because, a bit like the oracle, once he's said his piece he tends to consign it to some oblivion. 'I can't quite remember,' he'll say in response to my request for a reprise, 'how I framed it the first time.' Unless his thoughts are written down you may never get them back.

It's worth noting that (besides his wife, Pat) there's only one person who speaks to Peter more often than I do. That person is Bill Shorten.

If Peter is a political oracle, he is also a family man. He knows the importance of having balance in life. 'Peter's one of the toughest men in politics,' Paul Keating once told me. 'No,' I replied. 'I've seen him with his grandchildren. He's actually a softie.'

Having real friends—people who will happily listen to you when you need to talk about your weird dreams and creeping anxieties—is more often the exception than the rule in politics. I'm lucky to have come into the Senate with a supportive family as well as close friends. Many of those friends have known me since before I had anything to do with Labor—and that's saying something, considering I first joined in my teens.

Maladjustments of the personality seem to have reached epidemic proportions these days, but in political circles the ceaseless distraction of phones, emails and social-media alerts conspire to ensure that everyone is only ever half-listening to what anyone else has to say. Add in Parliament House's retro 1980s beeper system that alerts MPs and Senators when they're supposed to be in the chambers, and anyone who doesn't arrive in the job with a short attention span quickly develops it.

It's got to the point that the greatest mark of respect you can show someone is to perform coded gestures with your communication devices. For example, when you're paying high-grade obeisance to a demi-god, you ostentatiously put your phone out of reach; and to manifest a slightly lower species of reverence, you keep the phone by your side but indicate how captivated your attention is by turning the phone so that it's now face down while your face does what faces always used to do before the digital revolution purloined everyone's mind.

An inability to stay focused is one of the two big reasons why so many professional politicians now find it hard to connect one-on-one with the normal people who come into their constituent offices or bail them up in the street.

When your whole life feels like it's moving at a million miles an hour and every minute brings new information, new people, new stuff to process, the more sedate tempo of regular life can start to feel deeply strange. Spending forty-five minutes talking to a slightly offbeat senior about a local council issue that's beyond your jurisdictional reach, or an hour standing on a street corner where the best available stimulation might be two magpies fighting over rubbish and the occasional friendly sledge from passing commuters—these are moments in real life, instances of everyday sociability. But if you lose touch with reality, you yourself can't help but become a bit displaced. The upshot is that everyone else's reality—the daily patchwork of run-of-the-mill conversations and interactions—may itself become weird and unsettling to you, because your altered normality has estranged itself from the normality that you once shared with everyone else.

It's like a combination of FOMO (fear of missing out), withdrawal and acute self-consciousness when, for once, you have to be fully present somewhere instead of allowing your attention to pinball between five devices and the person in front of you. But people expect their political representatives to be present, to listen and look them in the eye. Pretty much everyone else can manage it: the GP, your kids' schoolteachers, even that surly woman on the checkout at Coles. So when politicians struggle to slow down for long enough to do the same, most end up seeming awkward and forced at best, or arrogant and aloof at worst. Neither exactly screams 'Like me', which, ironically, is exactly what politicians want you to do.

There's another reason why so many politicians can't connect, and it explains why genuine friendships are actually pretty rare in this job. It's the fear of revealing too much about yourself; the hypersensitivity that holds you back from exposing who you are.

Imagine this: you're a new arrival to Australia, having a tough time slogging your way through the incomprehensible paperwork and pettifogging bureaucracy involved in things like getting a Medicare card and enrolling your kids in school. You stop by your local MP's office for help, for a bit of a steer, or at least some hints on working the system.

If that MP were someone like me, in an ideal world they'd share their own arrival stories. I could easily give an anecdote about my mum or dad getting confused about something important when they first arrived here. I could summon up a cute story about something that I always thought as a little kid learning English but only found out later that it was wrong. You and this MP would form a small connection over the common frustrations and challenges of being new here. Maybe the MP couldn't help with your Medicare forms, but you'd still go away feeling a little uplifted, a smidge more bonded to your new community. You'd have acquired the impression that political figures in this country actually do give a stuff.

But see what's just happened? I've given up some facts about me. Some insights and details that people didn't know before. And when you do this all day, every day, you start to feel that a part of you is being given up each time. The business of the politician is not a zero-sum game, yet there is only so much of yourself you can always give. Why would that little bit of empathy that I showed in sharing my stories sometimes make me feel less complete?

It won't, of course—it *won't* make me less complete. But that's how politicians who've been doing this for a while think. Information is power; details are currency for trade. And so the goal becomes being seen to speak, without giving anything away.

That's why MPs will hastily resort to platitudes, counting on a few memorised facts and figures, being sure to say things that are boring and bland and so very safe. If it's something someone else already said; if it gives away nothing about what you actually think or feel; if it blends into the background noise so that there's no risk of its standing out—then what you say can't hurt you. It's the Humphrey Appleby twitch: at all costs, avoid being 'courageous'.

Of course, it won't make an impression on anyone either, nor convince people why you're deserving of their trust. But that seems to be a trade-off that professional politicians have almost uniformly decided to make.

I think we need less fear, and more exposure (this whole book is a testament to that!). I'm a married father of two who hasn't taken drugs or danced all night for far too long, though I do make a few social-media videos and sometimes I swear on camera. The fact that I'm considered one of the loosest units in federal politics today says a lot about how uptight and drab the whole show has become.

Maybe if we relax a little more and let people see past the buttoned-up suits and sound bites—maybe, if we could let ourselves dare to do that, politicians might connect again. We might connect with our communities and with each other. Here's one thing that I do know: it's bloody good to be able to drink wine and talk about your weird dreams and anxieties with some proper friends, to be *human* for a little while.

13

HALAL ELVIS

'It's not that we agree … but that she pays attention,' Alice tells me.

'What if it's the wrong type of attention?' I ask.

'Considering how isolated we are from the major parties, most people will take any attention over none.'

It was the best explanation of the One Nation phenomenon that I had heard, and it was given to me by Alice Milne, President of the Parkes Country Women's Association (CWA), who owned the Pink Orchid Café and Florist in which we were sitting.

After the 2016 election, Parkes won a slice of infamy. It had recorded the highest New South Wales per capita Senate vote for One Nation. The results showed that one in four voters in Parkes believed that Pauline Hanson's party would represent them best in Canberra. What I found amazing was that One Nation had achieved this result without running the type of campaign that would normally be required (by a major party) to achieve this level of electoral approval.

One Nation's appeal in the central west of New South Wales was part of a growing trend that caught the major parties napping. Only a couple of months before, at a recent by-election in Orange

(250 kilometres west of Sydney), the National Party lost big to the Shooters, Fishers and Farmers Party—their first win anywhere, ever.

Discussing this with Alice, I notice a knot developing in my stomach. In fifteen minutes, I was about to put on a Lycra jumpsuit and walk down the main street of Parkes dressed as Elvis. This was, certainly, one of my stranger weeks.

Wednesday (three days earlier)

'So … you are going to Parkes in the middle of summer for research?' Sharnelle Arthur asks me, as I again explain to her my travel plan. Sharnelle has been managing my diary since our early days together in the NSW Labor Party, and she is ferociously protective. My love for her is exceeded only by my children's adoration of her.

I repeat that my 2017 new-year's resolution is to spend as much time as possible in One Nation and conservative areas. I whine like a spoilt teenager. I need to break out of my inner-city Labor bubble.

'Then why are you going during the Elvis festival? Explain *that*. Wouldn't that be the worst time to go? Won't everyone there be from *outside* Parkes?' I was in the glare of The Inquisition.

I respond with a long monologue about the link between community and festival. I ramble on about how the Elvis week isn't really about Elvis—it's about bringing people together. The contrast between this inclusive event and Parkes' rejection of mainstream political parties is too tempting to miss. Sharnelle can tell that I'm making up my reasons on the spot. She's been with me for too long.

She cuts me off: 'You really just want to go to dress up as Elvis, don't you? *Don't you?*'

'You can have more than one purpose,' I sheepishly reply.

'You don't even like Elvis!'

'How dare you say that. I'm a huge fan of Elvis.' I'm not. Well, everyone 'likes' Elvis, but not once during the past decade have I mentioned him to Sharnelle, so she does have a point.

'Go ahead … name five songs then.' I feign outrage and aggression, the act of someone clearly in the corner.

'Don't tell me you're going to do something lame—like HALAL-VIS.'

'HALAL-VIS!' I hadn't thought of that. How *perfect*! A Middle Eastern Elvis. This is so beautiful and I jot it down in my notepad. 'HALAL-VIS'. No, that doesn't work. I try 'HALAVIS'. Too confusing. Then, in faint pen I write beside it—'Halal Elvis'. Done.

'Of course not, I would never do anything that shameless— anything that would embarrass me,' the bullshit rolls out.

'Halal Elvis,' delivered in my best Mississippi drawl … 'Thank you very much.'

Thursday (two days earlier)

Once you meet a guy in Parkes who is known locally as 'Al-vis' and another as 'Pel-vis', your life will never be the same.

I descended on Parkes in the middle of the afternoon. It was hot, dry and largely deserted. I found that everyone had unhelpfully disappeared into one of the nine pubs on the main street for the afternoon. Buskers crooned for the crowds on pub stages, bouffant hair immaculate. Less fortunate buskers were on street corners, in the sun, waiting for their chance to make it big, or at least earn some air-conditioning.

The dry heat was oppressive, but added to the anticipation. I saw a few Elvii (the plural for Elvis) walking around, but it was certainly not in sufficient numbers to qualify as 'a festival' (the collective noun for Elvii). I was told that the afternoon Elvis train would bring the main group of local Elvis impersonators and that Friday night was earmarked as arrival time for those from the capital cities. And there would be mass arrivals on Saturday. The Mayor of Parkes, Ken Keith, would later describe the festival to me as 'schoolies for oldies'. He was right.

The evening was spent at the Broadway Hotel, which was holding a karaoke evening. The room easily qualified for its 'schoolies for oldies' tag. Some patrons looked like they shared the same birth year as the King himself, and all were clearly enjoying time away from their normal lives. I asked the karaoke manager whether we could sing 'Suspicious Minds', as a nod to Tony Abbott.

'You know you'll be the twenty-fifth person to have sung that song tonight,' the karaoke guy told me.

'Is that a "no", then?'

He sighed. His immaculate Elvis hair wilting slightly. 'You'll be next after Shirley Bassey, and Pel-vis.'

Friday (one day earlier)

'I don't believe that this town is anti-immigration or anti-Muslim per se. It's just neglected.' This I hear from a local business owner who was surprised when I told him about the high result achieved by One Nation.

As far as he was concerned, Parkes was a safe National Party seat, so Labor did not really try, and neither did the Nationals.

'The people here are really close. So they can't be racist.'

'Really?' I ask, not totally convinced.

'Yeah, everyone knows everyone. That's why they aren't racist.'

This is an argument that makes no sense. 'Racism' can wrongly be imputed to you when you're distinguishing on the basis of socio-economic indicators, but you can legitimately be said to adopt 'racist' views of people whom you do, in fact, know—which is *not* to say that because you know someone whose ethnic heritage is other than your own you're necessarily going to exclude them, set them apart, ascribe particular motives to them or suspect that they're planning to blow up the town. Discrimination can work its malice subtly and indirectly.

The community in Parkes, I'm told, is pretty close. The business-man went on to explain that the local people voted for persons—for the personal character of candidates—more so than for policies. I was almost persuaded by this argument, until he told me that he had run for council and had missed out. Despite owning one of the largest businesses in the area, he had not made it. I later learnt that his campaign strategy consisted of reading minutes of council's meetings for the past two years. He might've done better had he conscripted some Elvii to hand out election material.

'Did you read about our nude dog?' the Mayor of Forbes asks me on Friday morning in his council office. 'It was a big story. My wife isn't a fan, but I'm comfortable with it.' I had travelled down to the neighbouring town of Forbes, Parkes' rival, in search of some answers. What I got instead was an exhaustive disquisition on names of dogs and how mean the mainstream press had been to Forbes.

'Nude dog?' I ask, thinking that I must have drunk more at karaoke than I realised. I felt like saying that I hadn't heard about a 'nude dog' but that certainly a dressed one would attract more media attention. I have two 'nude dogs' myself, hardly a story.

'It's very controversial. Dog and rabbit heads on nude human bodies. It was a big story in Sydney, or so I'm told.'

'At the zoo?'

'At the park. Forbes doesn't have a zoo.'

OK. By then I was convinced that something was amiss. Was this a practical joke they played on people, like drop bears?

'So you have human bodies with dog and rabbit heads walking around the park nude? Performing artists?'

'They aren't "walking around". They're statues.'

'Oh.' I'm not sure what I expected but this information somewhat disappointed me. I liked the small bit of Forbes that I had just seen and the idea that there were people who would walk around their park wearing animal masks while naked made the town somewhat more attractive to me.

My search for answers about the rise of One Nation was not really getting anywhere. Instead of the detailed discussion on social dislocation for which I'd hoped, the trip so far had descended into conversations about hairspray and naked dogs and rabbits. Perhaps Sharnelle was right. Perhaps all of this was a big mistake.

Saturday (Halal Elvis)

At first, the Christian children's books in the café spooked me. Not that there was anything wrong with the books, but they just seemed out of place in what was a fairly trendy café. On the right was what looked like a Dr Seuss imitation story explaining the holy trinity, and beside it was a book on creationism.

'The Christian book store shut down,' Alice tells me. 'So I told them they could sell their books here.'

'Oh,' I respond, clearly off-put. Meeting with the CWA in a café that carried these books wrongly played into a stereotype. It was a stereotype born of ignorance, but nonetheless the only one I had to rely on.

'Politicians live in bubbles, Sam, geographical bubbles. That isn't the real world. That's what separates you from us.' It is always telling when people move to the 'US and Them' language.

'I live in the inner west of Sydney, does that count as a bubble?' I fire back, knowing the answer but still drawing it out. My interlocutor is armed and ready.

'That's the *definition* of a hipster bubble!' Alice insists, exasperated with me though clearly relishing the exchange of views. I was burning to tell her that having an Elvis festival itself is fairly trendy, but decided to give it a miss.

'Tell me about One Nation. Tell me about why those out here vote for them in such large numbers.'

'People have to make choices. They might not like everything One Nation is putting forward, but at least they are talking to us. Where is everyone else?'

I didn't ask if Alice voted for One Nation. If I were to speculate, I'd say that she didn't. But, full of insight, she understood why her community did.

It was, as far as she was concerned, all about attention—namely, the *lack* of it from Sydney and Canberra. People in the bush had had a gutful of being ignored.

This was an important conversation. But, frankly, I had more pressing matters. It was, after all, the twenty-fifth anniversary of the start of the Elvis festival and I needed to get ready. My cheap, online-ordered suit was not really as impressive in Parkes as it was when I had tried it on in the comfort of my own home. No fewer than 25 000 people had come to the town that morning, and over 2000 of them were attired as Elvis. Many of them had paid more than $50 for their suit.

The Elvii were surprisingly ethnically diverse. There was an Indian Elvis, several Indigenous ones, a Korean and a Japanese Elvis; many Elvii had flown in from the Philippines. And, of course, dozens of Americans showed up. I'm not sure what I really expected. But it turned out that I was pleasantly surprised.

'The first thing you need to know is that they are not impersonators. They are tribute artists,' Anne Steel, the co-founder of the Elvis festival, fills me in as I prepare for the parade to begin. In fact, I learn even more than this. I learn that such persons belong to something like a guild, and that they are known as 'ETA'—Elvis Tribute Artists. There are THOUSANDS of them around the world.

The parade proceeds in three parts. We are broken up near a roundabout and each group goes in turn. The first group heads down and does its stuff, and obviously does it well. We can hear the screaming and the applause. These are mostly the professional Elvis tribute artists and sponsors. The pros are followed by the petrol heads, the many Elvii who went the extra mile and brought a Cadillac for the occasion.

Then come the walkers. I am with them. The crowd roars as we wind our way through Parkes. The sizzling heat makes it all somewhat unbearable in Lycra, but the adrenaline triggered by the crowd injects strength of purpose into flagging flesh.

The community has come out in force. The main street of Parkes is packed. There is a joyous sense of communal togetherness going on here; out here in the summer heat of a country town, I've happened upon a uniquely Australian expression of community—occasioned by the urge to pay homage to an American artist.

And as I walk down the street, kitted up as Halal Elvis, I'm greeted by the sheer enthusiasm of the locals. People are *here to support their community*. This is what impresses itself upon my mind.

It's what made Parkes, on that day, very special. Why was this the town in which One Nation had enjoyed its greatest electoral success in New South Wales?

Elvis in Parkes. It's an operative metaphor—a trope for communal glue. Festal togetherness in massed jumpsuits.

And that is the paradox of Parkes for me. I wanted to find justification for why these people had endorsed One Nation. I wanted to peer into part of the community that had some type of racist underbelly. I was searching for a section of the town that would conform to the stereotype that I had built in my mind. But I couldn't find anyone who fitted the identikit.

In one sense, I left Parkes empty-handed. The racists didn't exist. I didn't find what I was looking for—the Down Under outback rednecks. In fact, everywhere I looked all I could see was the opposite. I saw an open community that was embracing everyone from afar who had come to join them. In that sense, my hands were far from empty; I was clinging to the commonality of decent people.

Perhaps Alice was right. Perhaps I had it completely wrong. My outlook was skewed from the outset; I was trying to gratify my own hard-wired discrimination. I was looking for a cause to match my prejudice. Was I doing to the people of Parkes precisely what my school peers had done to me years ago—that is, zero in on 'difference'?

After fifteen minutes of walking, the parade comes to an end. I grab my friends and we decide that we need to get ourselves something to eat. Only the pubs are open; everything else shuts down for the parade. So the pub it is—suits me. The kitchen won't open for a few hours and all they have to offer, until then, is alcohol. So we do what any self-respecting men dressed in Lycra at a tribute festival would do. We drink.

After a while, the karaoke machine cranks up. I hear someone going up to the DJ and asking for a song. I can't hear what he asks for, but the response is clear enough: 'Oh bloody hell, not "Suspicious Minds" again'. And we stay in the bar, drinking with locals and singing the same few Elvis songs.

14

GO AHEAD AND HATE ME

Everybody needs a hobby. Some people collect baseball cards. Others find a fascination with coins or stamps. Personally, I collect hate. I'm well aware that this is rather odd.

'Why don't you just stop looking at it?' Helen asks whenever I start reading to her the vile messages that people post on social media or send as an email to me. Helen wants me to stop reading it not because it upsets me. Rather, she worries that it excites me.

'But look, Helen, they are being both homophobic and Islamophobic in the same message. In the same sentence. With just three words. Throw in a bit of racism and a dash of sexism and we have a winner.' This is my response to 'you Islamic cockeater', which, you have to admit, is beautiful in its brevity.

'It *is not* a competition to find the most offensive person in Australia,' Helen will protest. But she is wrong. It is. And for a long while, I thought I was winning.

I can't remember when I first started receiving so much hate. There must have been a moment when I received the first death threat, racist email or pornographic photo with my head glued on. But for some reason it didn't leave a lasting impact at the time.

That kicked in later, when the volume became so great that it was hard to ignore.

I do, however, remember when I began my collection. In 2011, I was the General Secretary of the NSW Branch of the Labor Party and had authorised the television advertisements. You know, that bit at the end of an ad that says 'authorised by someone or other' very quickly. Well, in that year, it said 'S. Dastyari'. The problem was that the only 'S. Dastyari' in the phone book was my cousin Solomeh. I was smart enough to get myself deleted from the directory. So Solomeh was the one who was receiving the fan mail, and she passed on to me my first package of hate letters. It was only when I had seen so many pulled together that I realised I was on to something.

I keep them in a plastic tub in a cupboard below my mother's bookshelf. It started with an ornate wooden box, the type that you'd imagine would provide perfect housing for a modest packet of love letters. But the swell in volume soon demanded an upgrade. I have to keep them at my mother's house because I can't trust Helen not to throw them out and, in the eyes of my ethnic mother, anything of mine is of value and to be protected, if necessary with swords drawn and until the end of days. Not even my father can be trusted with the treasure; Dad reckons that I'm a hoarder and has, over the years, moved in on my materials. I've considered buying a lock.

So a collection that started with a handful of written letters in 2011 has grown to over 100 pieces. Of course, the emails and Facebook messages have to be printed—an inconvenience but well worth the effort. The letters are preferably those that still have their original envelope. A handwritten letter is particularly valued. These are the rarest type of hate. I search for the holy grail: all in bold; all in capitals; all written with a red pen; randomly underlined words; verbose. I've kept about a dozen of those. Recently, when the volume was getting out of control, I established a rule of obsolescence. Every new piece needed to replace an old one. But I have to say, letting go has been so stressful that I keep breaking the rule. Call me neurotic if you like, but I find it hard to make hate obsolete.

Social scientists will tell you that the impersonal nature of social media emboldens people to write things that they would never say face to face. The digitising of speech removes the confrontational barrier to unacceptable behaviour. I'm sure that there is truth to this. But hate mail feels pretty bloody personal for the person receiving it.

I sometimes wonder if nowadays, in the age of social media, there's more per capita hate in the world than was once the case. Paul Keating used to say that 'if you don't have enemies, you are a nobody'. But that was before the internet. Now everybody has enemies. Now hate is freewheeling and cheap.

It's the one question that I always want interviewers to ask famous interviewees. Once the formalities and the niceties are out of the way, I want the interviewer to probe their guest's mail. I ache to know whether the well-known so-and-sos get the garden variety type of hate, or whether something really strange and exotic finds its way to their inbox or their mail box.

'Yes, Mr George Clooney, I do understand you have a new movie coming out next week, but we need to move on. Would you describe the messages you receive via social media as disproportionately homophobic in nature?'

I don't want to leave the impression that I get all that much hate mail. I get a greater quantity of repugnant letters than most politicians do, mostly about Islam and gay marriage. But I savour every one of them. Each is a speck of gold.

Anecdotally, politicians are mid-range on the hate-mail hit list. It appears that musicians get the least hate mail and athletes the most. I don't know any actors, so I can't number-crunch the anecdotes that might otherwise allow me to speak for them. Everyone hates politicians, but they, surprisingly, get less hate mail than athletes. I suppose some people assume that everyone else is already pulling hard against pollies in the hatred stakes, meaning that the composition of mail can best be left to others. Musicians somewhat self-select their audiences and are less in your face than are the recipients of high-volume detestation. Most abominated of all are participants in team sports, my sources of anecdote faithfully tell me. I hazard the guess that the competitive nature of sport brings out the worst in correspondents.

'It's not opponents that send you the most horrible attacks,' a school friend who plays football tells me.

'Who is it then?'

'Your own supporters. People who follow your team. You get some gentle sledging from opponents—but the really vile stuff comes from fans. They're the ones who really care.'

What I have also learnt is that women get it far worse than men. There is a sexually charged nature to the attacks that are inflicted on women through social media. It is repulsive, there is no doubt about that. I can't help but feel sickened, and baffled. I'm actually not interested in the messages themselves. I'm intrigued by the people who produce the crap.

Are there that many people out there who really hope a female politician 'bleeds to death at [her] time of [the] month'? Does one of my correspondents really want me to be 'fucked up in the biblical sense'? (I'm at a loss to know whether biblical idioms open themselves to this sort of translation, or whether a vulgar euphemism is being used to articulate any one of a multitude of scenarios stretching from the creation of Adam to the day of judgement.) For me, the personal touches to the vile hatred make the messages so memorable, so resistant to obsolescence.

I picture them sitting in their dens. All men. All in their forties. Angry. I picture them overweight. Smelly. Waiting for their retired mother to make them dinner. And she, poor soul, gnaws at herself—can't stop wondering what went wrong, why her son won't get a job and can't find a partner. But I know that this is the wrong stereotype. I know that because I've started stalking these people back. It's amazing how many will happily post from their own accounts. They don't even try to hide who they are when spewing vitriol.

Many of them are women. Most are parents and are employed, some are teachers and bureaucrats. And so rather than picturing them as dysfunctional trolls in their filthy dens, a more accurate scenario catches them dropping their kids off to school, stopping for a coffee to spew online hate, then having a civilised confab with the next-door neighbour before heading off to work.

These people are markedly distinct from the online conspiracy theorists. While the latter are fascinating in their own way, they are often more innocent than the vectors of hate. I've learnt not to argue anymore with the conspiracy nuts. If you genuinely believe in chemtrails (that the government is spraying you with control chemicals), that lizard people are running world governments or that 9/11 was an inside job, it is too late for my help. A fifteen-minute conversation online isn't going to change your mind. By the time you are reaching out to politicians, that ship has sailed. And while these conspiracy theorists will get angry that you don't see the world from their perspective, they don't normally spew hate the way the others do.

'You realise why you keep all this garbage,' my best friend Sam Crosby says to me.

'Because I'm a bit weird,' I respond, trying to take the sting out of what I think will be a joke.

'No. Because this is how you have decided to cope with it. It's your defence mechanism. This is the barrier you put around all that Islamophobia you get.' Totally ruining this insightful observation was the predictable rider: 'And also because you *are* weird'.

He is right (about both things). Why else would a grown man keep, in his mother's cupboard, a box of the most vile things people have said about him? Why do I laugh and print out the hate that gets sent my way? Because it's a way of dehumanising the hate. The same way the trolls on social media will strip people down—treat them as things, not as people. How is this any different? In the end, aren't I just trying to control a situation that I can't control?

What stuns me is that the hate, often, isn't passing from one tribe to another; rather, hate's flow is every bit as much intra- as inter-tribal in its circulation. With my athlete friend, I'm learning that the hate often kindles *within* the group. One is never 'pure' enough.

I'm not sure how to describe *Guardian* columnist Van Badham without resorting to the lonely description of 'pragmatic Marxist'. This is a really mean thing to do, because it angers everybody. The hard left get angry as 'pragmatic' implies that she somehow sold out. Contrariwise, for anyone to the right of Gorbachev the description is a polite way of saying, 'WARNING: The socialist streak is strong in this one'. But she is, after all, a 'pragmatic Marxist', so I'll stick with that title for now.

If my friends and associates ran a competition to determine who gets the strangest online hate, Van would be the hands-down winner. She gets attacked from both the left and the right.

'There is a reason why those on the left can't have nice things. It's because of the complete inability to accept that good change, while not necessarily perfect, should be grasped,' Van explains. And it is her tendency to express such arguments online that drives so many of the left into paroxysms of outrage.

'Too often, the left is allergic to winning. It's a lose addiction,' Van quips to me. 'It's how the puritan lefties are able to dine with their Tory parents.

'The left used to focus on winning, on getting things done,' she continues, having hit full stride. 'Now one big chunk of the left wants to focus on being outraged while leaving social democrats to make all the decisions around social policy; decisions that, inevitably, outrage them.'

Van has a love affair with baiting puritan lefties. It's her shtick. She is frustrated when people are trying to do good things and others sit on the sidelines throwing barbs at those who are trying to make things better. She calls it out. And that's borderline crazy in today's online environment.

Of course, her left-wing political outlook also gets all the regular hatred that any outspoken woman gets: the sexist taunts; the attacks on her integrity; the rape commentary. But it's the fact that she gets it from both sides of the fence that has me interested.

'Who gives it the worst? The left or the right?' I quiz her.

'I'm not sure it makes a difference when they are threatening to beat you up and rape you.' Should've expected that from Van. Her savage realism terminates the conversation.

I received a call from advertising executive Dee Madigan, asking if I had seen the Australia Day poster of the two Muslim girls that had been taken down as a result of complaints. I had.

An image of two Muslim girls formed part of a rotating billboard to celebrate Australia Day in 2017. A handful of right-wing trolls responded with a social-media campaign against the company responsible for the billboard. The company, in an act of cowardice, took down the billboard. In response, Dee had decided to run a campaign to raise enough funds to get it back up again.

'Do you know how much hate you will get?' I warn her.

I had had a few earlier interactions with these far-right groups. And when their crazy is directed your way, you quickly feel it.

Dee isn't what you would define as a defender of Islam. Quite the contrary, she is a staunch atheist. What's more, she can (and has) drunk me under the table. She swears and is closer to Shazza than Sharia. All of which made what she had undertaken to do perfect.

We get together and predict that she will succeed in raising the $20 000 needed to get the billboard back up.

I reiterate my warning. 'But you know how much hate you will get?'

'Sam, I'm pretty tough. I won't be broken by a few emails and messages.' And she is right; she is very tough. But what Dee got was not a few waves of hate. Descending upon her with grizzly intent was the entire Australian contingent of the Alt-Right.

The campaign itself was a huge success. Dee raised close to $200 000 and was able not only to restore the billboard, but to place full-page newspaper adverts across the country. It was widely acknowledged as a 'good-news story'. Everyone was lining up to talk to her about how successful her efforts had been. But I wasn't just interested in that. I wanted to know about the hate.

And she showed me some of it.

'Do you think this bloke called Steve Jones, if that even is his real name, really believes it when he writes to you, "I hope you feel as multiculturally embracing if one of your children is ever violated by one of these maggots you embrace with open arms"?' I ask her.

'I really just try not to think about,' she tells me.

Dee keeps trying to show me, and give me, examples of all the lovely letters she got, all the good wishes, all the words of support. But I'm not interested in that. And I explain to her about my tub at Mum's place, my flourishing tuckshop of ill-regard.

'Why do you only keep the hate?' It was something that I had never thought deeply about; it was a behaviour, I suppose, informed more by impulse than by purpose. My action was reactive, not providential. 'Surely you must get some nice stuff, sweet letters from old ladies and the like.'

And she is right. I do get a lot of positive letters—from people being sweet and supportive, often thanking me for things that I have done. I get a lot of really heart-warming correspondence. But I have never kept that. I keep only the hate.

'Is that healthy?' Dee asks. 'Just keeping hate. Is that a healthy thing to do?'

I know the answer to that but I don't want to acknowledge it. I know that deep down I hate it—'it' being the hate; it's an open question as to whether I hate hating the hate itself. But Dee has a point. I can sometimes dwell on things, as you may have noticed, and I can get self-conflicted. It can't, as Dee suggests, be good for me.

So while I joke about the hate to no end it will still, occasionally, keep me up at night. And while I try to use my morbid collection as a way of controlling my emotions, I can never successfully stop myself from wanting to be liked.

I take Dee's advice. I start a new tub. This one keeps all the lovely letters and emails of support. It's still pretty empty. But let's see how it goes.

15

HOW TO CONDUCT YOURSELF AROUND CHILDREN

I've been in some pretty rough mosh pits in my life. I've seen people be dragged down and beaten when crowd surfing. I've spent time at all-day festivals where drug-induced paranoia feeds the violent tendencies of middle-aged tattooed men. None of this, however, adequately prepared me for proceedings at the nativity scene in which, with her school companions, my 5-year-old daughter recently partook.

Frankly, I blame myself. All the warning signs were there. When the teacher rose to caution parents that, in the case of an emergency, they ought not to push children out of the way to get to an exit, I simply *should* have read the tea leaves. But I laughed, thinking that the teacher had made a joke, before realising how seriously this was taken.

Helen was working, which meant that she had to do her paid work along with the eighty or so other essential things that had to be done that day. In consequence, she couldn't get to the play until later. So she needed to delegate. I was the delegatee, meaning that I had the straightforward job. All that I had to do was to drop off

Hannah on time and reserve some seats. Sometimes things that at face value seem to be straightforward aren't, well … Let's just say that the designated task had its challenges.

The play was to start at 6:00 p.m. and the children were to arrive by 5:00 p.m. for costume. I thought that I could arrive at 5:00 p.m., drop off my daughter and still get decent seats. How naive. Seats, being a finite resource, would be sought after. They would be subject to intense competition, and those who got the good ones would be fiercely envied by those who didn't. By 5:10 p.m., the only seats that I could get were in the fourth-last row—row 17. People had been filing in from midday.

I had arranged seats for a friend, Lucy Mannering, who was coming with her two other children. Lucy has a daughter, Sybilla, in the same class as Hannah. It hadn't gone perfectly to plan for Lucy—she had to launch into crisis-management mode once it became apparent that the costume department was in a tizz.

Lucy had overlooked Sybilla's white socks, the required dress code for the 'naughty sheep' in whose guise both our daughters were to be appearing. I had to fight off parents trying to take the seats that I'd reserved for her and when she at last arrived was disappointed that she didn't appreciate the difficulty of procuring, and then of retaining, these shit seats. I'd needed to establish and patrol a beachhead. I'd deployed items of clothing—arrayed strategically on a series of seats—and had mustered my 3-year-old daughter, Eloise, to do guard duty by sitting across two seats that, had there been no bum or leg on them, would doubtless have fallen to the enemy.

'I need to ask you, politely, not to move your chair into the aisles, not to stand in the aisles, not to obscure the aisles and not to encourage your children to run into your arms.' The event MC, a teacher at the school, had commenced, preaching sonorously from the Book of Thou Shalt Not. This cautionary clause signalled the start of a briefing to the assembled parents and carers that made airport-safety procedures appear lax.

It was with the fighting words 'there are seats available up the front for anyone who wants them' that the calmness started to break down. As most parents come in pairs and leave individual seats between themselves and the next couple, a fair few individual seats were available but almost no pairs. No one was prepared to move. At this point, there were 462 parents in the hall, and it was getting hot. The frustration and the waiting were taking a toll. Arguments about seats began to break out. Spotfires of discontent were fanned into larger combustions. People were becoming less companionable; the milk of human kindness was beginning to curdle.

Society as we knew it forty-five minutes earlier was dissolving into Thomas Hobbes' state of nature, where life was 'solitary, poor, nasty, brutish and short'. The 'solitary' bit was inapplicable, but otherwise Hobbes had nicely captured the niggle on nativity night.

Straining to keep the mayhem in check, the MC morphs from preacher to prophet. 'We will start right on six o'clock.' Not fully persuaded, I glance at my watch. It's 5:56 p.m. Four minutes to go.

Watching the other parents skirmish for the remaining seats up the front, I settle in for some good old-fashioned judging of parents, a favourite pastime of mine. Lucy is with me on the judicial bench. (I plan, one day, to start my own reality TV show, in which parental contestants watch, judge and vote on the parenting of others. The degrading sociability to which Lucy and I were witnesses was looking like a chance for a perfect dry run.)

'Sybilla said to me she expected flowers because other girls were getting flowers at the end of this. I said it is not happening. I told her she was lucky we managed to get the sock situation fixed,' Lucy tells me.

As this information is being passed on, I'm thinking to myself that I too have turned up flowerless. Am I meant to get flowers for Hannah? These are the moments that make you question your own parenting. I look around and suddenly notice the many flowers that other parents are holding. Fuck. The guilt sets in. I'm both not prepared to fight for a better seat AND I don't have flowers. 'I think flowers are a waste of money. That money should go to charity,' I respond, leaving out that I hadn't bought flowers and wouldn't be donating what I'd saved.

HOW TO CONDUCT YOURSELF AROUND CHILDREN   147

This is my first nativity scene. I can't remember ever having performed in one, or watched one, during my schooling years. Hannah's school has been doing this for years, and the accumulated experience is telling. The statistics speak for themselves: seventeen songs, 200 kids performing and the whole thing going for twenty-eight minutes and thirty-two seconds (who's counting?).

To achieve this feat, a few creative liberties had to be taken. I'm not a Christian scholar, but there are not, to my knowledge, 200 people in any other version of the events surrounding the birth of the Christian Messiah.

'An inventive twist on an old story,' Lucy chuckles.

To be fair, the school had done an impressive job in coordinating all of this. There were thirty-nine angels, forty-six 'naughty sheep' (we will get to that later), twenty-six narrators, twenty-two camels and nineteen stars. The three wise men had brought a couple of mates, so they now numbered five, and were no doubt wiser for it. Why weren't their wives there too?

The role of Herod was politely whitewashed. The whole ethnic-cleansing and murder-of-children narrative, I conjecture, would really have dampened the festive mood. It was far too early in the evening for genocide.

The school understood what every parent really wanted—namely, a chance for their own child to shine. Let's face it, that was the only reason anyone was there that boiling December night. The school understood this. So all of the kids, all 200 of them, were on stage for the entire performance. Our kids were 'starring'; the liberties taken with the storyline hardly mattered.

The play opens with the welcome song: 'A Baby Will Soon Be Born'. Kids start walking, aimlessly, around the stage, totally forgetting their roles. It's gorgeous stuff. Or I'm sure it would be, *if only we could see any of it*. I understand that there are people who would want to snap the occasional photo on their phone, perhaps for an absent grandparent or a sick aunty. But it's news to me that you can film an entire play by holding up your iPad. Apparently, I am the only person who doesn't know this. I wonder if the messianic resonance of the scene before us has got the better of all of the other parents. What are they doing holding iPads and iPhones to the sky? Do they think that Jesus is descending from the clouds?

'I can't see shit,' I complain to Lucy. She's not listening to me, though—she's watching the play through the iPad of the person now standing up in front of us. Civility transforms into uproar as parents are cast into two camps, those who want the people in front to sit down and those who are doing the standing. As a member of the former group, I secretly cheer the parents yelling 'SIT *DOWN*!' though I'm nowhere near brave enough to do this myself. Instead, like a coward, I just sink back and bitch about it to Lucy.

'I think I should take Eloise up the front,' I announce. Eloise is very keen to see the play. She's not OK with the non-view from row 17.

'Are you sure it'll be safe up there?' Lucy jokes. But she has a point. I briefly pop my head up and realise that the front few rows are no place for children—which, at a children's play, is deliciously ironic. Helen takes the better option and decides to hold Eloise at the back for the duration so she can see.

My bitching pauses as we all turn to watch the Egyptian grandfather two rows behind us take a phone call. This develops into a heated exchange. His wife is trying to shut him up, a move that generates more attention as he puts his call on hold to yell at her. Sitting beside him is whom I can only suspect is his embarrassed daughter, hiding her head in shame.

It is minute 8 of the play and I can feel an internal transformation start to take place. According to what Hannah had told me earlier that day, the 'naughty sheep' song will soon be performed and I'm getting edgy that I can't see the stage. They will be singing 'Juicy Juicy Green Grass', an Australian childhood classic about hungry sheep. With this part of the play imminent, a metamorphosis has its way with me.

One moment I'm the casual detached observer thinking about the ridiculousness of how it could be that a natal procedure in ancient Bethlehem would find itself contending with an unruly flock of Australian sheep; and the next moment I've become the maniacal patriarch pushing a pregnant woman out of the way to get a better photo of his daughter. But, you see, this is who I am. Despite the judging, the mocking, the bitching, what I really want is to see my 5-year-old daughter as the star of the show. And, sure, her only role might be singing a song that has nothing to do with the story of Jesus. She might be only one of the unholy host of the 'naughty sheep', but damn it—she is MY daughter and I want to watch her nail it.

By minute 10, I'm not even ashamed anymore. The mania has conquered the conscience. I have a singular focus—get the photo. The kindergarten sheep start singing their song. It's a call-and-response arrangement. One sheep yells out 'Juicy juicy green grass' and then the group echoes the line. The children are set up stage right. It is then that I realise that the 200-and-something cameras are not filming *the play*; rather, each camera operator is filming *his or her own child*. The cameras aren't moving in unison with the action on stage. They are all fixed; the focus of each one is a single person. And that, of course, makes sense.

It's about being in the place, and in the moment—in the stifling heat of the school hall, towards Christmas at the end of kindergarten, with the most precious people in the world. You watch and film the precious one, each parent sending out secret rays of emotional support, hidden threads of guidance, protecting them from little mishaps, and riding the wave of their joy. I play my part, by being there and caring and taking photographs, and Hannah plays hers. And these are parts of a bigger play that will never, ever, in precisely this way, be performed again. It's madness—and it's magic.

Following the song, the play gets back on track. Shelter is found, a child is born, songs are sung, but I've lost interest. Hannah's role has finished.

'You were a great naughty sheep,' I praise Hannah afterwards. I go on to ask, 'Why were you "naughty sheep" and not just sheep?'

'Because we eat "juicy juicy green grass," of course,' she says, a statement in the matter-of-fact delivery of which Hannah fills me in and sorts me out, as if this will settle any other question I will have.

'I was so very proud of you today,' I let her know.

A smile creeps up on her face. 'Were you Daddy?' she asks, fishing for more praise.

'Oh yes I was,' I reply, having the same conversation that the forty-five other parents of 'naughty sheep' were having as they drove their children home that night.

I wonder if when St Nicholas decided to assume his Santa responsibilities he was aware that, in just a few generations, he would be walking the aisles of David Jones in Elizabeth Street, Sydney, under a new promotion called 'selfies with Santa'. If so, he was clearly comfortable with limelight, for the promotion encourages people to walk up to him in the department-store corridor and demand that he join them for a photo.

Call me a traditionalist, but back in my day you knew that you had to sit down with Santa, and you could safely assume that he was, at least, getting a cut of the photo sales. Now it's just workplace abuse. I'm not sure what I expect, but I find it somehow demeaning that Santa now aimlessly walks around with his elves, trolling the shops, obligingly complying with the whims of customers, begging for Facebook likes. Throw in a selfie stick and we might as well just give up on Santa now—his reputation is beyond repair. If ever there was an argument against intelligent design, 'selfies with Santa' is it.

I'm taking Helen and my girls for the obligatory Santa photo three days before Christmas. I'm at David Jones because I hate myself. Santa, when not walking around, is housed in the 'mystical magic cave'. It's hard to work out what the 'cave' is used for when it is not renatured for Christmas. Mostly storage, I suspect.

There are three identical Santa caves across Australia. The others are to be found at Bourke Street in Melbourne and Adelaide Plaza.

HOW TO CONDUCT YOURSELF AROUND CHILDREN   151

All follow the same basic design: a walk-through area that is elaborately decorated with fairy lights, a holding area that features window displays and a back area that has rooms for the different Santas—dressing rooms, I imagine, smelling of liniment, equipped with rub-down tables and staffed by physiotherapists. The battle for quality time with Santa can get physical.

But the real challenge lies in getting into the cave.

We approach the 'elf' that is running the rope line on the cave's periphery. She holds a clipboard and an iPad. A few years ago, I would line up like this to get into nightclubs. Now I do it to pay a bearded man to test the credulity of my children.

'Do you have a booking?' the elf asks.

'No. We thought we could just visit.'

'You really should have a booking.'

I notice that no one else is around.

'Let's create a booking for you right now,' she cheerily suggests.

'Can't we just go in?' I ask.

'Not without a booking.'

'They have a system,' Helen tells me, siding with the staff.

'Do they?' I not-so-quietly ask Helen. 'There is *another* Santa apparently just walking the halls taking photos with anyone.'

Helen responds with the look that says, 'Do not even try to mess with Christmas'. Helen's family takes Christmas very seriously. For them, the photo with Santa is a must-have item. Helen's mum, Pat, has a collection of kids-with-Santa photos dating back to when Helen and her sister Jennifer were little girls.

I learnt early on in my relationship with Helen that 'Christmas' and 'family' are inseparable. Pat starts preparing for Christmas in September, and every year she somehow manages to make it more magical than it was the previous year. My Iranian upbringing had not consolidated my own deep sense of family in quite this way, but it is a lovely thing to experience the sheer joy of a Barron family Christmas. My two girls, and Helen's two nephews, Liam and Rory, will no doubt grow up with treasured memories of Christmas, just as Helen and Jennifer have.

What's bothering me, though, is that we need to make a booking to see Santa. The spirit of giving doesn't feel quite so genuine when the elves are squeezing your wallet. 'You can buy the basic package, but the extra-value package is only $10 dearer and you "save" $30 by buying it,' we are helpfully informed.

I'm sorry. Have I, my whole life, completely misunderstood the concept of 'saving'? I wasn't aware that 'saving' was when you spend more for a product to receive a deduction from a different arbitrary price.

'We will take the extra-value package,' I tell her. Sold on the savings argument.

There are, on my count, nine green-shirted elves working the cave. At least eight other elves, attired in yellow, are on attendance at the cash registers and the Santa rooms. Around thirty people are in situ within the magical cave, which, I find out later from an elf, constitutes fairly quiet patronage in view of the day's proximity to Christmas.

By this stage, the elves have seen it all and are really just phoning it in. It only takes a minute to get them out of character and talking about their summer jobs. Their real job, here, is meant to be crowd control and up-selling products such as photo frames and the like.

'Soon there will be no Santas,' one of them tells me. 'Have you seen the digital stage?' In what is no doubt a glimpse into the future of Christmas, a green screen is available that enables you not only to get your photo taken but also to have Santa and his sled digitally imposed upon the image—which, frankly, is cheating.

A yellow elf calls out our number and prepares to take us to a Santa. There are four Santas working the caves today; at full capacity, the operation enables the simultaneous deployment of six Santas. 'We will have two more this afternoon,' the elf tells me. Would this be a sextet of Santas? I guess, strictly, they'd need to break into song or play some instruments to qualify.

We wait outside a room while Santa readies himself. A lot of logistical work goes into making sure that only one Santa is ever seen by the children at any point in time. How this is done when the sextet is up and about defies my capacity to imagine.

The room itself best resembles a prison cell. It is, at most generous estimate, a 5 metre by 3 metre enclosure that would usually be used as a cupboard. 'Is Santa being held hostage in an ISIS video?' I ask Helen.

The Santa is as professional as they come. He asks Hannah what she wants for Christmas (she is too shy to answer) and then asks Eloise (who has a complete list). Hannah eventually whispers what she wants to Santa and won't let us hear, not realising that her confidential monologue has sabotaged her chances of getting the toys that she desires.

'That's not the real Santa,' Hannah tells me afterwards.

'Oh really, why do you say that?'

'The real Santa is in the North Pole. That's just a costume Santa.'

Great, I think—a child with the insight to disabuse herself of one of childhood's principal fantasies. We leave immediately, taking full care to ensure that Eloise doesn't bump into the other Santa who's off the leash and roaming the store.

Col Macpherson lives in a town called 'The Rock', in south-western New South Wales. The Rock is about thirty minutes' drive from Wagga Wagga, and was clearly named by someone who knew that Col was destined to live there. At last count, exactly 860 people lived in The Rock. It's small, quiet and comfortable. Nothing much changes there, which is why the politics of the local pony club is so fantastic.

Col's appearance belies his seventy years. He is one incredibly strong and fit man. Having spent a lifetime as a shearer, he has seen strikes and workplace fights, and even played a role in the famous 'wide-comb dispute' of 1983, in which a proxy debate over the size of shearing combs got very ugly.

'During the wide-comb dispute there were bomb threats, bashings, two confirmed murders and the worst intimidation you have ever seen. But it still has nothing on the politics of the pony club—that's where things get really vicious.' Col tells me this, and I don't wish to disbelieve him. But did I hear right?

'Pony club?' I check.

'Yep. It's a nasty, nasty place,' he confirms.

What I later learn is that he is referring, specifically, to the Pony Club Association of NSW. There are twenty-eight zones and 285 clubs. The membership of this particular pony club exceeds that of major political parties in New South Wales.

Perhaps I have the wrong impression, and let's face it, I'm from the inner city, but when you say 'pony club', the images that I conjure up are idyllic and utterly devoid of the strife to which Col seems to be alluding. I think of small children riding around on miniature horses, with country mothers and aunties working together to keep everyone fed and happy, while, perhaps, the menfolk gather out the back to drink beer and play two-up. I picture floral outfits (not worn by the two-up players), warm summer days, little girls and cake stalls.

The way Col tells it, the club is a hotbed for psychopaths, the play thing of control freaks.

'I've seen the worst of Labor politics, I've seen workplace disputes where my friends got bashed for standing up for their rights, but nothing, *nothing*, is as brutal as the politics of the pony club.'

'How can the politics of the pony club be so rough?' I ask, not realising that this story is still raw.

'It's brutal, bloody ferocious.' The angst, it appears, is about power—the daily bread of voluntary organisations.

I go online and start seeing the faces of the pony-club management. While at first glance they look like nice parents, I start to think that perhaps Col is right. Maybe, deep down, something sinister is lurking. Perhaps the pony club *is* a place where psychopaths have mastered the art of espionage and where empires are built and toppled. Certainly, the rule book—judging by its impressive concatenation of regulations and by-laws—gives substance to the suspicion that many disputes have clamoured in the presence of local legislators.

'They act all sweet and innocent, but Sam, they are a vicious bunch. They use the rules, the system, the elections are rigged.' Col is now on a roll.

There is, of course, another explanation. To put it simply, when it concerns their children, people go a little nutty. Everyone knows of the overly keen parent at the sporting event, some of whom act like ratbags. When it comes to your own children, rationality is thrown out the door. The passion of a political rally holds no candle to the love that you feel for your kids. Even when the most minor of matters draws you in, you get caught up in feelings that you *cannot* control if, in some respect, your kids are involved.

That is the more sensible explanation, but I choose not to see it that way. I'm sticking with Col, and I call Helen to tell her to make sure we lock the doors that night, lest some posse of freaks from the pony club rides out to get us.

IV
THE MEAT

16

IDEAS IN STRAITJACKETS

'It's a Potemkin village. Never forget that.' It's July 2013, and Bob Hawke and I are on his balcony and he is describing the Australian Parliament to me.

I'd heard the term before. It refers to the fake villages built to impress Catherine the Great while she inspected the smoking ruins of occupied Crimea; nowadays it refers to a false front papering over deep cracks in the nature of things.

This was, and still is, the best description that I have heard of our parliament.

'Isn't that how it has always been?' I ask, the question posed with characteristic cynicism.

'It's worse than it used to be,' Bob says emphatically. 'There was more integrity in the business. That's gone. It's smaller. Politics is a smaller business than it used to be. Everyone is just always so afraid to give things a go these days,' he muses, taking another mouthful of beer. 'So afraid.'

He's right that there is a fear that permeates the corridors of Parliament House. The fear has suffused itself into the long, hushed rows of offices in that building on the hill. Pardon the metaphysics, but the fear is not only an agent, a something, but it ranges over many of the eventualities to which we give the name 'politics'.

The fear shows itself in different ways. Sometimes it's a fear of standing out, of being different. That kind of fear drives people who arrive with big ideas to make decisions that end up bland, watered down, weak. There's the fear of being 'caught out'—sprung for all to see in a 'gotcha moment'. This is the fear of being exposed. That's what drives the obsession with pre-defined talking points and the abhorrence for expressing personal views. And then there's the fear of not being taken seriously, of being laughed at by your colleagues, belittled. Gratuitous political violence often gets done when this fear starts to whisper in people's ears—the minister rolled for no good reason, the bright backbencher who gets blacklisted from ever getting a promotion.

But these fears are really one and the same. Each, ultimately, is an emotional shard of the fear of loss: of losing your spot in this strange house on the hill, of going back to what you were before you were a 'somebody'. That fear fills the building like smoke, seeping under every office door, wending through the ornate halls and chambers.

Parliament House is a place of contradictions. The building is lonely even when it is full. Everywhere you go there are talkers, people who have an endless stream of things to say. But if you actually take the time to stop and listen (which no one does), you'll realise that very little is ever being said. There is only the ringing of hollow words, the constant spray of garrulous guff: *Nice tie. Let's get lunch sometime. Loved your zinger on the news.*

There is a great emptiness to the building. You often feel that you've been cut adrift from everything that's important, for all that you're at the centre of the nation's governance. The sense of unreality isn't helped by the fact that parliament is never hot and never cold, it does not change with the wind, or the rain, summer or winter. Like an ocean liner or a spaceship, the building has services and supplies: a gym, a hairdresser, restaurants, a bar. The office couches are designed long and deep enough for sleeping on. One can enter the building on a Monday for sittings and not leave it until the place rises on a Thursday. I suspect that some *never* leave.

Apart from when the ringing of the bells calls members to vote, the building is mostly quiet. It looks peaceful and calm. Essentially, the place is a super-sized vacuum flask.

But spend enough time there and you begin to notice that the calm is really a tension, a wire pulled tight that countless occupants of the building want to break with a scream. That scream would give voice to a host of caged psychic states: frustration, panic, sadness, exhaustion, bitterness, sheer stir-craziness. And, no doubt, the screamer would be bearing witness to the fear that won't leave them alone.

But it doesn't matter how hard you listen, you won't hear that scream. People know how to bury the fear.

I could tell you plenty about Parliament House: for example, how many metres the corridors stretch; how many offices there are; how much carpet. All these things are regurgitated, time and again, to the thousands of children who walk through this building each year. But such details simply amount to more of the talk that means nothing.

They never tell the children about the fear.

If the fear only afflicted us as individual politicians, so what—right? Call your shrink; suck it up; if you can't take the heat, get out of the kitchen.

But, unfortunately, the fear affects everyone. And that's because it's fear, more than anything else, that corrodes ideas.

You begin with a big, bold policy idea. Maybe it's proposing a change that others have been afraid to touch before. There are surprisingly few entirely 'new' ideas, but there are many variations on existing ones.

The politician will walk into parliament with their big idea, full of conviction and determination. The fact that it is 'difficult' is part of the appeal. Others weren't prepared to see the big idea through, but this politician will tell you that they are different. They will tell you that they are bold. They might even use Gough Whitlam's famous line about having to 'crash through or crash'.

They will talk about their idea to their friends outside parliament. A chorus of the cognoscenti will sing as one. *This is a great idea. Our country needs this. You will be a hero for doing it.* And the politician will be further emboldened.

Then the politician will consult with parliamentary colleagues. This group will be more cautious, and notes of circumspection will be heard. Many colleagues once had their own idea that didn't make it. But the politician will ignore this. *They* failed, the politician thinks, because they weren't bold, they weren't strong, they weren't prepared to see it through. Not this politician, though— this politician will be different.

The next stage is that the politician will present their policy idea to their own team as a *fait accompli*. Perhaps they are already a minister, and will present it to their department. The public service, though, will have seen it all before. *That is a really brave suggestion,* they will say, *a bold way of doing things.*

Then the watering down will begin. *Have you considered this?* Bureaucrats will rattle off the inevitable spectrum of people who will be deleteriously affected by any change. *How much consultation has been done?* And so the politician will have to listen to those who don't want it done. They will start changing their policy, adapting it to appease the growing list of People With A View.

'Well, it doesn't need to be THAT radical,' the politician will say. 'Perhaps we can adjust it at the edges, make it less severe, a bit of give and take.' And those who like the status quo will agree. They will take these clawbacks but continue to push for more. Water it down. Always water it down.

But further dilution of the idea may happen. Perhaps the idea will somehow be covered in the media. Then the real outrage will

IDEAS IN STRAITJACKETS

begin. 'How can you possibly do THAT?' someone will say. This will intensify the scrutiny of the idea—aspects will be 'ruled in', and aspects will be 'ruled out'. The politician will defend their idea, but their colleagues probably won't. This wasn't, after all, THEIR idea. And the politician's colleagues will happily tell the journalists that (on the condition of anonymity, of course). But the politician doesn't want to give up on their idea. They want to push through, so they start accepting compromises. They make the policy as inoffensive as possible. Which often means that any remaining usefulness is negotiated out of it. Water it down. Keep on watering it down. Saturate it.

And so, having started with a big and bold idea, the politician ends up with a small change to the existing order of things.

Now, perhaps it was a bad idea to begin with. But sometimes the process that I've described wraps its tentacles around ideas that would make things fairer, and that would inspire more faith and hope in politics. Too bad. Ultimately, very few politicians are prepared to put it all on the line for their idea. You see, the fear of loss is far too great.

Of course, occasionally a politician is adamant. Once in a while they *are* prepared to put it all on the line—particularly leaders who have their legacy or a tight election in mind. When the fear isn't enough to kill an idea, then the professionals sweep in. That's when the idea gets sent to focus groups and pollsters.

If the Australian public truly understood how many government decisions are shaped by a few dozen people sitting in a focus group who are there to collect their $80, they would be horrified. These are people who, by the selection criteria, self-identify as knowing nothing about the topic at hand.

Here's how it works. People who have landlines will be cold called and taken through a questionnaire. The focus-group selection process is in motion.

164   PART IV: THE MEAT

'For whom did you vote at the last election?' the questioner will ask.

'No idea,' the candidate responds. 'All politicians are arseholes. Throw them all in a pit.'

'Great.' The questioner will not be put off by this. A clear opinion, after all, has been enunciated.

'Who is the Prime Minister of Australia?' This, let's be fair, is a very time-sensitive question in modern Australian politics.

'No idea. All politicians are arseholes. Feed 'em to the bloody sharks.'

'Would you be interested in coming to a focus group for $80 and to help shape Australian health policy?'

The respondent will hesitate. They want the $80, but are only marginally interested, if at all, in the topic.

'You can have as many free sandwiches and as much free soft drink as you want.' The clincher. And there they will be, a week later, sitting in a stale air-conditioned room with between eight and eleven other people sharing either the same postcode or the same demographic profile.

I have spent more time in focus groups over the past decade than anyone I can think of. I was, after all, once the General Secretary of the NSW Labor Party. And I have lost a lot of faith in the process.

Not that focus groups can't serve a role. The function of a focus group should be to decide how best to sell an idea. Such gatherings should be tasked with considering how to shape language and resources to convince people of the merits of an idea. But that is not how they are used in Australian politics. Too often their function is to decide *what* should be done, not *how* something should be sold.

The nub of the matter is that there are conflicts at the heart of every type of research of this kind. And when a potential policy initiative is controversial in some way, it is crucially important for the sponsors of the initiative to be able to communicate its benefits. Focus groups *could* be helpful were they to be assembled with this communication issue as their governing objective.

Every idea to increase a tax, of course, runs into some kind of opposition. A particular person won't like it if such an idea leaves them 'worse off'. Equally, every idea to increase spending will tend to garner support from the same person if it is clear to that person that they will 'benefit'.

I can sit in a focus group and ask, 'Should we cut taxes?' and be greeted by a unanimous nodding of heads. And the same heads will nod in concordance if I ask, 'Should we increase funding for our schools?'

In such venues, the merits of an idea are rarely placed under the searching glare of caring or focused minds. Sandwiches take priority over scrutiny. The focus group is where bold ideas go to die.

'Oh—you are just being a policy snob. This is real people vetting real ideas.' People will tell me such things. And on an idealistic level, that sounds great. But the reality is otherwise. The focus group is the search for the lowest common denominator. This is policy development by attrition.

And so we end up with the Prime Minister of Australia, responsible for the thirteenth-largest economy in the world, walking around like a headless chicken talking about 'jobs and growth' in a campaign without anything to back it up. Why? Because someone in between eating sandwiches and guzzling soft drink said, 'That sounds good'.

This is why you have slogans like 'Moving Forward'. A few people would have liked it and the rest of the country gets saddled with it for the longest three months of our lives.

Yes, I'm bitter and twisted; I'm also highly hypocritical. I've run focus groups. I've shaped the depressing outcomes to which they lead—presided over the tortuous process by which good ideas get killed because the politics didn't suit.

For a political party and for its leader, the first goal is this: win an election. And the second goal? Use the power that's been acquired for some beneficial purpose. There is no point in having the best ideas if you have no chance of implementing them. *That* is the politics of being eternally in opposition.

By the same token, what's the point in taking the trouble to acquire power if you don't intend to do something with it?

The challenge lies in getting the balance right. Party officials and party machines will always be more focused on winning, while the policy wonks will be animated by the opportunities that governing opens up. When parties are at their best, both kinds of objective will be achieved. That was the case for Labor in the 1980s and 1990s under Hawke and Keating, and then, dare I say it, under Howard in the period following.

When party machines become too strong, nothing gets done. This is the story of Malcolm Turnbull's prime ministership. The goal of winning becomes the only motive; obtaining power and hanging on to it together become an end, no longer a means. The rulers forget why they wanted to gain power in the first place.

However, when the party machine is too weak you end up with the Whitlam government, which relinquished the power that it needed to retain. Great things were done, but the government got kicked out before a genuine transformation could be effected in Australia.

I realised, during the second week of February 2016, how far my view of focus groups had shifted. Bill Shorten called me to talk about the negative-gearing policy he planned to announce at the NSW Labor State Conference that weekend.

Bill told me that he was planning to announce the biggest changes to negative gearing in a generation, making a policy shift that, though it risked being politically painful, would deliver an outcome we all knew to be necessary: more affordable housing. This is precisely the type of idea that, as General Secretary of the NSW Labor Party, I would have tried to discourage.

'Do you have any idea what this will do to Sydney seats?' I would have said. 'Sure, the policy won't be retrospective, but try explaining that to a couple who have invested in housing. Are you mad?' Then, in an effort to kill it completely, I would have said: 'Don't you have *any* desire to become prime minister?'

I would have done my best to kill it. And I would have been wrong. You can distinguish between, on the one hand, 'good policy' as an approach to governance, as a *modus operandi*, if you will, and, on the other, individual 'good policies', which are the bricks in the structure of bringing about change, the pieces of policy that get put into place over time. It's difficult to reconcile the two, but it can be done. They do not have to be mutually exclusive.

Being a strong leader brings rewards in itself; leadership is an intangible quality that can't be tested in focus groups. Leadership is much more primal than that, and it carries with it the nettling responsibility of coupling 'good policy' with 'good policies'.

'What do you think?' Bill asks me.

'I think it is great. I think it is bold. I think it is a game changer. I think it defines you as someone who will take action,' I respond. In spite of my initial reflex to play the idea-killer, I *am* impressed that Bill has pushed back on the nay-sayers. Bill tells me that Chris Bowen has laid the economic groundwork and that the numbers are watertight.

Bill is convinced that he can bring people on the journey. He believes that he can change people's views on negative gearing.

He is right. The focus groups are a snapshot in time. They don't demonstrate how you can change the public's mind. They don't measure how opinion moves once people have time to process an idea. They don't give enough credit to the intellect of voters—of people who will respond in a thoughtful and informed way.

Which takes me back to Bob Hawke's balcony.

I've come to Bob's house for his blessing to break my word and run for parliament. Three years earlier, in 2010, I told him that I wouldn't run for a decade. My focus, I vowed, would be on party rebuilding. And three years into the rebuilding phase, I'm finding a Senate vacancy too tempting not to fill.

'You have already made up your mind to run, haven't you?' Bob asks. He knows me well enough to understand that although notionally asking for his opinion, I'm really just seeking his blessing.

'Yes,' I respond.

'Just remember,' he tells me after a long pause, 'you may as well use the opportunity. You only live once.'

'YOLO,' I say under my breath.

'What?'

'YOLO.'

'What's *YOLO*?'

'You Only Live Once. '

'Yes, that's what I was saying,' Bob shrugs.

17

ONE NATION

I was thirteen years old when Pauline Hanson first came on the scene. Yes, only a child. I grew up being excruciatingly aware of my own *difference*. So, in a sense, I was front and centre of an emotive political happening, the told-you-so who fleshed out the Hansonian spectre—the fear of the other.

When she was defeated in the late 1990s we congratulated ourselves. We became complacent. We didn't tackle the causes of her appeal. We became arrogant. Dismissive. And her influence grew.

Politicians don't like to acknowledge the effectiveness of fear. But fear works. Hate is as powerful a tool as love. In fact, it's a far easier one to mobilise. Politicians are reluctant to tell you that the idea of the successful western nation at the bottom of Asia has always been permeated by the fear that someone was going to take it away.

In the Trump era, it has been popular to speak of this as some kind of new phenomenon. But it has always been here. Lurking not too far beneath the surface. It is the fear of *that which isn't us*.

The media cycle will write her in and write her off. But Hanson will always be there. Perhaps not as Pauline, but certainly as the

169

deep fear at the heart of the Australian condition. It satiates itself on reprehension of the outsider.

Her supporters think that we are out of touch, elitist. There is nothing elitist about the swathe of people who fear her making life for their children harder, who worry about the bullying in the playground. Hanson plays footsies with extremists, but keeps just enough distance to claim that she is not them. But she motivates and energises them. She makes them part of the discourse that becomes mainstream but is never defensible.

Australia is a place of openness, tolerance and acceptance. But it also has dark parts to its history: look at the treatment of Indigenous Australians, of early Chinese migrants, of South Sea Islanders. Yes, there is love, hope and joy at the heart of Australia. There is also a darkness. For now, that darkness is personified by Pauline Hanson.

'You are a real shit, Sam Dastyari. Here you are, coming onto my podcast and you are already making jokes about halal.' It was with those words of love that Pauline Hanson met me in the court-yard of Parliament House on 9 February 2017.

I wanted to correct her. I wanted to tell her that we were making a 'Facebook live video' and not a podcast, but that was beside the point. She hadn't taken my opening salutation of 'Halal to you all' very well. I knew she wouldn't, that's why I made it. We were going live in a few minutes and One Nation had made the mistake of inviting me on to their weekly round-up video (a strange decision on their part).

I had not spoken a word to Pauline Hanson since we appeared together on the ABC's *Q&A* program, on which she claimed that she didn't know I was a Muslim. Only once before that had I ever had contact with her: on election night in 2016, when I invited her on live television to join me for a halal snack pack. She rejected my invitation. Apparently halal is part of some kind of global conspiracy. Pauline Hanson's One Nation (PHON) wanted me on their Facebook live video for some light banter, perhaps even a fight on multiculturalism. I had decided I wouldn't do that. My only interest was in humiliating her.

The government's Minister for Communications, Senator Mitch Fifield, was also going to be a guest. But he had different motives. He was going on to tell her how wonderful he thought she was; he was sucking up, trying to win her support for future preference deals. I was going on to try to blow the show.

Pauline Hanson and One Nation, despite what most people say on social media, are not Nazis. Nazis are something else entirely. Trump is not a Nazi, nor are the French or Dutch far-right movements. These people lean towards fascism which, in my book, makes them downright repulsive, even if it doesn't make them Nazis.

'You can't call her a *NAZI!*' Brendan Bolton from my office exclaims, eyes boggling.

'No, not a Nazi, but a fascist.'

'There isn't a difference. As far as the media is concerned you are calling her a Nazi, and all hell will break loose.'

He was right. The world of Facebook videos offers no platform for the making of potentially fine-grained ideological distinctions. 'Fascist', there, would be elided into 'Nazi', simple as that. Even if that isn't the intention.

Pauline Hanson is a sensationally good politician, which is what makes her so dangerous. She's not new to any of this. Her first political break was back in 1996 and since that time she has finessed her brand. She started with an attack on Indigenous Australians, then Asians, and from there she moved on to attacking Muslims. I suppose that the subcontinent is next.

Other than the memorable words of greeting that she offered, Pauline does not say anything to me until we are live.

'I found your words on Vladimir Putin highly offensive,' I launch, knowing that she can't help but take the bait. On *Sunrise* a few days earlier, Hanson had strangely gone on about her admiration for the Russian leader. 'What do you say to the victims of MH17 and their families?' I add, throwing fuel on the fire.

'I said I like him as a person.'

'He is a murderous tyrant,' I yell back.

'What do you think? We have all been so perfect? Everyone has done something,' she says.

I'm sorry, I'm thinking to myself, but how many of us have actually killed journalists and shot down passenger airplanes? Is she really saying let those who have not shot down planes cast the first stone?

This is not what Pauline wants. She needs red meat to her base: that would be arguing with me on multiculturalism. My supporters would probably have liked it too. But that's not what hurts Hanson. Bizarre policies on fringe issues—they're the things that give her grief.

'It was weird,' I tell Brendan after the video.

Pauline Hanson's support for Vladimir Putin makes no sense. It's not as if she is someone who has a strong view, in fact any view, when it comes to foreign policy. It's also not as if there is a strong pro-Putin constituency even among the Australian far right that would welcome these views. In fact, there is no political space here in Australia for that at all.

Pauline's talking points resemble those that are mouthed by Putin's most ardent supporters from the Kremlin. Surely she can see that.

It's time to take the gloves off when it comes to Pauline Hanson and One Nation. The left has been as weak on her as the right. There has been a reluctance to challenge her. Our strategy on One Nation has at times been too tame.

There is a tendency among those on the left of politics to think that the best way to deal with Hanson is to ignore her. They say that fighting her gives her oxygen. They expect that the faults in her policy and agenda will naturally bring her down. In a nutshell, they hold that nationalist populists like her constitute no real threat. I don't think that such a view could be further from the truth. While I can't see a scenario in which Pauline Hanson could actually form government in Australia, that doesn't mean that she isn't dangerous. Hanson is shifting the political debate so far to the right that the Australia we currently know may become, before we know it, unrecognisable. She has the ability to transform the entire political debate in Australia.

She is the biggest political threat to moderates in Australia for a generation. And she has to be fought head on. I'm critical of the Labor Party here as much as I am of the Liberals. We have been too slow over the years in tackling the monster. We have been reluctant to fight in defence of multiculturalism, believing instead that the social and economic arguments are so strong that they don't need to be made.

The path to victory doesn't lie in a lame pandering to extremism; it lies in taking the fight to the opponent. It astounds me that so many of the more moderate members of the conservative party can even consider preferencing PHON.

Yes, people like Hanson will raise legitimate concerns, but their banal reflex to blame the last group of migrants is dangerous. Their platitudes, I think, are full of peril.

I remember that it was big, or at least bigger. 'How could it be so ... small?' I think to myself. Is this really where Pauline Hanson came from? A little fish-and-chip shop on the outskirts of Ipswich.

'I remember it being bigger on television,' I tell the new owners, who clearly consider this an odd comment.

'No. It's always been this size.'

'Well, yes, of course ... but it *looked* bigger!'

'No. It was this size.' The point is lost on them.

I'm not sure what I was expecting. For over twenty years Pauline Hanson has loomed as such a large figure that I am taken aback by the modest dimensions of this dark and dingy fish-and-chip shop. It's not as if I had ever been here before. It takes forty-five minutes to get from Brisbane to Ipswich and then another five to get to the town's outskirts, where this shop is situated.

There is nothing remarkable about the shop at all. In a country in which emphasis is sometimes placed on making everything stand out—we live, after all, in the land of the Big Pineapple—this shop blends right in. When I visit, it is being run by Vietnamese Australians. Say no more.

What impresses me about Pauline Hanson is that she emerged, from nothing, to become a significant voice in Australian politics. There is something very Australian about her rise from local chippie to household name. She has battled through elections, done a brief stint in jail and made a comeback of momentous proportions.

'Did you come all the way from Sydney to meet with us?' the shop owner asks me. I say yes. I tell them that I'm fascinated by the rise of right-wing parties and that I couldn't think of a better place to start than where it all began. They find all of this a little disconcerting. Two people are working in the shop today. It's not that they are not used to media and a bit of interest. Cameras have come in the past. It's too good a story to give up. The famous right-wing nationalist Australian politician who sold her shop to Vietnamese migrants; it writes itself.

The service-station operator from next door pops by. She is Indian and has a relative holding the fort while she grabs some fish and chips. Clearly, she is a regular. Aside from her, no one else comes by for the hour that I am there.

Marsdens Seafood is not, technically, even in Ipswich. I somehow expected it to be in the centre of town. Perhaps this is where the outsider mentality comes from, I think to myself. Perhaps being on the outside of the outside. No, no, I'm overthinking things. There doesn't *have* to be a reason. Life is not that structured. Causality isn't linear, even though we keep looking for clear causal lines. The fact that the fish-and-chip shop is not near the centre of Ipswich doesn't have to mean anything.

I'm surprised to find that the Lunar New Year celebratory cats are still on display, not only because they are tacky, but because Lunar New Year was done and dusted a month prior to my visit. 'Are you taking the Lunar New Year decorations down?' I ask the owners. They have decided to leave them there for good luck. Business is tough.

They tell me about Pauline. She has come there with cameras. She criticises the way in which they cook their fish.

'The fish?'

'Yeah, the fish. She doesn't like our batter.'

Pauline, they tell me, doesn't talk politics with them. They tell me their very Australian story about the Vietnamese who fled Vietnam.

And, of course, they tell me the story of the shop. Perhaps they have told the story so many times that the irony of their shop's Hansonian provenance has been erased from their minds. But here they are, another set of migrants trying to do their best in life, and their story is always going to be overshadowed by Pauline Hanson.

18

THE GATEWAY AND THE VICTIMS

Everybody has a breaking point. As Bernard sat in his car under the flightpath near Melbourne airport, shortly before Christmas in 2014, he knew that he had reached his. There is only so much that anyone can bear. The pain, the pressure, the heartache take a huge toll. The years of fighting, the calls from creditors, the court battles—all of it erodes the sense of self-confidence, and triggers feelings of isolation, helplessness and loneliness.

Bernard just wanted the pain to stop. In his left hand he held a bottle of pills as he agonised over whether or not he should simply end it, take his debts to his grave and, with the help of his insurance, give his children a chance at moving on without him.

As is often the case, Bernard's marriage had not survived the pressures that come from being a victim of financial crime. A back injury sustained at work left a legacy of its own. Bernard was unable to ever work again, and the pills were the only means he had to dull the pain that came from having a 'cage' inserted in his spine during a bone-fusion procedure.

We don't often hear from the victims of financial crime. Their stories rarely claim our attention. They battle the stigma that they

THE GATEWAY AND THE VICTIMS

carry every day: they 'should have known better' than to have acted on such advice; they were 'greedy'; they 'brought their misfortune on themselves'. How can they have been 'so foolish'? How can they have 'believed the lies of the financial advisor'?

Bernard knew that he had been lied to and conned. He knew that he was a victim. He just wasn't sure if anyone cared. He wasn't aware that his situation wasn't unique—that there were tens of thousands of other Australians who had been swindled. Bernard's financial advisor, Peter Holt, had left a wreckage of hundreds of victims, many living in Bernard's vicinity. I met Bernard, at his home, later on the day on which he considered suicide near Melbourne airport.

The bloke who greets me at his front door is confident, charming and funny. I've come to talk to Bernard about Timbercorp and about the financial advice that brought him to breaking point. I'm running two hours late but Bernard, a kindly soul, doesn't mention it. His nondescript street in Craigieburn, a suburb twenty-five kilometres north of the Melbourne CBD, resembles the Australia of a bygone era. The street is filled with children playing cricket and celebrating the start of school holidays.

'If my son hadn't called me and come to pick me up, I wouldn't be here now,' he says, almost nonchalantly, alluding to the dark state into which his mind had sunk a few hours before, while he sat under the flightpath. I struggle to balance the seriousness of the topic at hand with holding back his boisterous staffie-cross puppy, Nelly, who has decided to use me as a launching pad. Enticed by the sheer volume of food that has been laid out for my visit (Bernard is a former caterer), Nelly has decided that something is in it for her.

A few weeks earlier, on 12 November 2014, I met Bernard at a Senate hearing that I was chairing into the collapse of Timbercorp. 'My story,' he told a group of assembled Senators, 'is that I am just a simple family man who went out to invest, because we had a bit of equity in our home. I was hoping to be a self-funded retiree.' He explained, 'I have always prided myself on working hard and supplying for my family and living as a good Australian'. His subsequent tale is harrowing and, unfortunately, not remotely unique.

At our meeting in Craigieburn, Bernard tells me that he was advised by a relative to look at making the equity in his house 'work for him' by meeting Peter Holt, a financial planner working in the leafy Melbourne suburb of Kew East. 'I did my homework on this bloke,' says Bernard. 'I did my due diligence. I spoke to my bank, I spoke to ASIC, I spoke to the ACCC to confirm that he had a reputation. They said that they had nothing on record to show that he was anything but upstanding. He wasn't going out there changing his phone numbers or anything like that.'

The victims believe that Peter Holt is the villain in the Timbercorp saga. To them he is a financial planner who epitomises a culture that has taken hold of sections of the financial-advice industry. Beginning as a small-time accountant in a firm comprising just himself and a business partner in the 1990s, he has ridden the wave of financial-advice fees and become a multimillion-dollar success story. His office in Burke Road has around a dozen staff.

It is hard to get an exact handle on what Peter Holt has made from commissions alone. He perhaps made over $3 million from the Timbercorp group of companies. Internal documents suggest a figure as high as $7 million, though the accuracy of this may be questioned. Holt, however, was not operating only on behalf of Timbercorp. There wasn't a managed forestry investment scheme (agribusiness) that he didn't get involved in selling. Even by the standards of reckless financial advice offered on the back of sales commissions—characteristic of a financial-industry culture that became prevalent in the years preceding the global financial crisis—Peter Holt's behaviour stands out for its brazenness.

In September 2012, the Australian Securities & Investments Commission (ASIC) banned Peter Holt for three years from providing financial advice. The ASIC banning order gives us a picture of Holt at work. Examples of Holt's clients are provided: a football coach, a technician, a young family and even some of his own friends. In each instance, ASIC found that people were given the same advice—to invest in agribusiness products such as Timbercorp. In every instance, the same advice was provided, regardless of the circumstances, of the facts, of the needs of the client. Take out as many loans as you can and invest in agribusiness—preferably Timbercorp. This was Holt's chant.

Peter Holt left a trail of destruction in his wake. For himself, though, business was booming. In many instances, Holt was receiving commissions of up to 15 per cent for every dollar he could bring into Timbercorp. The incentive to get someone to take out a \$200000 loan and invest in Timbercorp was an immediate payment to him of up to \$30000. Not bad for a few hours' work. Long-standing tax clients whom Holt had advised over decades made for perfect targets. 'We trusted Peter. We knew Peter. He was a friend,' one of his former clients revealed. 'He was a charming guy. We didn't all just walk into his office one day—most of us knew him for years.'

The story of the failure of financial products like Timbercorp and other managed forestry investment schemes is also the story of the handful of financial planners who were able to benefit from them.

Why? Because without a steady stream of victims, these products would never have lasted. Like any structure that contains a Ponzi component (whereby investors receive returns not from profit, but from fresh capital paid by new investors), there was a constant need to get more and more people to invest in order to keep the projects afloat. The planners like Holt served as the gateway for potential investors. Once the tax-exempt status for these projects was pulled in 2007, the pressure to tap this line of money became greater. Inexperienced retail investors were being pushed towards complicated geared products and no one batted an eyelid—surely a state of affairs indicative of regulatory and policy failure.

Once the investment schemes collapsed on the back of the twin blows of the removal of tax exemptions and the global financial crisis, Peter Holt's investors were left to hang. Holt had already received his commissions. His clients were no longer of any use to him.

The sad reality is that Peter Holt will most likely walk away. His actions, however unconscionable, have not yet been proved to have been in breach of the law. While ASIC found that it was 'a serious failure' not to 'make sound investigations into the subject matter of advice' and not to pay due regard to clients' 'circumstances and objectives', ASIC gave Holt only a slap on the wrist. A three-year suspension was all that Holt was obliged to suffer. As one whistle-blower says to me, 'It really makes you wonder what it takes to get a life ban in this country'.

While he is supposedly bankrupt, Holt still drives a big Mercedes, still operates his business from his Kew East offices and still lives in his sprawling Melbourne home. His victims have not been as fortunate.

On a monthly basis, Holt's victims get together in a cold, damp room at the athletics hall in a Coburg clubhouse. One of the participants described it to me as the equivalent of an AA meeting. 'I started going because I wanted to find answers. In truth, I found some friends. There is something cathartic about sitting around and talking to people who have felt the same pain, who know what I am going through.' The group gets together to share their stories, plan their campaign and organise.

As one victim put it to me, 'We are asked repeatedly, "Why were you investing in a scheme like this and not in real estate?" We were told that this was a government-backed scheme. We trusted this man. He is a professional. It is like when you send your children to school: you put your children's future in the hands of their teacher and the educators at that school. We put our trust and our future into this man's professional practice—some might not call it that and I certainly do not now. But he has decimated our financial future. Our children do not have a financial future.'

'Do you want to hear his voice?' Bernard asks me.

'What? Like on TV,' I reply.

'No. I have a recording of him that I made two years ago.'

THE GATEWAY AND THE VICTIMS   181

'Is that even legal?'

'I don't know. Oh shit. Perhaps I shouldn't have mentioned it. I took a tape recorder in my pocket—it was nine days before he got barred. It shows how he planned for me to go bankrupt.'

'It's fine,' I reassure him, trying to sound confident but unsure of the legality.

The recording is scratchy and unclear. This wasn't a professional sting. Nonetheless, it provides a rare and fascinating insight into Peter Holt. What is surprising is the lack of confidence in his voice—the ums and the ahs, the pauses and the gaps. 'That's how he speaks; he's a qualifier,' Bernard contends. Given what we know of Holt the operator, the equivocations in his speech are disarming.

The tape itself is not flattering of Peter Holt. At no point is there any acknowledgement from Peter that he is in any way responsible for getting Bernard into this mess. 'Well, he always had chutzpah,' Bernard reflects.

It's difficult to even know the veracity of these tapes, but I never had a reason not to believe Bernard.

The audacity to brag in front of one's own victims reflects a rare confidence. But that is exactly what it sounds like on the tape. 'I have spent a lifetime in politics,' I tell Bernard. 'I have heard and met some arrogant, cocky, detestable pricks. But this guy really takes the cake.'

Bernard simply responds with, 'Welcome to the last six years of my life'.

You can see the change come over Bernard when he talks about Peter Holt. I've seen that change in victims before. He is not simply dealing with anger. There is a pervasive sadness about Bernard when he holds Peter Holt in his thoughts. The *emotional* consequences of being a victim of financial crime are often overlooked. What is remarkable—considering what he has been through—is the faith that Bernard has in people. 'Don't get me wrong; all of this has been horrible. But I have met some of the most amazing people … Perhaps not in the most favourable of circumstances.'

Bernard quickly cleans up lunch and spreads out a series of documents on the table. They are his loan-agreement documents with Timbercorp finance. The forms are photocopied and pasted together. The format changes from page to page. The handwriting keeps changing. It is clear that the documents have been pieced together by someone in Peter Holt's office, filling in parts of the documents as they go. Nonetheless, there remains one undeniable fact that continues to haunt Bernard—on about four different occasions, you can see Bernard's signature on the documents.

'Yeah, that's my signature,' he tells me in a defeated voice. 'That's how the bastards got me.'

'Did you read the documents?' I ask.

'No. That's my fault. I just trusted it was going to be OK. I'd get a call telling me the deal was about to close. He would say I needed to race into the office to sign the forms or I would miss out. I dutifully did it every time.'

I didn't have the heart to tell Bernard that creating a sense of urgency is a classic trick. I'm sure he knows that now anyway.

All up, Bernard owes around $170 000. When Timbercorp went into liquidation, that figure was around $80 000. A heavy toll has been taken by compound interest of 13 per cent tied to penalty rates of 18 per cent. 'At the start I was told by Peter Holt not to worry—that we would win a class action and that everything would be OK. I feel like an idiot for believing him.'

'Are you losing the house?' I ask.

'Hopefully not. My daughter lives here with me. Breaking the news to her would kill me.'

Bernard's daughter has acted as a carer since his work accident. 'She's amazing. She might be only twenty-one, but she has the maturity of someone in their forties.' He swells with pride when talking about her.

Lamentably, the outlines of Bernard's story are not special. Too often people playing the gateway to opportunity have been able to exploit people seeking financial assistance.

Bernard, like the others, sought professional advice so that he might put something away for his children. He is one of the good guys.

Four years ago, Bernard was at the brink of ending his life. Now he is full of energy—taking the fight to those who used and abused his trust. 'I don't want you to see me as a victim. I'm a fighter, I will fight on. I went to the brink. I nearly jumped off the cliff—but I fought on. I will continue to fight on.'

He stresses the imagery of ongoing battle that the little people must wage: 'I had always felt like we would never be heard, because we are not a big, powerful group of people, but I need to show my children that you do not give in without a fight'.

I leave Bernard's house and his suburb to catch my flight to Sydney. Now running three hours late, I pass under the flightpath on my way to Melbourne airport. As I settle into my chair on the plane, I consider the numbers that I need for an inquiry, the backs that I will need to scratch to attempt some change and the resistance that I can expect on the way ...

19

BANKING ON CONTROVERSY

'Do you think she will even come?' I ask my advisor, Brendan, as we wait in the coffee shop for the whistleblower's arrival. She is only just late, but whistleblowers are never late. They are always early. So I begin to worry that she will not show up at all.

No one becomes a whistleblower from a place of peace. You don't wake up one day and decide to spill the beans. Usually, there has been a build-up over several years. It will have been like the pressure of two continental plates moving together, and suddenly there's an earthquake that knocks down a village or causes a tsunami. In this case, Brendan tells me that the whistleblower is ready to knock down the bank, its management and its culture. It sounds electric, though even with my help I have my doubts about how successful she will be.

Australians, like the continent that we occupy, don't appreciate seismic shifts. We are not used to them, nor are denizens of our political class ready to embrace them. It's different in the United States, where uprooting the bad guys and sending businessmen to jail play a customary part in the theatre of politics. But Australians seem content to blame a junior fall guy/girl, and so limit the seismic potential of any scandal.

The strategy that Australian organisations use to discredit whistleblowers is well practised. I liken its efficiency to the prowess of our national rugby-league or women's hockey teams: few opponents stand a chance. The accused group finds the flaw in what the whistleblower has said—there is always one factual inaccuracy or embellishment—and pounds them with it. Even easier is to find a personal flaw and feed that to the media. There must be some *schadenfreude* to be relished as the executives watch the whistleblower's life being torn to pieces. Find an email or a comment, dredge up some complaint about the whistleblower. Use that one weak time in their lives to portray them as being a serial liar, an adulterer, a stooge, a drunk, a gambler or all of the above. Destroy their reputation, and if their family suffers too, then so be it. Nothing can be more important than protecting the organisation and those who run it.

It is the corporate equivalent of 'slut shaming'. Organisations find something that can totally discredit the whistleblower in the eyes of the public, and it lets that overtake the importance or the nuance of what the whistleblower is trying to expose. Journalists love a yarn about a flawed character, something juicy and salacious. Tales of systemic corruption don't so easily draw the eye and hold the interest. The whole thing is brutal. It destroys lives. But when there are millions and perhaps even billions in share-price value at stake, it is hardly surprising. History is littered with examples of people who have killed for a lot less.

Against this background, it's amazing that there are still whistleblowers ready to take on the status quo and fight back. Some are prepared to wear the backlash on their own, while others are subtler and put their faith in the political system to help. By the time that a whistleblower is looking into the eyes of a politician in a quiet café, they have wrestled internally and exhausted every other angle and option available to them. They are nervous, tired and overwhelmed.

Somehow, this has become what I now do with my time: meet with whistleblowers, take down their stories and use the information to help build the case for a royal commission into Australian banking. This is incredibly important—but something more clandestine than I once imagined.

Brendan nervously checks his watch. She is now seven minutes late.

'She will come,' Brendan reassures me. 'She's been pretty keen to talk to you for a few weeks.'

He says this, but I know he isn't sure. He keeps checking his phone to see if there is a message there or some kind of contact. Nothing. Another minute goes past.

'She's been briefed on what she can expect from you. I've straightened out her expectations, but she will need to hear it from you. She has seen you on television and thinks *you* are her white knight,' he advises.

It is February 2017, and Brendan Bolton has been working with me for a year. He has the ability to stay calm in the face of anything. 'The gentle giant,' his friends from school used to call him: 6 foot 5 inches tall, and around me he looks even taller. He does not have my anxiety, and despite sharing the 'Bill Bus' with me for two months during the 2016 election, I still can't get under his skin. Formerly, he was with the Department of Foreign Affairs and Trade (DFAT), and had a posting in Japan. At his interview in a Woolloomooloo pub a year ago, he told me that he wanted out of DFAT as he was tired of other countries' problems and wanted to focus on Australia's. Why he wanted to work for me, I will never know. Such poor judgement should have been a disqualifying decision.

'Is that her?' I ask Brendan. A middle-aged woman enters the café. Brendan had been meeting with her for a few weeks, getting her ready to sit down with me.

The meeting had taken time to organise. At first, the woman was nervous, and wanted to feed me information only via Brendan. A few public statements from her bank's CEO changed her mind, and she's ready to go nuclear. If the bank knew that she was talking to a politician, she would lose her job.

Brendan has explained parliamentary privilege to her. This, a protection that Australia's federal and state parliaments inherited from the Westminster system, helps to enshrine the separation of powers between the legislature and the courts. It means, in effect, that anything the woman tells me is protected, that she can divulge information without fear of reprisal.

However, in reality whistleblowers are pitifully protected in Australia. Were we in the United States, this whistleblower who was about to meet with me could expect a share of the money seized from the errant organisation or the satisfaction of seeing fines issued, and her job would be reinstated had she been sacked. In Australia, whistleblowers get thrown to the wolves if exposed, regardless of the gravity of their revelations and the degree to which they serve the public interest. Previously, and on more than one occasion, I have talked whistleblowers out of going public and encouraged them to report their information anonymously. On these occasions, it was my judgement that the devastation likely to be wrought upon their lives would not be worth the wrongs that they were trying to expose and correct.

There is a woman approaching the café now. Unusually, she appears eleven minutes after the agreed time. I know that this must be her: she is betrayed by the three large ring-binders that she carries; such accessories, I've come to know, are routinely lugged about by those who are fighting an organisation. People like this woman become hoarders of paperwork. They know that documents can be made to disappear instantly, that evidence needs to be carefully gathered. The whistleblower slowly collects and builds their physical files as if the assemblage of documentation amounts to some sort of protective talisman.

The waitress at the café goes straight to her. The waitress knows her, which makes sense: we're meeting at a place of her choosing.

She is clearly unsettled, and I walk over with my hand out. My face wears the best politician's grin in the repertoire. The look is meant to put people at ease, but, because I am so socially awkward, it just comes off as downright creepy.

I say her name, and I get half a look back. Her look back at me says, 'I'm not meant to know you!' Only two other people are in the café (a couple drinking coffee). She is worried that someone—I don't know who—will see us together.

She is negotiating with the waitress for a private room. It appears that she had previously called to organise a private room, called to cancel the same room and called earlier this morning to book it again.

I figure that she had, at one point, decided to bail on the meeting, but then decided to see it through.

'Do you have WhatsApp? Or use Wikr?' The first question. There is a paranoia that comes with being a whistleblower that moves people towards the world of secret-messaging apps. Even Malcolm Turnbull uses them. I explain that I don't, and wonder how people develop their expertise.

'OK,' she finally says as she relaxes in the private room. She opens the folder and turns to me. 'Have I got a lot to tell you!'

Those who know my history in the toughest school of the Australian Labor Party machine—the NSW ALP Right—always ask about how life was growing up in the ALP. Before I became a Senator, I used to tell them that it was the best training that I could have had. I thought that I would come to parliament as a beast somewhat different from most already there. I was not going to be some naive community activist, or a corporate lawyer looking for a stage. I would come as the former general secretary of the largest branch of the party, and as a veteran (if a young one) of one of the most tumultuous periods in the party's history. I told them that I understood power. I understood how it was exercised.

Coming into parliament, I was quick to realise that I really had no idea what power was, and what it actually meant. All my life I had thought that parliament, and political parties, were the ultimate decision makers in Australia. It was a rude shock to see how much influence that business and industry wielded in Canberra—incredible! Chief among the cadre of the influential corporates were the bankers.

The first time that I met with the CEOs of Australia's big banks, in 2014, I was struck by the splendour of their sartorial display; their suits and ties grabbed my notice. Tens of thousands of dollars of refined merino wool made to measure in various Italian cuts: I was staring at a banker-look that comes straight out of central casting. Only it wasn't a casting call for the 'Wolf of Pitt Street'; these guys were the real deal.

The banks' CEOs appeared before me as chair of the Senate Economics References Committee—my stomping ground for a few years. We came across a little-used power of the Senate: the power to summons witnesses. It was a power often used to compel bureaucrats but rarely applied to corporate Australia. We exercised it ruthlessly. (Not that we actually summonsed the CEOs of Australia's banks to appear before the Senate. We just threatened to use the power. The banks fought back, hard.)

The CEOs couldn't have been more reluctant to appear. If it wasn't for the nervousness of the banks' respective boards, they probably would not have appeared. I knew that this was the case, because one of their lobbyists had been asked to tell me: 'Tell that Dastyari that I won't let him parade me across the cameras like some type of common criminal!'

When they eventually did front the cameras, all smiles and handshakes, I knew how much they seethed deep down. I also picked up that they were 'backgrounding' some of the media about me.

'He's so reckless.'

'He's anti-business.'

'He's a socialist,' as if, after a lifetime in the Labor Party, this was a title that would scare me.

I knew that they had been calling those above me in the Labor Party. I knew that they had gone to Chris Bowen and Bill Shorten, both of whom made the point that it wasn't their place to rein me in. I knew all of this because everyone talks.

The wood-panelled committee rooms of Parliament House do have the feel of a courtroom. Except that instead of playing the part of the judge, the committee that assembled during 2015 played that of 'the firing squad'. Firing the questions were seven committee members from across the political spectrum. The drama was something to be savoured: bright lights, cameras poised to capture every angle, the buzz of expectation, the icy facial expressions.

We had seen it all in these sorts of inquiries. The Senate inquiry into multinational tax avoidance brought to light some of the shenanigans and instruments around payment of tax that had been exercising minds in high places within corporate Australia. But we weren't prepared for the deluge of stories of victims of the banks. Once the committee started to get some publicity, a trickle of these stories turned into a flood. During the hearing into the banks, the victims sat in the back row. They were the individuals steamrolled by the banks. And the banks, it seemed to them, had done whatever was necessary to crush them.

The financial papers called the banking inquiry a 'show trial'. Not true, but there certainly was an element of sensational exposé. This is the era of television and social media, after all. If you want to achieve cut-through in the public, you have to make it worth watching. That was something that I learnt early.

Jeff Morris is still dealing with the ramifications of being a whistle-blower. He lost his job, his career and almost lost his family. He lost it all because he blew the whistle on systemic issues at the Commonwealth Bank. His revelations triggered the creation of a $50 million compensation scheme and a complete overhaul of internal controls in Australia's biggest bank. He achieved this despite the total failure of the regulator, ASIC, to take his concerns seriously.

In October 2008, Jeff, aided by a small team dubbed the 'ferrets', sent an anonymous fax to ASIC, citing fraud at Commonwealth Bank's financial-planning division and an alleged 'high-level cover up' at the bank. For sixteen months, ASIC sat on this explosive fax. ASIC failed to deal with the issue—so complete was ASIC's failure that a bipartisan Senate committee found that the only way to get to the bottom of the scandal was through a royal commission.

Jeff Morris had revealed that rogue financial planners working in the Commonwealth Bank's financial-planning arm were committing fraud with the full knowledge of senior management. Jeff identified the planner at the centre of this activity, a person named Don Nguyen.

The fax from Jeff warned ASIC that Don Nguyen was currently covering up the paper trail. 'There is some urgency required,' Jeff stated in his fax, 'to secure evidence as they are being "cleaned up".' No action followed. In fact, it took a series of follow-up emails from Jeff Morris to get any response from ASIC. While ASIC claimed that the matter was being investigated, there was no attempt by them to seize files.

Recently, I met with Jeff, who lives in North Sydney. He told me that 'ASIC was a complicit non-participant, not interested in taking on the big players. Not interested in taking scandals on. Not interested in rocking the boat'.

Jeff went on to outline the treatment that he received from ASIC. 'The organisation totally failed me. It was too slow to act, the process lacked transparency, and it was too trusting of the big end of town.'

Jeff and his associates became very frustrated by ASIC's evasiveness. They could do little other than make gadflies out of themselves. 'We even had to physically start showing up at their office,' Jeff winced, 'just to make sure they were taking our concerns seriously. Even when we met with them, while we were told that we would have "whistleblower protections" they were keen to point out that "this wouldn't mean much".'

He's older now. It has been a decade since he decided to speak out. He is quieter than he used to be. The years of fighting have inflicted inner damage. Look carefully, though, and you sense that within him a fire still burns—fire kindled in outrage at injustice. Jeff Morris knows all too well that there is a wrong at the heart of Australian banking that needs to be righted.

'You're going to bang on about the banks in your book, aren't you?' Sam Crosby asks me.

'Just a bit. A tiny bit,' I respond, playing loose with the truth.

'Don't make it boring. You get obsessed when you talk about banks.'

He *is* right. I'm not sure that 'obsessed' is correct, but I certainly get angry. I think that there needs to be a complete overhaul in Australian banking. This will begin with a royal commission to expose the activities of the banks. Whistleblowers need to be compensated. I believe that we need to shake up the banking structure in this country if we are to make it better. The shake-up needs to be comprehensive in scope—we need to probe into structures, not simply apply spit and polish to surfaces that already shine and glitter.

I tell Sam, 'I'm going to argue that we should be using institutions like Australia Post to shake up the banks. Why can't we develop a low-fee, low-rate credit card and give consumers access to an affordable, "no-frills" product through the government? Set a benchmark and make it clear to the banks that if they don't clean up their acts, real change is coming. That would shake up the entire credit-card market—the biggest rort in Australian banking.'

The lecture goes on. 'I would start with credit cards and if the banks didn't get their acts together in other areas, I'd be making them compete with more affordable products across the board.'

Sam cocks his eyebrow. 'Riiight … and you think there is a way to write that and keep your book interesting?'

'Probably not,' I concede. 'But by that stage the reader is half-way in, so some water will have passed under the bridge before I start ranting. Anyway, I'll only crap on for a few paragraphs.'

The Australian Government has not been a direct participant in the banking sector since the privatisation of the Commonwealth Bank was completed in 1996. Under the Banking Act, banks must hold capital in particular ratios relative to the riskiness of their assets. Australia Post would therefore be required to hold significant capital reserves against its credit-card balance sheet. This would be provided by the Australian Government's balance sheet. I'm not pretending for a moment this is not a radical change from current orthodoxy. It's also not Labor Party policy. It's a major change—but a major change is what we need.

So why credit cards first? The rorts in credit-card products, the rates of interest of which never seem to fall, could easily be corrected by government intervention, and this could be done in a way that would introduce real competition into the banking sector. And it would prompt a change for the better in the behaviour of the banks.

Of course, some will argue against this. They will say that it is too hard, too risky, too interventionist. My argument is simple. The system is ripping off consumers—let's shake it up.

And with that, I close my rant.

'What will change the whole banking industry will be the introduction of digital currency! This is how you shake the industry up!' Ron Tucker tells me, with a look that says there's more to be said—so listen hard. But it's hard to hear him over the early '90s dance music that is blasting from the student bar in Canberra, where we are trying to enjoy a quiet drink. In our defence, this is the only place still open late at night.

Ron is the President of the Australian Digital Currency Commerce Association (ADCCA), the peak body for digital currencies and blockchain technology in Australia. Think bitcoin.

Everybody wants a piece of Ron. The banks, venture capitalists and payment-system providers have joined his association, as has Australia Post. Ron looks very much like the future that he preaches. Dressed impeccably (he previously had a line of fashion stores), he converted me to the digital-currency cause a few years ago after I conducted a Senate inquiry into digital currencies. He talks with a Canadian accent and with a charm that comes from learning how to win over investors in a few minutes.

We exchange stories. I tell him my concerns over the rorts conducted by the banking sector. I ask him to meet with a few victims to make sure that the system he creates doesn't cause the same sorts of consequences with which they've had to contend. He agrees to do this, then looks me straight in the eye.

'Why don't we be daring? Why don't we be first?' he asks. 'Why is Australia waiting for the rest of the world? A world-first government-backed digital currency is there for the taking, and we would be able to write the rules.'

Ron wants the Reserve Bank of Australia to take the leap and have Australia produce a fiat-backed digital currency. He wants us to make good on the promise of new technologies like blockchain and have the world follow us.

I know why we won't. We are too cautious, too hamstrung by vested self-interest, too afraid of risk. We will sit back. We will wait for the Americans or the Europeans. The Asian financial giants will all be there before Australia is ready to proceed. Then we will scramble and regret not crossing the threshold when we could have. We don't back ourselves—and that is wrong. Ron has a point. Australia has so much to gain from being more bold.

But then I'm distracted by another thought.

'Ron,' I ask, 'are we the two oldest people at the bar?'

'No. There's that creepy guy with the beard.'

Great, I think to myself. We're barely distinguishable from the bearded bloke glued to the bar, as if the bar were his living room and alcoholic liquid the only fluid that passes his lips. So we order shots, and leave ambitious thoughts of a revolutionised financial system to another day.

Brendan continues to meet up with our whistleblower. She is afraid of being seen with me, which I understand.

'Should I go to the media with this, publicly? Put my name to it?' she asks.

I tell her no. I tell her not to do so because they will chew her up and spit her out. I tell her no because they are bigger, meaner and more ruthless than she can imagine. I tell her no because they have all the power, and she has none. I tell her no because until we can properly protect people like her with a royal commission, what right do I have to throw her under a bus?

The bank in question was soon to announce a giant profit. And every one of the executives who featured in her evidence would take home record bonuses.

She wasn't lying at our first meeting. Her information is explosive. Fake banking structures; drunken parties billed to clients; rort after rort: all of her material supports the case for a royal commission. All of this will duly be submitted to the regulator—and, I fully anticipate, be left to watch on as nothing happens. Watch this space. I'm getting sick and tired of *watching*. Something needs to be *done*.

20
TWENTY-SIX MEN

On 17 November 2016, twenty-six men filled a small room in Victoria's La Trobe Valley, 500 metres from the power station that would soon be closing. Each man knew the date at which he would become unemployed, a few months from now. This, we are told, is the price of progress. But when decisions get made in places like Canberra, or in this case, Paris, there are real human lives that are affected.

'I'm worth more dead than alive,' Jason says, his wife by his side, comforting him.

'He's a positive person, but it all messes with your mind,' she continues on his behalf. 'We had four kids based on the promises that we were given by the company. We made decisions based on what they promised us.' Everyone in the room is nodding.

The population of Morwell is 2500, and around 750 of these people are either directly or indirectly working for the local power station, Hazelwood, the imminent closure of which has been announced. This is a power-station town and it is dying.

'It's just another fucking multinational company squeezing us out,' says another worker, Peter, breaking the directive that has been given by the organiser that since 'there are kids in the room, nobody swear'. The staff were informed by SMS. There is an indignity and brutal efficiency in using text messages to tell your employees that their lives are about to be turned upside down.

I notice the kids for the first time: a 4-year-old boy fixated on his mother's iPhone and a baby in the corner, fast asleep.

The Hazelwood power station is an evocative place. It was first opened in the 1960s and was designed a decade before that. While the machinery inside has been updated over the years, the brickwork steadfastly recalls the 1950s. The contrast between the idyllic countryside and soviet-style brutality of the power station is breathtaking. 'They are beautiful pieces of engineering … they will never get built again,' I'm told by a local the next day.

A man in his late thirties starts speaking. 'That's Mackie,' someone whispers to me. My look gives away that I have no idea who that is. 'You know, played for North Melbourne.' I consider explaining that I'm from Sydney and that AFL is lost on me but there isn't time, so I just agree. 'Oh wow,' I manage to mutter.

'Four weeks ago I got the keys to my new house. A house I purchased after being told the power station would continue operating until at least 2025 and perhaps even 2033,' Mackie tells the room. 'Two weeks ago I was told I would be losing my job. Having only worked there for three years, I will be lucky to get a few months of redundancy. You can't imagine the pressure that puts on you.'

Mackie is actually Troy Makepeace. He was drafted by the North Melbourne Kangaroos in 1999, made his debut for the club in 2000 and was delisted at the end of the 2006 season. He's a loved figure, having played with a local side before making it in the AFL. He maintains his involvement in local football.

The building the workers have gathered in used to house the offices of the State Electricity Commission (SEC). The SEC once was the administrative headquarters for thousands of people working in the power industry. But that was a generation ago, before privatisation and the many rounds of job cuts. In the end, the building was purchased cheap by the union and they have made it their office.

While the details vary from speaker to speaker, all of the stories related in the meeting share similarly structured threads. Misinformation and lies from the owner; French-Government-owned multinational, Engie; economic devastation; family stress; depression and shock: the workers take their turns on these themes.

Most of the men in the room are younger workers; the older men will be taking redundancies and leaving the workplace earlier. The younger workers are the ones in real strife.

Morbid themes are touched on in muttered voices. 'The work-site is like a wake,' one of the men says. 'There are just not enough jobs to go around. You can't get work anywhere.'

Hazelwood is the dirtiest power station in Australia. It alone is responsible for 3 per cent of Australia's greenhouse gas emissions. It's hard to have tears for a project that is so terrible for the environment. Environmentalists, economists, power companies, trade unions—pretty much everyone will speak of the inevitability of the closure of power stations like Hazelwood. The closure will be a brick in the wall of Australia's economic restructure. It is, then, a matter of *how and when*, not *if*. The banks won't lend for these types of projects anymore. It's done. Over.

But when these decisions are made, the system often forgets—or doesn't care—that people are left without work. It's easy to sit in a boardroom or a university lecture hall and have the theoretical discussion about jobs and displacements, but it's another thing altogether to speak to the people impacted directly. When you speak to those people, you watch on as their lives fall apart.

The policy purists will talk of collateral damage—taking the human factor out of play. It is simply to pay the 'price of reform' that closures are made. 'Oh it's inevitable,' they say. But is there no plan in place to fill the void? Do we have to be a country that manufactures *nothing*? (Is it a mere coincidence that regional Victoria has one of the highest suicide rates in Australia?)

It's not only at Hazelwood that workers are treated like so many units in a 'price of reform'.

'You can't understand what it feels like,' a car worker in Melbourne tells me.

The car worker makes the point that things used to be done differently. 'There used to be rules. There was a system. We knew if our plant was making money. And we knew that if the plant was failing it would eventually shut down. But now the board in Tokyo makes a decision and they shut down the plant without anyone here knowing a thing about it.'

Everyone is making the same joke. You come to expect this at a Labor Party conference. Overhead, a helicopter descends and lands on the banks of the Yarra River. It's a tourism promotion. As the rotor blades fall silent, someone pipes up, 'Hey, I think Bronwyn Bishop has arrived', and everyone chuckles. It isn't all that funny the first time. By the fifth time it has lost any charm.

It is 11 a.m. on 24 July 2015—the first morning of the Labor Party National Conference, and it has been deemed far too early to start drinking. Well, far too early for everyone but me. I've ordered a beer, but none of my colleagues at the table has followed my lead; they're all asking for an assortment of coffees. The mould has been broken—I'm not in the company of the hard-drinking Labor types of old. But there's a time and a place for elbow-bending. As in all Labor conferences, the real business will be taking place outside, in the bars. Some might also get done in the cafés.

The conference proceedings will follow a format. At some point, all of the delegates will head in. Bill Shorten will give a speech and there will be a standing ovation. These things are pre-determined. But, for now, I am outside the convention centre with an eclectic group of trade unionists. Tara Moriarty is there as the head of the Liquor and Hospitality Division of the United Voice Union. Sitting around the table are Gerard Hayes from the Health Services Union; Graeme Kelly from the United Services Union; Mark Morey from Unions NSW; and Alex Claassens, Bob Nanva and Luba Grigorovitch from the Rail Union. It is as large a table of union leaders as you can imagine.

The conversation, however, breaks the old-Labor mould. 'I go to nightclubs for the music,' Graeme Kelly tells the group.

I jump in to set him straight. 'No one "goes for the music." That's not the point of the music. Is that even a thing?'

'Then why do you go?' he asks me.

The truth is that I don't anymore. But when I went it was never for the music.

Graeme has spent the previous fifteen minutes giving a detailed explanation of why privatisation of electricity assets will lead to economic devastation and thousands of job losses. He speaks, with eloquence and passion, from the perspective of the workers, the people who will be left behind. The issue at the conference that has bobbed its head up again is free trade. The recent free trade agreements with China, Korea and Japan have made the subject topical. The likelihood of a Trans-Pacific Partnership (TPP) is adding spice to the concerns about job losses.

'What people never understand is that when the jobs go—they go forever. It's only in one direction.' Gerard Hayes is running with the theme. 'How on earth are we to compete with the wholesale importation of labour? It's a race to the bottom.'

While free trade agreements will not impact workers in the healthcare sector in the same way as they will those in the blue-collar trades, that is not the point. You can't begin to understand trade unionism without understanding solidarity.

'The perverse incentive of getting bonuses for cutting jobs instead of creating them is irrational,' Tara Moriarty asserts. The short-term-bonus culture means that many of the executives responsible for the worst behaviour never have to be around for the consequences of the decisions they make.

As Mark Morey goes on to say, 'You have no idea how huge an issue this is out there. Job losses, apprenticeships. You have no idea.' And it's true, at that moment I have no idea.

If you live in the bubble of economic arguments and theoretical job replacements, free trade makes sense. Not so, however, if you take into account the people who have lost the dignity of being employed and who are stripped of the capacity to provide for their families. For economists, the debate is about graphs and numbers. They never have to transpose bloodless statistics with real people.

I should have listened closer to what the unionists were saying. If I had done so, I would have seen the backlash coming. They were talking the language of the disaffected working class before Donald Trump turned it mainstream. They were telling me what the people with whom they deal on a daily basis were telling them. It has become fashionable in some Labor circles to talk down the trade-union movement. Some even argue that the *success* of the movement in achieving workplace protections and justice *now makes the movement itself redundant.*

The conservative press rewards anyone making these arguments. The idea that a group of political professionals, myself included, are more in touch with Australia than those dealing with people on the coalface is laughable. The unions constitute a unique point of connection to those people, and it would be madness for the Labor Party to throw away this crucial differentiating element.

Tony Sheldon arrives. He is the National Secretary of the Transport Workers Union and a mentor to me. He starts talking about the TPP and its impact globally. He places emphasis on how dangerous agreements of this kind can be for tens of thousands of workers. 'When people realise how bad these deals are—they won't stand for it.' And with that, we get up to leave. Bill is due to speak. We are late. There's another helicopter preparing to land, and the 'Bronwyn Bishop' gag gets trundled out again.

'Has anyone ever told you that you look like that bloke from the movies?'

'Hugh Jackman?' I ask.

'No. Rowan Atkinson.'

Fuck, I think to myself. This isn't going well. Not that there was any reason to think that it would. Here I am, never having been on a ship before, and I'm sitting with the professional crew of a freight company crossing Bass Strait.

The Maritime Union has helpfully managed to find a way to transport the 'Bill Bus' across the strait, the flip side being that I'm travelling with the crew. It's an overnight trip from Port Melbourne to Burnie, a port city on the north-west coast of Tasmania.

'Do you get sea sick?' I had been asked a few hours earlier.

'I don't know. I've never been on a ship.' This was not an answer that had filled anyone with confidence.

Members of the crew were incredibly stressed. Over the past few months, they had repeatedly seen the crews of other ships be replaced by foreign workers. Deploying a business tactic called 'flags of convenience', a shipping operator will base itself in another nation, usually one that appears on a list of tax havens, fly that nation's civil ensign and hire a foreign crew at a cost lower than that of an equivalent Australian crew. Operating expenses are thereby reduced, and regulatory obligations minimised.

As Jack puts it to me, 'You register in the third world. Pick a country. You use third-world labour. Get a single-voyage permit and keep trading on the coast.' After forty years in the industry, Jack presents a weathered face to the world. He speaks in a deep, authoritative voice. The twelve members of the crew who dine with us go quiet when Jack says something. It's a mark of respect.

The younger members of the crew, like the young men at Hazelwood, worry about the debasement of their industry and the resultant threat to their livelihoods. 'The bastards,' one bloke laments, 'are getting rid of everything. They have taken over our coast. Bass Strait is pretty much the only part left. Who knows how long that will last.'

The foreign crews that are placed on these ships are themselves victims. They are exploited by the operators. 'They're cheap labour. Hardly trained. I feel sorry for them,' the seamen, as if in chorus, tell me.

We now give advantages to those companies that go offshore. Now you are rewarded for not being an Australian company.

You get ahead by being a company that exploits foreign labour. Your returns improve when you shift the jobs elsewhere. It makes no sense.

'Disempowered.' It's a bastard of an adjective to apply to a group of workers—*Australian workers*, indeed. But, as I travel around the country, this is a word that keeps battering my ears. And not surprisingly, since 'disempowered' is a word that fittingly describes what so many workers have become. So it's a collective noun as well—you can call a group of retrenched workers 'the disempowered' and wink at the absence of a word that stands for shattered members of the human race who now cannot work to feed and shelter their families. The one word, both noun and adjective, says it all.

Doubtless, 'disempowered' is a word that finds no place in the lexicon of the policy purists, although, if I asked them, they could probably plot a line of notional increments of disempowerment on one of their bloody charts.

I'm face to face with deep crisis at Hazelwood and in the heaving middle of Bass Strait. It's individual, personal, painful. It's also communal; the crisis of 'closure' and 'convenience' ruins communities.

'Innovative' is another adjective that doesn't tell the whole story. It's a buzz word that fails to capture the devastating effect that industrial rationalisation can have on people's lives. It's all well and good to push ahead by discovering new ways of doing things. But who counts the *personal* cost? Who thinks about the loss of livelihood, and who appreciates the stripping away of a worker's dignity? The unionists do; the retrenched do. Counting the cost—it's a job for the disempowered.

21

FROM AWAY

Broken Hill is a town in western New South Wales that you have probably heard of but never visited. Which is a shame. Because it is, you'd be surprised to know, one of the best places in Australia. Aside from its significant mining history (think 'Broken Hill Proprietary'), it is famous for being the set for *Priscilla, Queen of the Desert* and *Mad Max*. The town is ruthlessly milking the result-ant notoriety for its tourist potential. And good on them for that. Each September brings the 'Broken Heel' festival, destined, I hazard the prediction, one day to rival the Sydney Gay and Lesbian Mardi Gras.

Broken Hill is also very, very remote—over 1000 kilometres west of Sydney and around 500 kilometres north-east of Adelaide. But it's a great place to find yourself. And finding Sam Dastyari was exactly what I was doing there at the end of 2016. Ostensibly, I was going bush to learn about the effects of post-mining-boom eco-nomic inequality and the plight of Indigenous communities. What I received was life advice. To be more precise, I was the beneficiary of three bits of information.

Revelation ONE. Never warn someone you will shoot their dog.

'If you're going to shoot your neighbour's dog don't warn them first. It works against you in sentencing.' These were the first words that Audrey said when she joined our table.

It's difficult to explain how the conversation got to this point. Perhaps it was the 35-degree heat, perhaps it was the free-flowing alcohol, but, really, no explanation will do this situation justice. I can only say that 'this is Broken Hill' and hope that such a semi-evasion is good enough.

I'm sitting in a friend's back yard having an afternoon drink with a group of young professionals mostly working in the legal-services and healthcare sectors. I'm fascinated by what uproots people from safe and stereotypical careers in places like Melbourne and Sydney, and transplants them out here, where they work with the disadvantaged members of rural communities. Frankly, it's something that I convince myself I would have the gumption to do, but in reality I've always been too much of a coward to up-end my life.

Roughly 10 per cent of people in Broken Hill are Indigenous, but they make up 90 per cent of the prison population. I want to know why, and a group of lawyers has agreed to talk to me about it.

But that is before Audrey, the aunty of one of our group, comes to share her own experiences with the law. She is short, with fading blonde hair. I'm not sure what I love most, her stories or the fact that her nephew is desperate to get her away from us, knowing how this will end.

'You shot your neighbour's dog?' I ask, totally losing track of the conversation up to this point.

'Well, I didn't just walk up and shoot it. I warned them first. I called, I wrote. That was a mistake.'

I assume that the mistake was shooting someone else's dog, but I confess naivety in these matters. Audrey was working the night shift at her job and the barking dog had been too much to handle, so … she shot it. Which apparently is what one does.

She accepted the charge for discharging a firearm but refused to accept a fine for cruelty to the animal, and because she wouldn't pay the bill, she landed in jail.

'I kept telling him "I'll shoot your stupid dog," and when the dog got shot, it was hard to deny it was me. But I wasn't cruel. I shot it in the face. It died immediately. What is cruel about that?'

'Isn't just killing the dog the bit that is cruel?' I mean, if you are going to take a stand on a point of principle, would you be wanting to erect palisades over the right to shoot dogs? Hardly worth the effort—so if you ever shoot someone's dog, make sure you do it without warning.

Revelation TWO. There is something called 'desert hot' and it is a real thing.

'There is hot and then there is desert hot and they are not the same—you can't understand what it means to live here without understanding this key difference.' Rachel Humphries, one of our group, is explaining to me a wafer-thin distinction of potentially life-transfiguring importance.

'You mean the weather—the dry heat?' I ask. Sweating uncontrollably in the 35 degrees of relentless solar misery.

'Not that type of hot—the other type.'

'Oh, like "sexy hot"?' I ask, embarrassed at how stupid that sounds.

'Yes—but not in the creepy way you just said it. Someone is "desert hot," when distance, isolation and the sheer boredom mixed in with heat means that they are decent enough … but that I would never date them in Melbourne.'

At first, I'm suspicious of this new phrase. To be irreverent, it just strikes me as an excuse to lower your standards and blame isolation for it. But I soon learn that this is an all-encompassing life doctrine.

Wishing to address my initial scepticism, another member of the group, Eliza Hull, jumps in with a helpful incantation that, though delivered with the conviction of the convert, leaves me no less bereft of comprehension than I was before she opened her mouth. 'It's shorthand. Someone will ask, "is he hot?" and I'll just say, "he's desert hot" and they will know exactly what I mean.'

Eliza has spent the past few years working with disadvantaged (mostly Indigenous) communities. I'm impressed by this, though what I find equally intriguing is the fact that she has, in her house, a document that explains exactly what 'desert hot' means. This is a document, I'm politely told, that I will never be allowed to see.

'In a town of 20 000 you aren't about to meet Ryan Gosling at the Palace Hotel [the main bar] on a Friday night. But you will find "desert hot,"' Eliza continues.

I've spent a fair bit of time in Sydney bars and I've never met Ryan Gosling either, but I'm not sure that I want to burst that bubble, so I stay quiet.

'We didn't create "desert hot," but we are living it,' Rachel intervenes, going on to illustrate the blessings borne by the shimmering mystery. 'It got my parents married. I asked Mum, "Why Dad?" And she said, simply, "He was better than his friends." They were living in rural South Australia at the time. If it wasn't for "desert hot," I would never have been born.'

'Aren't you just rating the men?' asks my friend, recovering from the fact that his aunty Audrey had joined us. He has the exact look on his face that you would have on yours if you'd just now realised that all your female friends subscribe to a secret system for assessing people and you were never told.

'You are making the mistake of viewing it only through the prism of physical appearance. There is more to it than that. That's why we wrote the manifesto.'

Somehow the document has become a 'manifesto', which makes me want to get my hands on it even more.

I sit back, open another drink, and secretly plot how I will one day get my hands on this document.

When the document arrives in Sydney a week later, I'm mildly astonished. I can only imagine that the decision to share this philosophy of living with the outside world must have involved even more drinks and perhaps a meeting. I imagine a fight breaking out. Some, the evangelists, would have wanted 'desert hot' to be a gift to world, while others, cultishly inclined, would have pronounced gravely upon the 'power' and the 'secrecy', and admonished the devotees that the one cannot be decoupled from the other. But all of that was now irrelevant; the manifesto, enjoyably ungrammatical and littered with ampersands, had been made manifest.

Desert hot
|dezart-hat|
adj.

1. There is a phenomena we dubbed 'desert hot'. It's a term used to describe the effects of a remote exile in a small town, where you survey men & wonder what they'd look like tangled in your sheets. However it's well known that if you encountered them anywhere except Broken Hill you probably wouldn't feel a degree of physical attraction. It's not just about looks; those who are labeled 'desert hot' usually have starkly different interests, values, outlooks, plans & lives. Men who pass through Broken Hill from 'away' almost always encapsulate 'desert hot', with an added element of mystery that comes from never having seen them before. You have interactions you'd never usually come across in a more densely populated area, & small quirks & strange behaviours are easily justified when the gender balance in your life is heavily skewed.

This 142-word statement, I'm told, best divulges what it is like to live as a young professional in Broken Hill. One hundred and thirty words fewer than Lincoln's famous Gettysburg Address. Bush speech has an economy all its own.

'I have heard the term "from away" before.' The mother of my daughter Hannah's best friend, Rose Jackson tells me this after politely asking why I have a printed photo of a document entitled 'Desert hot' on my kitchen table. I tell her that it is 'for research'; this somehow satisfies her.

'People from the bush are always saying that so-and-so is "from away" …' Rose, who grew up in the eastern suburbs of Sydney and now lives in the inner-west, is about as strong an authority on these matters as I am.

'You realise this is just the same thing as "teacher hot" and "politician hot,"' she tells me, and my whole world comes crashing down.

'What do you mean?' I profess ignorance. But I know exactly what she means.

'It's all relative to your environment. We go on about hot politicians, but that's not really a thing outside the world we all live in. And let's face it, the reason everyone had the hots for the same physical-education teacher wasn't because they were some superstar—it was because they were just there, every day, in shorts.'

Revelation THREE. I really should know more about Indigenous incarceration and it shows what a sheltered world I live in that I don't.

Indigenous incarceration is a tragedy and, even though people talk the talk, no one is doing enough about it. In part, this is because it poses a difficult challenge; and in part, it's because it is a problem whose solution is not given sufficient priority. I understood little more than this of the issue before going to Broken Hill. That in itself is worrying.

We all live in our own bubbles. As an inner-city migrant from Sydney raised on that city's politics, I can draw you a breakdown of each migrant community and ethnic group. I can tell the difference between a Sinhalese and a Tamil Sri Lankan by their surname; I can navigate the politics of Greeks and Macedonians; I can recite *Shahs of Sunset*. But personally confronting something as important as the plight of Australia's Indigenous people has been removed from my daily experiences.

The rate of Indigenous incarceration in western New South Wales is a disgrace. Broken Hill is not unique in this regard. Any town where almost the entire prison population is Indigenous, which is a lot of country Australia, will be contending with very nettling socio-economic issues.

Not that that makes the crimes that have been committed any more acceptable; but surely you have to wonder what the root causes are of a situation in which people from one group make up virtually the entire prison population.

The young lawyers I'm with talk of what we all know: intergenerational poverty, social disadvantage, inherent intolerance. Like me, they are outsiders. They come into town to do a job, in this case represent Indigenous communities. Unlike me, they are doing something about the problem.

Much research has been published. It will tell you that the high rates of crime and violence have many different, overlapping and combined causes, including intergenerational trauma and other impacts of colonialism. In the mix are poverty, alcohol and drug abuse and their long-term consequences, such as foetal alcohol spectrum disorders, child neglect and abuse, and absence of opportunities stemming from lack of education and employment.

Broken Hill has mineral resources that have made billions of dollars in profit. The town itself has been a huge success story. But the benefits have never been equally shared.

I ask a local lawyer to take me to the Indigenous community within Broken Hill. While predominantly Indigenous communities are further away in places like Wilcannia, the Indigenous population in Broken Hill—one in ten—isn't small.

The Indigenous people live largely on the outskirts of town. There is a department-of-housing feel to their streets. I see smashed windows boarded over with plywood, yards that have been burnt, cracked buildings. It is certainly not the worst that I have seen, but the trademarks of disadvantage are there.

'Indigenous communities are always outside of town. That's how they were built,' my friend informs me. 'We could be in Broken Hill or any other country town; the Indigenous communities had their houses built far from the centre. It's a legacy of "out of sight–out of mind."'

I get angry and decide that I should do something about this.

I spend a week asking around for Indigenous-incarceration figures per prison. I want to know the exact percentage at Broken Hill jail. I ask the attorney general, who is another Senator. I ask the head of the Attorney General's department and I even engage the parliamentary library to investigate. No one is able to obtain the percentage. Various excuses are offered, none of which speak favourably for claims of 'transparency'.

I spend a few days doing some research. I track down various figures. In the Australian justice system, as of June 2015, Aboriginal and Torres Strait Islander prisoners accounted for just over a quarter (27 per cent) of the total Australian prisoner population. The total Aboriginal and Torres Strait Islander population aged eighteen years and over in 2015 was approximately 2 per cent of the Australian population aged eighteen years and over, meaning that Indigenous Australians are thirteen times more likely to be incarcerated than non-Indigenous Australians (on an age-adjusted basis).

I learn that the Senate itself undertook to report into Indigenous incarceration, and that the report came down only a few months ago. This report I never read; I did not even know that it had been produced. It barely got a mention in the media—I ask why and I'm told that it wasn't 'sexy' enough. This despite a royal commission into the Northern Territory treatment of detainees, with clearly overlapping issues of Indigenous incarceration. The number of reports, trials and government-funded programs is staggering; all the while, the statistics are appalling and getting worse. Between

2000 and 2015, the imprisonment rate for Indigenous adults increased by 77.4 per cent.

The experts say 'get in early', they say 'deal with alcohol', they talk about family violence, and their programs do get funded on an ad hoc basis. And still nothing changes.

A few words stick in my mind: 'out of sight' and its companion 'out of mind'. In public discourse, the Indigenous communities are not front and centre. The communities are remote; most of us will not see them. Speaking politically, they are not located in the handful of seats that determine elections. And so, they are forgotten.

Governments set goals, they throw money. Inner-city lefties like me argue for the need to 'do something', but how many are really prepared to do what the young lawyers whom I met in Broken Hill were prepared to do—namely, up-end their existence and take their skills to the bush?

22
OF HOUSES AND DOGS

It is truly difficult to know how you will cope under interrogation. Action movies often feature a scene in which the protagonist undergoes some form of exquisite torture. The lead character is always tested, by steadily intensifying increments of physical pain, to blurt out some information. The modern equivalent is how well you can bullshit to a real-estate agent before, during and after a rental-house inspection.

'Oh that stain, don't be silly. Wasn't that always there?'

'What do you mean you think more than one person was staying in the room ... no ... he just likes to cross dress. I'm not one to judge.'

'I can't explain the dog smell either. In fact, why doesn't the owner pay to get that fixed?'

In a bid to build up enough money for a deposit, I spent four years at the onset of my adulthood living with my friend Josh McIntosh in a series of shared houses. By the end of this small odyssey, our friendship had acquired all the hallmarks of a marriage. We fought and argued about cooking and cleaning, and nobody had sex. But all good things come to an end and, eventually, it was time to move on. A few months after first dating Helen, I used the

213

prospect of living with her as a bridge to something new—which was, of course, also a slamming of the door on something old.

What I didn't realise was that my leaving, in August 2008, would send his housing arrangement into a downward spiral.

'You got me kicked out,' Josh screams down the phone a few days after I have absconded to a rental property with Helen.

'How is this my fault?' I respond.

Earlier that day, a decision had been reached between Josh and our real-estate agent that it would be 'best' that he move out of the house and that he not think about the bond ever being returned.

'Hang on. I lost my half of the bond too!?' I ask, with the reality finally hitting me that this is not all good news.

As far as Josh was concerned, this was my fault for two reasons. Firstly, I would have checked the mail and alerted everyone to an impending inspection, and secondly, once the real-estate agent called me to arrange it, I would have been able to deploy my irresistible resources of charm and verbal ingenuity to convince the hapless agent that, really, there was no need for an inspection at this juncture and that we, being experienced and responsible tenants, were always mindful of the obligation incumbent upon us to maintain the pristinity of the abode, its contents and its amenity. I didn't ask Josh if 'pristinity' was a word or if he made that up.

I had purchased a surprise Siberian Husky pup just before I was getting ready to exit the house, and Josh matched me by getting a cattle dog to go with the German shepherd whom we were already illegally housing. By this stage, we had kept dogs for long enough to have our real-estate-agent routine down pat. When inspections were about to be done, we would just move the dog(s) between friends. We would also spend the week ameliorating the squalor that had accrued. As Josh's girlfriend used to remind us, heroin den chic is not a thing.

As I had been the person checking the mail for the past four years, Josh had just let it pile up since I left. He had missed the inspection notice.

Upon arriving at the house, the real-estate agent thought it strange that three bags of puppy food were sitting out the front,

OF HOUSES AND DOGS 215

right against the door. Apparently, there had been a sale at the local pet outlet and Josh had stocked up.

As she opened the door, both the full-sized German shepherd and the new puppy appeared, tooth and claw primed to attack this potential intruder.

A couple of observations might usefully be made here about how having a pet is something that many people take for granted, but that when you're living in space owned by someone else, your decisions about pet ownership become their decisions too. As rents get more expensive and as good-quality rental accommodation becomes harder to find, landlords really can lord it over people who are seeking shelter. It's not just to do with having pets—little things like decorating a kid's bedroom or doing up a back yard have become controversial; we've come to accept that if you don't own your own home, then you don't have the right to occupy your domestic space in a manner that's most agreeable to you. That's not how it works in countries where long-term leases are much more common and where a tenant will get to treat their property as a *home*. In my view, our shoddy treatment of renters illustrates the imbalance that exists in the Australian housing market. Investors are being given unfair priority over people who just need a home.

Faced with barking dogs and an empty house, the real-estate agent had tried to contact Josh, but when this came to nothing she called the other tenant, who had replaced me. Being completely unaware of the backstory, he blurted out, 'The dogs have nothing to do with me, they're Josh and Sam's'.

'He got us evicted,' Josh declared, self-exonerating and passing on the blame.

'Well, not me—you,' I corrected.

'Technically, you too. The lease never got changed.'

'What do you know about asbestos?' my friend Bob Nanva asks me. 'And what do you know about lead paint?'

This, clearly, is a conversation that will not end in a good place. The truth is that at the time I knew nothing about either of these two things, and neither did Bob, although that was about to change.

In a bid to break into the housing market, Bob had purchased a dilapidated semi-detached house in Burwood, a suburb a dozen kilometres west of Sydney. The house was in serious need of renovation before it was liveable. Bob and his wife, Sally, were expecting their first baby and, rightly, they considered the gaping holes in the floorboards too much of a safety hazard for the baby, especially once it reached the crawling stage. The place had potential, but to buy into an overheated market, Bob had overcapitalised and was trying to get the renovations done as cheaply as possible.

'They tell me it's the good type of asbestos. But I'm not really sure there is a "good" type,' Bob goes on to say.

'I didn't think so either,' I reply, not knowing.

'The builder is suggesting we burn the lead paint off, but the internet says that's the dumbest thing you can do.' While I would normally lean towards going with the advice of a professional builder, there was nothing 'professional' that could be attributed to the one-time acquaintance who was overseeing Bob's renovations. (It turns out that a person can suffer lead poisoning by breathing in the fumes given off by burnt paint, and that this, in turn, can cause severe adverse effects, including death.)

People freak out whenever new data rolls in showing that house prices in Sydney, and in other capital cities, have jumped another 10 per cent over the year, but we don't step back and realise that large price leaps have been happening every year for over a decade. My conversation with Bob took place in 2008, when the close to $1 million he paid for his place in Burwood seemed like an outrageous amount. Today, you wouldn't get change from $2.5 million for the same place.

Back then, Helen and I were still renting, trying to get our finances in order so that we, too, could know the unique stress of owing a bank many times more than your annual income.

Bob's dog, Wednesday, had been staying with Helen and me in the property that we rented while Bob and Sally were living with relatives and frantically trying to get their new home habitable.

Wednesday was not toilet trained. This was a key fact that perhaps should have been shared with us before we agreed to have the dog. The dog was a 'spoodle', which means that it annexed the stupidity of a spaniel to the energy of a poodle. The fact that it didn't shed hair—apparently its selling point—just made it dirtier. My dogs wanted nothing to do with it.

While Helen and I were meeting with a mortgage broker to work out just how much irresponsible debt someone would be prepared to lend us, Wednesday jumped on the dining table and onto our paperwork. This did nothing to make us look like the type of people to whom a financial institution should be lending money.

Not that this affected the person working on our application. It was early 2009, and although the world was heading towards the peak of the global financial crisis, the lending practices that caused it had still not been shut down. Nothing was going to deter this guy from throwing money at us that we would forever be indebted to repay.

'So, there is a car parked out the front,' asks the broker. 'Is that *your* car?'

'Not really. It's a work car,' I reply.

'Yeah. But is it *your* work car?'

'Yes. But I don't own it.'

'Sure ... but how about we just list here that you have a car. Now Helen,' he says, turning to her, 'would you say you have 20k in jewellery?'

'No,' Helen replies, 'I would say I wouldn't have 1k.'

'Would you say you had 20k if you realised no one ever checked?' he brazenly asks.

'No. No, I wouldn't.'

He kept winking, giving no indication that he was concerned that there was a dog on the table.

PART IV: THE MEAT

'Well, that went well,' I told Helen that night. In hindsight, it's hard to believe that anything ever went wrong in the financial markets.

Bob's builder went missing for weeks on end, jobs were not completed and precious time kept passing. In the end, the baby was born before the house was ready and, having exhausted their welcome with his relatives, he and Sally moved in with us. That's how Helen and I ended up living in a two-bedroom rental house in Five Dock (not far from Burwood) with two other adults, one newborn human, three dogs, three cats and around forty-five fish.

It was, I am happy to admit, a strain. It was student-living all over again—the drugs, the drinking and the exams did not return, but the grime and the muck and the stench did.

The house was not designed to cope with four adults, and the electricity switchboard gave up within days. Considering that we had six illegal pets and three illegal people staying with us, there was no way that we could get an electrician in through the home's owner.

If the cramped conditions and the emaciated electricity weren't bad enough, there was the constant noise that emanated from six animals living in far too close proximity to one another. The solution was that Wednesday was deemed an 'outside' dog, which, considering that she wasn't toilet trained, should have been a no-brainer and therefore should not have required a full-on dialectical thrashing out within the solemn forum of a household meeting.

Wednesday, however, was not OK with this new development. She spent all day scratching the back door, begging to be let back in so she could poo on the linoleum in the kitchen, her favourite spot.

When we finally vacated the house, the landlord turned to me and asked, 'What are these scratches on the back door?'

'Oh, them, they must be the birds,' I lied.

'The birds?' he repeated in an exasperated voice.

'Yeah, they keep coming up to the glass and pecking on it.' This answer had not been workshopped with Helen, who was not impressed by my improvisational skills. Two years of theatre sports clearly wasted.

Nonetheless, the house was being demolished, so a potential problem was conveniently bulldozed.

Bob, Sally and the baby moved elsewhere, and, finally, Helen and I were able to enter the property market. Even on great incomes we were only able to purchase with family support. Most people aren't fortunate enough to have the support we had. Our share-house days make good dinner-party fodder, but it's the sort of fodder that many people can regurgitate nowadays. The overcrowded juggle is becoming more common in our capital cities.

Few people really want to live this way. But when even renting a free-standing home can eat up almost all of an average income, some city dwellers simply don't have a choice. Much of the conversation about housing affordability focuses on people's ability to buy a home. But we've also got a problem with rental affordability for people with families and those who do the jobs that keep our cities running—the shop assistants and cleaners, the nurses, teachers and firefighters.

'Do you want a beer?' I ask Chris Bowen as he takes a seat on one of the leather Parliament House couches. I ask this while I am already going through his fridge, which is quite rude considering that I'm in his office.

'How can you know so much and yet never have heard of "Cristal champagne"?' I quiz him again.

The whole conversation is going around in circles. We are meant to be talking about strategies to promote Labor's housing affordability policy but I can't get away from the fact that there is footage of Chris in the parliament asking his colleagues, 'What is Cristal?', following a jibe from the prime minister.

'I grew up in Fairfield. We didn't have expensive champagne. We were working-class kids,' he answers.

I could tell him that in the western suburbs of Sydney they all know what Cristal is—firstly because they can't afford it, and secondly because it's the basis of dozens of American rap songs.

'Are we going to talk about housing or are you just here to give me a hard time?' Chris asks, not so much asking a question as declaring the innings closed on the talk about booze and rap music.

The truth is that I intend to do both. Chris Bowen for the past few years has been obsessing over the same issue that all of us have, the near impossibility for first-home buyers to purchase a house in any of Australia's capital cities. Chris wants to shake up negative gearing, to level the playing field for first-home buyers. It's a big aim, and a controversial one.

The insane, million-dollar average price of a house is the thing on which people focus when they talk about the affordability problem within our market. But there are further problems that ramify from this issue, and they deserve more attention too. Rental affordability for people working in low-paid jobs in our cities is at crisis point; our rental laws make millions of Australians feel like unwelcome squatters in other people's properties; and mortgage costs are such that those who can get into the market take a huge hit to their standard of living just to buy an often very substandard home.

These problems all stem from the fact that we've come to think about housing as a financial asset first and a place of shelter only second. And, to boot, all of the incentives and advantages in the system are skewed towards investors.

'It's not just a BBQ stopper,' I say to Chris. 'It's the issue stopping avocado brunches across Australia', testing out a line I want to use.

'Sam, that is lame. Don't use that.' Coming from a guy who has never heard of Cristal, this is a devastating blow.

23
DRUGS AND THE LAW

A small neon-yellow capsule is placed on my desk in my Parramatta office in Western Sydney. It looks as though it could be something nefarious, but I'm not sure.

'What's in it?' I ask.

'Nothing,' I'm told.

'Okay,' I say. 'How can I help you?'

A constituent has come to my office to talk about the current illegal-drugs curse. 'Well,' he answers, 'if this were a Friday night, and if we were out in the city or at a music festival, this capsule would be full of drugs. I didn't think bringing a capsule full of drugs to a Senator's office would be a very good idea.'

I nod in agreement, pleased that my interlocutor's instincts accord with my own. I'm not squeamish about drugs—over the years, I've tried as much as most people my age—but my eagerness to learn about the dynamics of the illicit-drugs market in Australia would hardly constitute an acceptable defence had my companion been questioned by the police.

I'm concerned that our use of law-enforcement resources is doing little to counteract the burgeoning market for illicit drugs in Australia. Much of the debate surrounding drug prohibition strikes me as rank hypocrisy. Parliamentarians who preach an abstinence policy often conveniently forget about their own school and university experiences. The objective of keeping people safe, we are told, requires us to accept the attendant collateral damage— namely, the higher-than-average rates of incarceration of people from Indigenous and relatively low socio-economic backgrounds for drug-related convictions. But I consider this scenario to be *unacceptable.* Drugs policy stands still; it's a deliberate no-go zone for modern politicians. In the meantime, Australia continues to make money for international illicit-drug manufacturers.

'These capsules are sold down the road,' the man continues.

'Empty ones?' I ask.

'Yeah. You buy the empty capsules and pack in the drugs. A dissoluble capsule containing drugs in powder form delivers a faster hit than a solid pill.'

Like most things that are said about illicit drugs, the truthfulness of this statement is unknown. But people believe it and simply 'go for it'—they pop the capsule in the expectation of experiencing a quick high.

'And what exactly is put in these capsules?' I ask.

'It varies. Which is the problem. Some variation of MDMA and speed, padded out with rock salt, sugar or ketamine. Meth-amphetamine is used to keep it going longer, and occasionally a dealer will slip in some ice to get you addicted quicker.'

The man is not a drug dealer or a drug taker; he has come to my office to talk about making pill-testing kits available at music festivals. I can see the benefit of this suggestion. The capsules about which he speaks give even the most hapless of drug dealers the wherewithal to create a cheap, pre-packaged, marketable and brightly coloured product. Without risking border-control hazards to import cocaine or heroin, the distributors will play out the latest Australian version of *Breaking Bad*, without needing any of the chemistry nous. The harmful effects of whatever dodgy knock-up next arrives on the market won't be known until the luckless naive soul who swallows the capsule ends up in an emergency ward or worse. This is why I believe in the value of drug-testing kits.

I accept that it would be better if no one took drugs when attending music festivals or other events, but research shows that we ought to assume that drugs will be taken at particular kinds of gatherings. What interests me is that the experience of countries that have adopted pill-testing techniques suggests that people take notice of what the pill tests show. If a test records a lower-than-expected quantity of active ingredients, the user tends to ditch the pill because they're worried about what else might be in the mix. This seems like common sense. It also seems like common sense that we should give people access to information that will protect them, rather than deny them the opportunity to protect themselves.

The yellow capsule on my desk gives me pause to consider that policy makers are always too late when it comes to new drugs on the market. We focus intently on one drug; in the meantime, another is taking hold. It's like playing an endless whack-a-mole game, but the moles don't go back into their hole so easily.

The campaign to highlight the dangers of ice has success-fully portrayed it as the new heroin, a taboo drug. It highlights to potential users that ice isn't a recreational drug that can be used on weekends without likelihood of long-term consequences. Typical meth is about 20–30 per cent pure. Ice is closer to 70 per cent or more. So it's no wonder that we are seeing a much sharper and faster decline in the wellbeing of ice users. Whereas a heroin addict might have been able to hide their habit for years before hitting rock bottom, many ice users reach the nadir in around six months.

A person might try ice once at a party and, well within a year's time, find that they're penniless, outcast, alienated from family and friends, and caught up in criminal activity.

I find it interesting to compare the campaign against ice and heroin with the reality of the rates of addiction to prescription opioids. We don't really understand the extent of opioid abuse in Australia because, at a national level, we don't have any real-time monitoring of prescriptions. However, according to the Centers for

Disease Control and Prevention in the United States, more than 30 000 people died from opioid overdoses in 2015. To put this into perspective, the number of people who died as a consequence of overdosing on prescription opioids exceeded the number of people who died from HIV/AIDS in the worst year of that epidemic.

It is right to talk about ice as the new heroin and to scare people away from trying it, just as it is right to demonise the abuse of prescription drugs. But we need to do more than draw attention to the dangers of misusing drugs. We also need to assist people whose drug habits are jeopardising their wellbeing.

'Don't get me started on depression,' my drug expert interrupts my thoughts. 'Everyone is getting depressed. Drugs are an easy-to-come-by relief.'

A lot of intelligent people have written volumes about the subject of substance abuse and mental health. There is a huge amount of published material out there, a lot of it regarding disorders brought about by the previous generation of drugs, but very little about the effects of new drugs.

'Is it the depression that leads to taking the drugs or the drugs that lead to depression?' I ask. It's an unfair question. My companion doesn't know the answer. I suspect that no one can answer definitively, though I assume that the subject has been researched ad nauseum.

What should we be doing about the drugs problem? The objectives can be simply stated.

We should be protecting the kids.

We should be locking up the drug dealers.

We should be creating safe environments in our cities and towns.

These policy aspirations are so obvious that you'd think, by now, that they would be well on the way to implementation.

What we do, instead, is provide no protection (pill testing) to the kids who are taking the illicit drugs and watch on as the real drug dealers (who use desperate kids to do the selling) get away with it.

I pick up the empty capsule on my desk and study it.

'What do they call these things?' I ask.

'Caps.'

'Caps,' I repeat to myself, getting to know the enemy.

It was my sixteenth birthday party and my cousin Samira was meant only to drop off her younger sister, Sayna.

'Hang on. Your parents are letting you hold your birthday party at night in a park?' Samira challenges me. 'Sure,' I reply, playing fast with the truth.

'I'm going to stay around,' she says, letting me know that she realises I am lying through my teeth. While having her sister around was really going to dampen Sayna's style, I knew that Samira loved me and wouldn't dob to my parents. Samira was in her mid-twenties and, despite having better things to do on a weekend, she knew that it was a smart idea to stay and keep us out of trouble.

The truth is that my parents had no idea that I was having a party. Considering that I'd invited around 100 people and that I didn't want the house to get trashed, I decided to go offsite. The local park in Cherrybrook seemed as good a place as any. That'd do for a gathering of a horde of the young and the very restless. The whole thing had been organised in twenty-four hours, which, in those days, added to the excitement. This was the end of the 1990s, after all. Before Twitter and Facebook, even before Messenger, we had ICQ—the first, and in my opinion the best, social-media tool.

Kids whose parents wouldn't let them just be dropped off in a park were taken to my house, whereupon the drop-offs would sneak out and head to the park.

In the end, around 250 people showed up. Not a bad return on the invitational outlay. No one—bar two or three of the girls who had older boyfriends—had access to a car.

We thought we were tough. We knew we were cool. We possessed the confidence engendered by upper-middle-class privilege.

We were secure in the knowledge that our parents would get us out of any real mess. The truth is that no one had ever been in a fight. Most of us attended a selective public high school.

But this is my contention: if we weren't in suburbia, in the heart of Sydney's Bible belt, this story might have ended differently. If the police had found 200 drunken teenagers at a park in an Indigenous community, would they have laughed and politely told us to stop being silly and go indoors? Would they simply have disposed of the alcohol and guided the group back to someone's house, as they guided all of us to my parents' house that night?

And what if the police had found the drugs? Those who attended the park in Cherrybrook didn't even check. We had nothing more than some low-grade cannabis, but we were good-time harmless kids from prosperous backgrounds. How differently would we have been treated had our goings-on been going on somewhere else—say, for example, in south-western Sydney, in the shadow of a housing-commission project? Might criminal charges have been laid?

'Yeah. That's not how it worked for me,' a fellow Sydneysider tells me over a beer.

'I was in Glebe at Wentworth Park with a few friends. The police entered the park. Many groups of people were there. The police bypassed all of the other people and approached me and my friends. They said a lady had seen drug use in the park earlier. My friends fitted the lady's description of the people doing the drugs.' All of the people in this story, including the man telling it, are Indigenous Australians.

The case for legalisation of low-level drugs like cannabis isn't about encouraging young people to take drugs. Many are taking drugs anyway. We aspire to live in a society in which everyone is 'equal before the law'. There's a catchphrase to warm the heart. But the catch in the catchphrase is that some have means of accessing legal assistance, and ways of finding justice, that are simply denied to, are unavailable to, others. Reform is needed for the sake of those people who do not have 'equal access' to the law. We should be ensuring that all people have the same sorts of opportunity to get ahead and prosper, and the same capacity to be treated justly.

People who are poor, who come from migrant backgrounds, who are Indigenous—they are the ones who tend to get caught up by laws aimed at making low-level drugs illegal. They are the ones who end up having criminal records.

That about 50 per cent of the prison population is made up of non-violent offenders makes me wonder why we lock so many people up in the first place. Over 35 000 Australians are in jail, a number that has tripled since the late 1970s (during that forty years, the national population has increased less than twofold). The government spends $300 per prisoner per day. It's a stellar figure. And it's money that could be better spent.

I'm in favour of legalising low-level drugs like cannabis and of lightening sentences for non-violent offences. I get that I'm an outlier on this. But I'm happy to be that.

Surely our limited resources can be better spent on tackling the drugs that are devastating society than on locking up cannabis users. Surely.

24

MY FRIEND STEVE

I'm quickly learning that there isn't really a protocol to direct the behaviour of neighbours when they see that the photojournalists are out in numbers and prowling around the locale.

'Steve,' I repeat in pure shock, 'you threatened to call the cops.'

'Well, of course. Imagine him parking in our street to take photos of you taking your kids to school. I told him I suspected he was a paedophile and that he was being creepy. I did it to get rid of him.'

My first instinct is to explain that when accusing someone of being a paedophile, 'being creepy' is an unnecessary descriptor. But I let it go. I am too distressed and Steve is being supportive. I also don't have the heart to tell him that the photographer in question was probably legally entitled to get the photos he was after.

He continues, telling me of his plan to play pest to the plague. 'By the time all the TV cameras pulled up in front of your house, there was nothing I could do. Still, I was going to come out and mow your lawn and water your garden—just to piss them off.'

By 'them', Steve was referring to employees of many major news and print-media organisation in the country. These people had arrived; they were outside my house.

In the days leading up to this moment, I had been, as we professional politicians call it, 'in the shit'. My house had been the centre of a media bubble for over a week. I hadn't quite come to terms with the commotion that I'd created in the street. Everyone, I'm now learning, came out to participate in the spectacle, and Steve was the ringleader.

Steve is fifty-five years old and has been living in the house next door to mine for over thirty years. He is a tall man with somewhat dishevelled, longish hair. Sporting a goatee and with a penchant for ripped t-shirts, he looks like a bassist from an '80s rock band (any '80s rock band).

Until she passed away in 2016, Steve was the primary carer for his mother. For eight years he took care of her after a mishap at a hospital resulted in a stroke. The stroke, compounded with Alzheimer's disease, rendered her entirely reliant on Steve's care. Apart from repeated hospital visits, Steve's mother did not leave her living room for the whole time. For years, Steve hadn't spent more than two hours a week away from his mother.

We live in a normally quiet suburban Sydney street in a little-known suburb called Russell Lea. The houses are overpriced (naturally, being Sydney), and everyone is mortgaged to the hilt. All the neighbours tell me that they voted for me at the last election. Statistically, that cannot be true. Our street is lined with what a real-estate agent once described as 'boxelder trees'. A quick google proves that this is not the case. But whatever they are, they're big. One such tree sits directly between the front of my house and the front of Steve's, and it is at this spot that we usually meet for a yarn. People, here, get on; there's a friendly vibe about the neighbourhood.

This wasn't the sense of community that I had been promised. As a child of the 1990s, I was raised on American television. I imagined myself living in a New York- or Seattle-style apartment (the type of structure that I now know exists only on television or in Trump Tower), or, better still, in a converted warehouse. I realised quickly that puppets with a penchant for cookies were unlikely to greet me in the morning as I left our loft, but the idea that Helen and I would be holding flash dinner parties at which people would laugh at my witty jokes, and we would discuss books and world affairs, took longer to dispel. If life couldn't be *Sesame Street*, it should at least be *Frasier*. Or so I once thought.

Steve's house is twice the size of mine and sits on a 600-square-metre block. It's a 1970s, double-storey brick home surfaced by fading yellow paint. There had been tension among the neighbours, and Steve relishes the opportunity to rake over the coals. When Steve speaks of the previous owners of our house, his words register a deep-rooted, visceral contempt. 'Those arseholes,' he begins, and proceeds with the story of how he spent years fighting against their planned redevelopment of the house. Despite having never met the aforementioned, and despite being the ultimate beneficiary of their redevelopment, I share Steve's hatred of our house's previous occupants—because that appears to be the done thing.

The ethos that sets the emotional tone of our street is indebted to the story of Steve's ill-tempered relations with our predecessors. We're bound together in amicable bonds by the legends passed on from times when neighbours were consumed by mutual disregard. In no particular order, Steve and the previous occupants of our house had floodlights trained on each other's bathrooms, music playing at full volume, cameras at the ready to catch every act of trespass and patrols at the fence line that bear comparison with operations along the Demilitarised Zone that borders North Korea.

On the day of the departure of our predecessors, Steve purchased a giant neon board, wrote the word 'CELEBRATION' on it, and played, at full volume, six different versions of 'Celebration' by Kool & the Gang. It was, I'm reliably told by another neighbour, 'fucking epic'.

It has also become abundantly clear why the previous occupants were so keen to sell before the auction. When I ask Steve what he had planned for the auction, he goes quiet, smiles and gives me a look that can only signify that he has entered a dark place.

Steve isn't married and doesn't have any kids. That's a shame, because he would've been a great dad, judging by how much he sacrificed in order to care for his bedridden mother. Steve's example of selfless giving prompts me to wonder whether many of us would be prepared to devote, and I do mean *devote*, a large slice of our lives to the care of another person. When push comes to shove, how many of us would give up everything for someone else?

Politicians live in the shadowy region between selfishness and selflessness. There is honour and decency in wanting to use your life to contribute to public policy and effect change. There is also something quite narcissistic in the need that politicians have for public adulation and admiration. We politicians, almost all of us, are insecure.

And we are extremely selfish. Politicians constantly expect their families to make sacrifices. The politician's presumption is that one's nearest and dearest will 'do the right thing'. You can see the spouses, wearing the perfected smiles and performing the obligatory handshakes; and you can see the children, being used for the Christmas-card and campaign photos, struggling to look interested—all the time wondering when exactly they signed up to all of this. I'm not sure that a politician could ever make the kind of sacrifices that Steve has made.

What Steve does have, and it's something of which I am incredibly envious, is the ability to slow down and take time. He can pause, and for a while stay still. That's what I want Steve to teach me.

In the afternoon of 2016 I was outside my house with Steve, sitting under a tree and drinking cheap wine while conducting what had been, so far, an incredibly unsuccessful garage sale. We had far more toys than anyone could possibly need or want. Hannah had decided to create a store out the front of our house from which to sell her toys. Recalling the American utopia of my childhood dreams, I decided that this was a 'cute' notion, and set the stall up. I imagined Hannah's stall as being akin to a lemonade stand without a permit, the kind of arrangement that was an ever-present trope in 1990s sitcoms.

Hannah and Eloise were able to talk me into bad ideas like this stall because I had recently resigned from my positions of Manager of Opposition Business in the Senate and Shadow Spokesperson for Consumer Affairs. 'I'm resigning to spend more time with the family' is a much-heard political euphemism that normally means 'I'm jumping before I get pushed'. But there was no point in my trying to paint my resignation as anything other than a big dose of humble pie.

The day after my resignation, my house became the scene of a hipster wake. Friends came by in dribs and drabs, and strangers showed up with halal snack packs. The Halal Snack Pack Appreciation Society ran a '#putoutyourhsps campaign' following my resignation. I felt supported and almost relieved that the controversy was over.

Sitting out the front of my house the next day, contentedly surrounded by toys, I have no idea that my relief and contentment won't last—that within a week, I'll crash and feel as though I'm at rock bottom, and that the phone calls and messages telling me that 'you'll be right' and 'everything is going to be OK' will stop. I don't at that point know that my assistant, Sharnelle Arthur, will be calling my friends in parliament, Anthony Chisholm, Jim Chalmers, Tony Burke, Joel Fitzgibbon and Tim Watts, to make sure that they maintain their regular visits to my parliamentary office to keep my spirits from entering a dark space. Then, when others are moving on with their own lives while I'm at home and consumed by self-doubt, only Steve will have the time or the desire to be there to help me confront my demons.

'So how did you get it so wrong?' Steve asks me in my back yard after I give up on the garage sale. The question is phrased with refreshing bluntness. Steve is not one to sugar-coat his speech or to tiptoe around sensitive issues. I'm relieved by this—I know that when I talk to Steve I'll get the truth and nothing but the truth, however brutal that may be. Steve won't deliver the standard lines of facile comfort, that 'it's only a setback' and that 'I'll be back in no time'. He knows that I don't need to hear this from him.

And his straight-to-the-mark question will prod me to think, with due honesty, about my predicament.

I resigned over a $1670 office travel expense that I had arranged to be defrayed by a donor, and declared on my parliamentary pecuniary-interest register. I treated the payment like I would a campaign bill—raise the money, declare it and then pay. In the context of the sensitive atmosphere that surrounds China–Australia relations, it didn't help that the firm that paid the expense had Chinese links. It was a stupid way to handle an office expense that I should have paid myself, and it allowed my political opponents to suggest that my integrity had been compromised. The fact is that I hadn't thought it through. I hadn't considered the consequences. I hadn't been well enough attuned to the environment.

'I messed up,' I tell Steve. 'It was the payment, tied in with some loose language about Chinese matters that I knew far too little about that sunk me. I didn't think it through. I rushed—like I always do, and that was foolish.'

'Yeah,' Steve nods. 'I knew you were cooked when you held the press conference the day before you quit. A hundred journalists showed up.'

On 6 September 2016, the day before my resignation, I held a train wreck of a press conference at the back of the Parliament of New South Wales. The reality was that it didn't matter what I said at that point. There was blood in the water and the journalists were circling. From the moment that I stepped up and saw the looks on their faces I knew how serious a mess I was in.

'They said you were a Chinese spy,' Steve recalls, laughing into his beer.

'Yeah, I know. It got a bit crazy. They said a lot of things. The allegation was that I contradicted ALP policy on the South China Sea. I'm not sure that I contradicted it. But that doesn't matter.'

Of course, it hurts when you have your integrity questioned. It hurts when you love your country and you have your motives questioned. But the pain penetrates even more deeply when you realise that you brought it all on yourself.

I knew the Sydney Chinese community leaders like the back of my hand. I also know the Indian, Middle Eastern and even the Nepali leaders too. The Chinese Australian population exceeds one million, and I pride myself on having developed a close relationship with this significant community. Frankly, I always held the view that Australian politicians ought to do more in reaching out to migrant communities, and this was an aspect of public life that I seized as an opportunity. I thought that I could make a difference. Why wouldn't I do what I could to connect with, and to help, the migrant communities of our nation?

But I was naive. I made a mistake in letting someone sort a bill. This was a bill, as I said, that I declared, but I should have had the prudence to foresee that opponents might run with the payment of an expense in order to question my motives. It was an error on my part to think that it wasn't inappropriate to have a bill paid on my behalf. And so I paid the price. In my case, the price was high, but right. Justice was done.

'So what did you learn from it all?' Steve asks me at Christmas in 2016, a few months after my resignation.

'I learnt that politics is a tough business,' I say, failing to honour the question with a thoughtful answer. Not that politics isn't a tough business—it certainly is. But I already knew that.

What I learnt was the importance of knowing *when to keep my distance*. I learnt how much *perception* matters in politics. Once your actions are painted in a particular way, and once the speculation begins about what precisely motivated you to do what you did, it becomes very difficult to defend yourself. If you are widely perceived to have acted in an improper way, your honesty will be questioned and, ultimately, your standing will be tarnished. We expect high standards from our elected officials, and those officials need always to be aware that they should not act in ways that may jeopardise their reputation. It doesn't matter how high you are flying, you cannot afford to think that you can't do wrong. If you don't think about the consequences of your actions, you will let people down. These are the lessons that have been driven home to me.

The garage sale has been a disaster. After five hours, the only buyer has been Joe from across the road, who purchased two toys for $10 out of pity and a sense of neighbourly niceness. Eloise started to cry at this development. The concept of money means nothing to her (she is three years old) and she was shocked by the realisation that Joe's act of kindness would result in the loss of her toys. I promise to take her to the shops the next day and replace the two toys that we just sold. Steve believes that this represents a socialist tendency. I'm not sure that he understands what socialism is.

Politicians tell you that they have a lot of interests outside politics. They like to pretend that there is a whole host of normal things that they like to do, and that politics is just a small part of what makes them who they are. This is, of course, complete and utter bullshit. Politicians do politics 24/7. They live and breathe it. That is why every profile of a politician desperately tries to search for the one thing that makes them 'normal'—the thing that connects them to others and which, it turns out, most of them do not have.

I'm coming to the realisation that Steve is probably my only friend who isn't in some way connected to politics. That's a pretty worrying thought.

Politics can be a prison. And it's insidious; it cunningly disguises itself—so that those whom it imprisons don't realise that they are locked in it. I'm yet to meet a politician who actually feels content with their lot. Of course, they don't aspire to contentment; that would be too near to complacency, and it might abut vacuity. Politicians are driven to do things. As a politician, you're always active; you don't stop. If you seek power, you'll be on the ever-turning roundabout, and chances are that your objectives will always be ahead of you, attainable yet out of reach. This may eat away at you, white ant your confidence, and leave you feeling weak and afraid.

I don't know if this plight is unique to politics. I imagine that musicians and businesspeople, motivated by an insatiable drive to succeed, would share with me a sense of—at least sometimes—being imprisoned within a self-made cage.

That cage is unknown to Steve, which is not to say that he doesn't wrestle with his own demons. He, daily, processes memories of his mother, and faces the challenges of letting go and moving on after a decade of being a carer. But, as I've said, he has the ability to exist 'slowly'.

I'm learning that I have more to learn from Steve than I realised. I wouldn't say that he's 'happy'. But he accepts things for what they are. I don't. He understands and values real human connection. What I'm starting to understand is that the willingness to accept the world around you, and the ability to make genuine human connections, are linked. I'm finding out that you can't be with someone if you are constantly running, and you can't sit with someone if you are trying to get to the next thing. I've not yet made up my mind about this thing called 'acceptance'—is it a virtue or a curse?—but what is dawning on me is an appreciation of just how much *real connection* with people matters. It seems to me that the constant chatter of social media, the deluge of phone calls and the routines of the rat race haven't made anyone happier.

In this world of Twitter, Facebook et al.—in which, so we are told, everyone 'connects'—why do we feel so alone?

Memories are notoriously unreliable, but in my memories of growing up in Western Sydney in the 1990s, *everyone had time*. I can now acknowledge time's blessedness. And what I'm referring to is a blessedness writ small; I'm savouring, in the storehouse of my memory, the little joys of a different age. Time to play in the street, time to hang out with mates, time to complain with whoever will listen, time to sit contentedly with someone you love: I used to do such things. The neighbours even had time—Oh what a scandal—to get each other pregnant.

Now it's different. I give a quick wave as kids are packed into the car in the morning. There's a rapid-fire 'g'day how-ya-goin?' while I'm on the move, hurtling from one event to another. Perhaps, just perhaps, I'll find time for a brief conversation about noise. But it's all done in a gallop; there's no time to slow down and feel the day's delights. But Steve, bless him, is showing me a better way.

If it weren't for Steve, no one in our street would have anything to do with one another, and no one would own a neon sign.

V
THE SAUCES

25

BILL CREWS: THE ONE I ADMIRE

The Reverend Bill Crews is sitting on my couch in the Senate wing of Parliament House. He's wearing his typical outfit: a black shirt, black jeans and a jacket.

'You have to piss in every corner,' he tells me.

'You have to what?' I ask, assuming I misheard him.

'Not what, *where*. Every corner!' he repeats.

I have never heard this phrase before. Later I ask around and find out that no one has. It has the ring of a saying to it, but it isn't one.

As Bill puts it, 'People say you can't piss in that corner because it will upset so-and-so or you can't piss here because it's so-and-so's patch.' After thirty-three years of regular bladder movements, I had no idea that I was doing it wrong.

As far as life mottos go, it's a pretty good one. So, I decide I'm going to keep it and make it mine. I take to telling this to people around parliament, mostly to get their reactions. It's a good way to check if they are actually listening to me. 'To what? ... I have to *what*?'

This is what passes as a pep talk from Reverend Bill Crews. Bill is known for being frank and fearless. He's more Robert De Niro in *Sleepers* than your stereotypical man of God. Faith is a means, not an end, which isn't everyone's cup of tea.

Bill is sixty-eight years old but has the energy of a twenty year old. He has wavy white hair, big blue eyes and would measure 5 foot 7 inches if he didn't stoop so much. He's thin, bearing the physique that comes from always being on the go. What you first notice about Bill is his smile; he's always cheery. I often think he would make a good Santa.

These days, Bill is not afraid of much. That wasn't always the case, as he's had a fair few of his own battles over the years. I like to picture Bill as he appears in the Archibald portrait of him that sits in his hall—a young man driven by faith, not yet jaded by years of bickering with church bureaucracy and fighting with government, and by the constant tragedy and loss that surrounds his life. His son is in the background of the painting, then still a child, smiling wryly at his father.

I had stopped listening to Bill talking in my office and I tune back in.

'And there I was with a group of drug addicts sitting in the Jungle de Calais refugee camp with a young Iranian bloke who reminded me of you.'

You have to keep up with Bill; he doesn't need an active audience to keep talking. I find it endearing but that's probably because it is a trait that we share.

'You were where?' I ask.

'The refugee camp near Paris, Jungle de Calais. And there was this Iranian bloke, who looked just like you. He was running a program.'

Bill had just returned to Australia from visiting Syrian refugees in France. The camp of which he speaks is the last leg of a long journey for people trying to get to the United Kingdom. He'd left London with nothing but his passport, 40 euros, a train ticket to Dover and a boat ticket to Calais.

'I asked the driver at Calais how much to get to the camp. He said 20 euros, which was great because it meant I could come back.' I wonder what his alternative plan actually was.

The refugee camp is notorious. Built on a chemical waste dump, it is polluted and covered in mud. The makeshift accommodation has a shanty-town feel to it. Houses are made out of cardboard and tin.

'I was sitting there, and I saw a sign which said NA meeting,' Bill continues.

'Twelve-step program? Narcotics Anonymous?' I ask.

'Yep, yep. And I thought, I'll go to that.'

'Hang on; you just decided to randomly go to a Narcotics Anonymous meeting in the middle of a refugee camp?'

'Well, there was a sign!' Bill protests. 'Anyway,' he continues, not to be thrown off by the interjection, 'I'm sitting on a carpet on the floor with probably thirty people and there were people there from every nation. There were Saudis, Africans, Syrians and Iraqis. All sitting in a circle. And they're all telling their stories, right? And I couldn't understand a word anyone said in their native tongues. The guy running it was Iranian and he was translating into French, which I didn't understand either. But I didn't need to understand. I could tell from their faces.'

At this point, the bells at Parliament House start ringing, meaning that I'm required to vote. The bells will ring for four minutes. It takes two minutes to get from my office to the chamber.

'Do you need to go?' Bill asks.

'I've got two minutes,' I reply, feeling guilty.

'It went around and it got to me and I thought, what am I going to say? And I said, "Hi, I'm Bill from Australia. I've got two failed marriages and I have trouble with my kids." And they replied, "Welcome, Bill," and I cried. I felt more at home there than I have ever felt anywhere in the world. These were refugees and they were drug-addicted refugees. In the eyes of many people, they are the lowest of the low, and I'd found a home.'

As I race to the chamber, I can't shake the thought of the camp, and that was Bill's aim. This is how Bill talks. It is always through stories and there is always a point. He won't say it explicitly, but what he is telling me is that there was the Iranian volunteer in a refugee camp with no money and no power doing what he could for drug-addicted refugees, and here you sit in a cushy office of the Senate wing of the Australian Parliament and you should be doing more. But I wasn't even giving Bill the twenty minutes he needed to talk to me because I was racing around, desperate to ensure that I didn't miss an insignificant procedural vote that would soon be forgotten.

For thirty years, Reverend Bill Crews has run the Exodus Foundation, located on a busy road in the suburb of Ashfield, in the heart of Sydney's inner west. While the demographic of Ashfield has been transformed through gentrification, those seeking help have not.

'We did a health profile of our guests.' Bill always calls the homeless and helpless who come to him his 'guests'.

'And it is exactly the same today as it was thirty years ago. Nothing has changed. The profile is the same: above middle age, chronic illness and usually a mental-health problem like depression too.'

The site of the Exodus Foundation has grown as its activities have increased over the years.

There are two main parts to it: the Uniting Church structure that was built in 1864 and the Loaves and Fishes restaurant, which is Bill's food kitchen. Twice a day for around thirty years, Bill has fed and clothed anyone who walks through the foundation's door. He averages 400 a day for lunch and dinner, and the number continues to grow. What is shocking is that Bill needs to be doing this *even* in a wealthy part of the wealthiest city in one of the wealthiest countries in the world.

In addition, Bill runs an education service, and provides health facilities and support services. He's engaged in a constant battle with local residents, many of whom think his shelter lowers their property prices. They like to cite 'parking problems' as their concern. As Bill points out, most of his guests can't afford to eat, let alone drive. 'I don't see much difference between my life and the lives of people who come here to get help. Most of them are on their own and I'm on my own. And they struggle through the day and I struggle through the day.'

I first met Bill when I was twenty-two years old, and we have stayed friends ever since. He officiated when Helen and I were married at a ceremony in Bowral, where, as a trained Christian pastor, he assisted by meeting our peculiar requests.

Helen and I pulled up to the Uniting Church in Ashfield on a Sunday morning, just as Bill was completing his service. While Bill and I had known each other for years, Helen had met him once, briefly, and our wedding was fast approaching.

'Are you sure he will be OK with this?' Helen asks.

'Of course, it's Bill!' Helen shoots me the same look she gave me earlier that day when I said that I didn't need an electrician and nearly burnt down the house.

Bill leads us up to his office on the second floor of the Exodus Foundation office building. The building is in desperate need of renovation, but Bill would see that as a waste of money. The walls are cracked and the carpet, though recently replaced, serves simply to delineate the unevenness of the wooden floorboards beneath. Bill's office, utterly colonised by papers, has a mad-professor feel to it. It's small and overcrowded, but not in the quaint sense.

'So the wedding,' Bill says, getting straight to the point. Bill is shortly to race off to a commitment ceremony for a lesbian couple and has only a few minutes to spare.

'Yes, about that. We were thinking about what would be said at the wedding,' I ramble sheepishly.

'Ah … you want to do your own vows, well sure, why not? It's very fashionable these days.'

It was not fashionable and that was not the purpose of our visit.

'No, not that. It's about God,' I say.

'God?' This has caught Bill's attention. 'What's this got to do with "God"?'

'Well, that's kind of the view we have, so we were hoping you could perhaps not mention him at our wedding.'

'Righto,' replies the only Christian minister who would agree to officiate at a wedding without mentioning God. He follows it up with a 'God bless you,' as we leave.

'Are you a Muslim?' Pauline Hanson asked me as I sat beside her on the panel of the ABC program Q&A.

I had just made the observation that her suggestion of a 'Muslim ban' would have meant that, as a child, I would not have been permitted to come to Australia.

But Pauline didn't care about that; she was fixed on one fact, the 'Muslim' part: the idea of the 'other'—that some strange creature was sitting beside her.

In the green room afterwards she expressed her disgust, claiming that she had been 'ambushed by Muslims' on the program. Later, on a different television program, she would claim that she keeps a copy of the Koran with her for reading at all times, which is just downright weird.

Having been born in Iran after the Islamic Revolution, I am regarded as being a Muslim. While I have never been a practising Muslim, it is hard to deny at a cultural level that Islam is part of my identity.

My maternal grandmother was a devout Muslim. She prayed at the necessary times, wore a headscarf, ate only halal food and never let alcohol pass her lips. My grandfather was a staunch atheist. This caused tension in their relationship. Domestic bliss was hazarded when—he being a former doctor—my grandfather got his hands on the alcohol that was severely limited after the Islamists seized control. What he drank, a watered-down version of pure alcohol used for medical procedures, shared more properties with methylated spirits than it did with Grange hermitage.

'But how can you be a Muslim and be non-practising?' I'm often asked—by people who claim to be Christian but last went to church in primary school, and even then under protest.

I'm as good a Muslim as most of my friends are good Catholics. Most people I know are a 'non-practising something or another'.

But if you've been born in Iran, saying that you are 'not a Muslim' is as politically charged as saying that you *are* one. If I'm 'not a Muslim', isn't that a rejection of my heritage? My cultural identity? While I don't have the faith that others might have, isn't it still part of who I am? It would be easy, and perhaps politically convenient, to run away from it all. It would also be dishonest.

'I couldn't give a shit what religion you are,' Bill Crews calls to tell me after the program. 'But tell me, was she faking it that she didn't know you were Muslim?'

I pointed out to him that my Muslim heritage was on the bio given to all the participants, but I can't say for certain that she ever read that. Perhaps she was too busy reading her Koran.

It was less than twelve hours before voting began at the 2016 federal election and Bill Shorten was getting jittery. While the polling had consistently kept us in the race, the popular wisdom was that Labor didn't stand a chance.

'It will be fine,' we kept telling each other in the makeshift campaign headquarters that were being run out of Shorten's Sydney hotel room.

While Bill would be making a final election-day blitz through Sydney, there wasn't all that much left to do. No one sleeps on the night before an election, so there's little point in trying. It's a waiting game.

'Can we do something?' Bill had asked a few hours earlier. 'Rather than just sit around a hotel room, let's go do something tonight.' The advancers who go to places before Bill in a campaign, the media team, everyone—they had left the last night free, as is traditional. The campaign was over for all intents and purposes, and their jobs were done.

As the Sydney resident travelling with him in the final days of the campaign, the job fell to me to find 'something' to do.

I threw up a few ideas, and still in campaign mode, my mind turned to the images that we might still be able to squeeze out for breakfast television.

'No TV; no media.' This was Bill's instruction, which made finding 'something' all the more difficult, particularly as there were camera crews parked out the front of his hotel.

'You're friends with Bill Crews, aren't you?' I ask Bill. He was. They had met years earlier, and the politician had visited the pastor's Ashfield food shelter.

I knew that Bill Crews would be in Woolloomooloo at Boomerang Place and put him on the phone to Bill Shorten. Every Friday night, in the shadow of St Mary's Cathedral, Bill Crews feeds several hundred homeless people.

It was a solemn occasion. After the highs of the campaign, the zigzagging across the country, the television interviews, appearances, speeches—here Bill Shorten was quietly, at the end of it all, feeding people with Bill Crews.

And while Bill Shorten had been on every television station every night for the past year, the real celebrity was Bill Crews.

Bill Crews is the one who is there for the needy, week after week. Sure, some of them recognised Bill Shorten; they were all polite, but mostly they didn't care. They had their own struggles, challenges and issues to deal with. Bill Crews, in his own way, was teaching Bill Shorten.

Bill asked me what I thought of it the next morning, as he blitzed the last remaining seats during the campaign. In the course of a discussion about our chances that night, I told him, 'It's called pissing in all the corners'. And he gave me a strange look.

26

RICHO: THE ONE FOR LUNCH

Graham Richardson walks into the Golden Century restaurant at 393 Sussex Street, Sydney, like he owns the place—which, I learn later, is how Graham walks into most rooms. He shakes the hands of thirty people on the way through, calls me 'a prick' to my face and then sits down to lunch. It was 13 March 2009, and it was, to quote Humphrey Bogart, the 'beginning of a beautiful friendship'.

Graham is universally known as 'Richo', and is the legendary hard man of the Labor Party in Sydney. Prior to being a media commentator and a politician, Graham was the General Secretary of the NSW Labor Party, a position I ended up holding from 2010 to 2013. If the Labor Party were Microsoft, Graham would be our Bill Gates. Prior to our lunch I had completely ignored him for the previous decade of my career in NSW Labor. From what I had heard around the traps, my reticence had not impressed Graham and so I was dreading this meeting. More than one serious figure in the Labor Party had given me the same advice: 'Don't mess with Graham, he will eat you alive'. Considering how much food he was about to order, this was a distinct possibility.

There is a performance art to how you enter a room. If done correctly, you create incredible stage presence; you command respect and you turn heads. But if you do it wrong, you resemble the lead character in a Mr Bean sketch. With my physical attributes, I naturally fall into the latter category. That is not the case with Graham.

We were to meet at 12:30 p.m. Graham is twenty minutes late. With Graham, it is always hard to tell if lateness is calculated or if he's just been tied up; more likely, he's been making these entrances for so long that being a little late is ingrained in his character. Lateness, for Graham, has become customary.

The Golden Century is a hugely popular Chinese restaurant. Without a booking, or the right connection, it's hard to get a seat there from around the middle of the day until the early hours of the morning. Graham had booked the table. Or so I thought. I later learn that Graham doesn't book at the Golden Century; rather, he calls them to inform them of his arrival time.

The bottom floor of the two-level restaurant has two parts. The higher part is where you enter; a 15-metre stroll takes you to a sharp right turn and a handful of stairs—descending which, you dip into the main eating area. One entire wall is filled by fresh seafood, as is the tradition in fancy Chinese restaurants. It's a grotesque tradition, picking your own fish, but at least there is an honesty here that connects prey to predator. The carpet and walls are faded, strategically; the owners are well aware of their reputation and aren't in the business of messing with their golden goose. Even a paint job would be too much change.

Graham walks to the top of the stairs and casually waits for five seconds. The waiters see him and pandemonium breaks out. Three people rush up to him to walk him to his table. They know where he sits. They ALL know where he sits. It's not off in a corner, or in some private room; it's the third row from the back to the left, dead centre, as they know that there will be a row of people coming to see him while he eats. His shtick is to complain that he is never left alone and how it bothers him. If that were true, he wouldn't be coming *here*.

'So not even a phone call,' Graham says. 'I keep hearing about this young upstart. Running around the place in a huge rush. But I guess you don't have time for advice from an old bloke like me.' This is a not-so-thinly-veiled swipe. In Labor speak, this is interpreted as: 'Who the hell do you think you are?'

For over a year, I had been dating Helen, the daughter of Graham's oldest friend, Peter Barron. Helen has known Graham since she was born; he has always been a part of her life—like an uncle.

'About time we talked,' he continues. I apologise profusely, setting the power dynamic that will remain in our relationship. We are about to get to something meaningful, but are disturbed by the battalion of waiters circling our table, as one of them, finally, has built up enough courage to interrupt him. I had been nervously waiting for Graham and hadn't had time to consider the menu. Not an issue: Graham launches into the order.

'We will start with spring rolls. Then we will have the Peking duck and san choy bow. After that, salt and pepper squid, then half a kilo of drunken prawns. I want a steamed barramundi with ginger and shallots and crispy skin chicken.' Graham pauses. 'You got that?'

'Yes sir,' replies the waiter.

I'm in a state of minor shock. Did he just order for me? I've had, by this stage, my fill of lunches in Sydney, and no one has ever ordered for me.

'Oh, and we will have this bottle of wine,' Graham says, pointing somewhere on a list. 'Bring two beers to get us started.'

Did he just order me a drink too?

A minute later, two beers arrive. At this point, the real conversation begins. Over the next three booze-filled hours, Graham proceeds to go through every element of my career. Whom I had pissed off, who thought I was an arsehole (a worryingly large group that has only continued to grow), what I needed to do and where I was headed.

'Oh, and don't mess things up with Helen. She's a good girl, too good for you, and Peter and I will kill you,' he concludes, as one does. Just casually threatening homicide in a Chinese restaurant.

This becomes a ritual, the regular long lunches with Graham. It's a nod to a bygone era, before the urgency of mobile phones and the pressures applied by twenty-four-hour media cycles made the ability to disappear for an entire afternoon something that can only be imagined. The 'smoke-filled back room' where political deals were made no longer exists. Who has time to smoke a cigar, let alone meet face to face? The group text message is the method of choice nowadays.

For every major milestone of my career, Graham has been there, in some shape or form. He was there for the highs and the occasional low. Always there, always a few steps removed, waiting to order lunch and pick the wine.

When I was twenty-six years of age, and with the position of general secretary available, Graham helped pave the way with the older generation of Labor stalwarts—people who were naturally sceptical of this young, ethnic upstart who had been on the scene for five minutes.

'He's too young. He's not ready,' they'd say. And Graham would point to his own tenure in that role, at that age, a generation ago, when it meant a lot more.

When I was leaving the NSW Labor Party to take a Senate vacancy, both Paul Keating and Bob Carr hit the phones to stop me, saying that the NSW Branch head office, following the 2011 election disaster, needed stability and that I should stay to see the job through. But Graham was there, saying that there was a place for me in Canberra and that I should go—though, privately, he was seething, and agreeing with Keating and Carr that it was the wrong time to leave. Graham's loyalty and friendship, on this occasion, outweighed his better judgement.

I knew that he was sick, and that he was getting worse. We would talk about his health, from time to time, but for all the social presence, the media, the bravado, Graham has always been an inherently private man about personal matters. While he would tell me bits and pieces, I knew where my place was, and I knew when it was not my place to ask.

I did know that the surgery would be major, we all knew. Graham had tried to avoid it with experimental drugs, but when that approach had failed by 2015, there was no other option but the operation. He had the first diagnosis over fifteen years earlier, and since then the cancer had only grown. They were taking out his bowel, bladder, prostate and rectum. 'The ultimate tummy tuck,' he'd say in jest.

If he was afraid, and how could you not be, he didn't let on. Graham tackled it with the stoicism that comes with that generation of men, for whom setbacks and challenges are private matters. While my peers will spend hours posting on social media about the smallest headache, hangover or cold, a previous generation would summarise something as serious as terminal illness by simply stating, 'It's not looking too good'. This was the way of Graham Richardson.

Three days before he walked into surgery, a small group of Graham's friends had lunch with him at the Golden Century. There would have been no indication of the enormity of what he was about to undertake. The laughter, the jokes, the theatre, this was all Graham at his best. And then he vanished—into the mist of the operation and the long recovery that followed.

'For God's sake, go and see Graham. You haven't called him in three months and he nearly died twice,' my father-in-law, Peter, said to me over the phone.

I was walking through the main street of Kalgoorlie at 9:00 p.m. on 17 June 2016, and I could tell that Peter wasn't impressed. For the preceding few days I hadn't had reception, crossing the Nullabor on a bus emblazoned with a giant picture of Bill Shorten. But that was hardly an excuse for not having called or seen Graham for three months. For the first month, the reasoning was simple—Graham had made it clear that he didn't want visitors. He needed to focus on his recovery and understandably didn't want the distractions.

For the next two months I'd been crisscrossing the country on a bus. But that was really just an excuse; it's not as if I hadn't passed through Sydney on more than one occasion.

I hadn't seen Graham because I was scared. This is nothing to be proud of. There is something eerie about seeing a friend who is ill. And while the age difference between Graham and me exceeds that between me and my parents, he is both a mate and a father figure. And still I avoided going to see him. That was an easy decision to make in the midst of a campaign—there is always the mitigating distraction, the event, the place to be.

But Peter was right. I needed to go and see him, and so I did.

The Royal Prince Alfred (RPA) hospital is its own bustling metropolis of activity and action. Nothing stops. And, in all of this whirling to and fro, there was Graham, more at peace than he had ever been. The young doctors, almost all ethnic, bustle around looking at their watches, too stressed and too pushed for time in a hospital system that is always under-resourced. They all blur into one; the thin physique, the stubble on the men, the dishevelled hair on the women. They know that there is someone famous in room 39, but they aren't all that sure why all these people keep coming to see him.

This is the man who made Bob Hawke; the man who, with John Ducker, drove the support behind Neville Wran; the man who paved the way for Paul Keating. Environment Minister Graham Richardson radicalised Labor policy, was the subject of a thousand stories, was the greatest show in politics. But all of that would mean nothing to the young doctors at RPA. For them, Graham was a name on a list of old men jousting with death; they had no time to get to know the person behind the name.

The nurses understood. They treated Graham like royalty. Privately, once he was asleep, they would tick off the politicians, media personalities, athletes and celebrities who had been in to see him. And there were dozens of others as well; his hospital-room door was forever revolving.

By the time that I saw Graham he was past the worst of it, but it would be wrong to say that he was well. He certainly wasn't. The human body can endure only so much punishment—or medical intervention—and it reaches a point at which it, essentially, gives up. At such a point, all that keeps you going is a *will to fight on.* Graham has always had that will. He wasn't going to lose it now.

He looked older. He still had the trademark grin, the dry sense of humour. He remained the same Graham that I had always known, but the body was giving way. The hair had been shed—that was on the way out anyway—but the sudden loss of weight is what threw me.

One can only imagine how hard the preceding months must have been for Graham's wife, Amanda, and his son, D'Arcy. Watching the ones you love struggle with pain and illness is a burden you would not wish on anybody, and they certainly didn't deserve this. On two occasions, the doctors thought that he would not make it through the night, and the family was called to his bedside.

'I'm through the worst of it,' Graham says. 'I'll survive this. But it's a real kick to the guts. I want a small life after this. I'll still do things, but it will be smaller. I want quiet. Some time with D'Arcy.' I wasn't sure if this was the exhaustion talking. But since his operation, this is how he has been.

'I've seen Graham go through everything,' Peter tells me. 'I've seen him come through the toughest political fights. But they were always mental—he has the strongest mind you can imagine.' The difference here is that the fight was with his own body. And you can fight your own body only for so long. It, eventually, will win that battle.

The theatre, the action, the bravado, the show—all had paused. And there lying on the hospital bed was simply Graham the man, the legend stripped away. He was exposed in the face of death—a mortal man struggling with a dark present and a very uncertain future—yet he was at peace.

And I stand at his door and want to tell him that I'm worried about him. That I love him. I want to tell him that I didn't see him because all of this scares me. That I was a coward. I want to say that I'm sorry. But we don't do that as the supposed hard men of the NSW Right. We don't shed tears. We don't show emotion.

So I do what it's *traditional* for us to do. I bring him Chinese.

'What did you get?' Graham asks.

'We will start with spring rolls. Then we will have the Peking duck and san choy bow. After that, salt and pepper squid, then half a kilo of drunken prawns. I then got a steamed barramundi with ginger and shallots and crispy skin chicken,' I reply.

'Good ordering,' he says with half a smile, not realising that I learnt from the best.

He takes a few mouthfuls and asks if I can pack up the rest and put it in the fridge; he's not that hungry anymore.

27

RUDD: THE ONE WHO WAS KING

It's the middle of winter, yet I'm sweating. I'm sweating as though it were 40 degrees. The more I stress about how that is going to look, the worse the problem becomes.

I'm also suddenly very conscious of how poorly I'm dressed. I've somehow managed to get drenched between my front door and the car, and I have raced out in whatever I was wearing in a moment of panic that I might be running late (I wasn't).

'What were you thinking—wearing torn jeans?' I interrogate myself as I sit in the car, waiting for the arrival time. I whisper back: 'Kevin won't care, he won't even notice'. And now I realise that I'm arguing, audibly, with myself. This is what Kevin Rudd can do to me.

A drenched shirt, torn jeans. I decide I can't possibly see the prime minister like this. I need to go home to get changed. It is 8:12 p.m. and I'm not due to be at Kirribilli House, the prime minister's Sydney residence, until 9:00 p.m.

I've arrived early. Too early. I tell myself it is because I was justifiably worried about Sydney traffic. That is a lie. I'm not afraid of that at all. I'm late to everything, usually. I'm just nervous when it comes to Kevin and I think that being there early will help me calm down. Madness.

Now I have too much time to sit and do nothing except think. So I start to catastrophise. What does he want to see me about? Is he angry? Did he sound angry? I start to think of all the reasons why Kevin could be angry. I decide that he must be angry.

Is he trying to stop me going into the Senate? He did encourage me to take the vacancy and it will be filled in a few weeks. Perhaps he's so angry he will try to stop me going into the Senate. I decide he is definitely going to try to stop me going into the Senate. Fuck him, I think. Where is the loyalty?

'If he wants a fight—I'm going to fucking give him one,' I text Chris Bowen, who doesn't respond. This makes me even more worried. Chris must be avoiding me. I don't know that Bowen is actually already inside with Kevin, that he too was summoned, but for an earlier meeting.

All I know is that Chris isn't answering, which makes me more nervous. So I decide to ring. He doesn't pick up. I ring again. Still doesn't answer. So I start ringing non-stop. As if that will make any difference, as if he will suddenly decide to pick up or call back if he has ten missed calls instead of three.

There is a knock at the window. It's the Australian Federal Police. Apparently I am also making them nervous. Perhaps a white SUV doing laps of the prime minister's residence and pulling up at the front, only to wait a minute and drive on, isn't the most inconspicuous behaviour. Particularly with tinted windows, boxes in the back seat and a Middle Eastern driver.

'I'm waiting for the prime minister,' I tell them.

I don't think the police officer quite buys this explanation— I must look like a nervous wreck by now.

'Are you OK?' he asks.

'Oh yes. I'm seeing the PM at nine. I'm just early.'

I give him my name and details. He calls the house. Kevin hasn't told them to expect me. Having worked with him, if I'd been thinking rationally … this wouldn't have been a surprise.

'What's in the car?' he asks, pointing at the boxes. I tell him that they're election flyers. Now a second officer has arrived, and then a third. They ask if I will let them see inside the boxes, which I do.

A call comes through. This seems to settle things. It is decided that I will be allowed to wait. I am expected.

Now my paranoia completely takes hold. Why didn't Kevin tell them I was coming? Is he so mad that he doesn't even want to think about it? Of course this makes no sense. But my anxiety is out of control and nothing makes sense when that happens.

'Do you know what being this anxious feels like?' I tell my friends, stealing a description that was once given to me by my sister. 'You know when you trip and there is that split second before you catch yourself? The anxiety feels like that moment will never end. That you will never actually catch yourself. Stuck in the moment before the fall.'

It is too late to go home. To get changed. A text message comes through from Anthony Albanese: 'You aren't going to like it, but just do what Kevin asks'. Fuck, I think. This really must be bad. He MUST be trying to stop me taking the Senate seat. Why else would Anthony be texting me that? So I start to call Anthony. Once, twice … and a third time. No answer. I decide it must be so bad that Anthony doesn't want to be associated with it, that he doesn't want to be the one to tell me.

I shouldn't be here at all. I should be with Helen and Hannah. It is Saturday 28 July 2013, and the night of my thirtieth birthday. We were meant to be at dinner. But I cancelled that. Instead, I'm parked out the front of the PM's house, suspected of being a potential terrorist and erratically trying to call anyone who might have any idea what Kevin is up to.

Kevin had returned as PM just over a month before. The polling had improved, and there was a hope, albeit a faint one, that not everything was lost. I was among a handful of people urging strongly that we call the election and just go for it. Kevin wanted to get his policy ducks in order first. In hindsight, it wouldn't have made a difference, but we didn't know that then.

Earlier that day, I had been told that Kevin would be calling me from his private line on the plane. He was returning from visiting troops in Iraq and wanted to speak to me. This made me suspicious. What could be so important that it couldn't wait until that night? Was he calling just to wish me a happy birthday? Surely not. I had known Kevin for a decade and that wasn't what he did. There must be a purpose.

'Soon-to-be Senator,' Kevin had said on the phone. 'Happy birthday.'

'Thank you,' I responded.

'What are you doing for your birthday?'

'Oh, just an early dinner with Helen and my daughter. Helen's pregnant so it won't be a big one.'

'Well, send my love to Helen and Hannah,' he said, deliberately using Hannah's name, to show me that he knows it. Kevin is a pro.

'Look, this line is bad. If you are having an early dinner you will surely be free by nine. Swing past and see me at Kirribilli then. Take care.' And with that, he hung up.

So I had spent the afternoon stressed out and trying to identify what he wanted. I replayed the conversation in my head over and over, trying to remember his exact tone. I repeated it to anyone who knew him, wondering if they could tell what he wanted.

'Do you think when he said "soon-to-be Senator," he was being sarcastic, like it's something I want but will never have? Do you think it was a warning about tonight?' I ask Helen after the call. This is the fifth variation of the same set of questions that I've asked her during the course of the day.

'Stop it,' she tells me.

'Stop what?'

'The panic. You obsess over anything to do with Kevin. He loves you. It won't be anything bad. It never has been with Kevin and you, and yet you do this every time,' she reminds me, shitty that I've already cancelled our dinner so that I can do laps of the prime minister's house like a madman.

RUDD: THE ONE WHO WAS KING   261

Of course she is right, I tell myself as I count down the seconds until 9:00 p.m. Helen is always right about these things. But reassuring myself makes little difference.

The last time I was at Kirribilli House it was also all about Kevin, except that then there was a different prime minister in the room. Julia Gillard had ostensibly invited me over for a cup of tea as the General Secretary of the NSW Branch of the Labor Party, but that wasn't the real issue. She had invited me over to see what was going on with so many MPs from the NSW Labor Party so openly supporting Kevin's return.

'You don't know him,' she tells me. 'You weren't there in government.'

'If it comes down to loyalty to you, or winning their seats, they will ultimately choose their seats. As John Howard used to say, "politics is governed by the laws of arithmetic".' The irony of quoting Howard at the house in which he lived for eleven years was not lost on either of us.

At some point between 2007 and June 2010, everyone in the Labor Party seemed to have turned on Kevin Rudd, which I never understood. He was always good to me. He never shouted. He was never unreasonable. I had heard the stories, everyone had. But I never saw any of it. Kevin was always supportive. He supported my taking over as secretary of the NSW Branch. He supported my going to the Senate.

I wasn't a peer. I wasn't a protégé. I wasn't a friend. But I was a supporter. And in 2013, when he was returning to the prime ministership, there were so few of us left that it made us close.

A mythology has since developed that Kevin was popular with the public and Julia with the party, and that neither one could find support from other groups. While there might be a little truth to that, it hardly captures the complexity of what was going on. It was also a mythology that was quite unfair to Julia.

Yes, Kevin's polling numbers were better than Julia's. But that was partly because he wasn't the PM. Grass is greener and all the rest. And Julia's support was deeper. The public who supported her loved her. And while there is no doubt that Julia was much more in line with what the party wanted on a policy level, there remained a sense that what had been done to Kevin was wrong—that he was never given a proper chance. It was a complicated cocktail.

We all still carry scars from that period. No one who was at all involved escaped unscathed. Friendships were destroyed and people still don't talk to each other years after the events. The Labor Party was never able, really, to choose between the two of them, and yet everyone had to pick a side. I was firmly in the Kevin camp, which made me unique insofar as party apparatchiks went.

I never really knew Kevin. I'm not sure that anyone really ever has, or will, for that matter.

What I do know, however, is that there is more than one Kevin Rudd. I suppose that it is common for people of his intellect to be able to transform themselves into whatever persona the situation requires. There is Kevin the charmer. This is the Kevin of breakfast television, the most telegenic, engaging campaigner I have ever met. He's the guy who can make a self-deprecating joke in any environment, disarm the angriest constituent and make himself immediately likeable. This is the Kevin 07 who made winning the election look like child's play.

There is Kevin the policy wonk. This guy needs to know everything about everything before he will comment. He constantly searches for more information, as if there is something hidden in the details of the data. This is the Kevin who kept demanding policy papers and briefings. This is where the stories of the 3:00 a.m. phone calls to staff come from. While most leaders ask for a one-page brief, Kevin would want all the supporting documentation. He yearned for documents that most people would never be able to read, and he'd stay up through the hours of the night devouring document after document.

And then there is Kevin the ruler. This man is iron fisted, unwavering, painfully short with people. He will not tolerate nonsense; he is incredibly loyal to his supporters—but only his supporters.

I can't explain a man whom so many of us have tried to understand. But what I do know is that there isn't one simple explanation. Everyone is complex, but Kevin is more complex than most.

When he was on top of his game, when he was at his peak, he was brilliant. And when it was all taken away from him in 2010, of course it changed the man. How could it not?

There are forty-two steps from the security gate to the front door of Kirribilli House. I know, because I counted them. I count things when I need to calm down and focus.

As you walk through the front door, you pass by the stairs; you turn left if you're going to the sitting area, or right if you're headed for the dining room. I'm led to the left. A clearly tired Kevin Rudd is holding court in the room. With him are Anthony Albanese, Chris Bowen and Bruce Hawker. At this point, Anthony is deputy PM, Chris is treasurer and Bruce Hawker is Kevin's principal advisor. They are huddled around the fireplace. I suppose that this is why they aren't taking my calls.

Everyone else is also wearing jeans. This calms me down a little.

'Do you want a drink?' Kevin asks.

I decide that this is a good idea.

It is Kevin the charmer, which is disarming.

'How are you? How is Hannah? Thank you so much for coming out tonight.' This is Kevin at his best. He tells me how he flew into the country a few hours ago, and that he hasn't slept—thanks to time zones and international flying. He tells me about the troops he met, about why he wanted to visit them before he called the election. He's giving me information he doesn't need to give. I'm in the room with sweet, charming Kevin.

Then he turns to the issue at hand. It is impossible not to notice the silence of the other three around the fireplace. I can sense the tension. Has there been a fight? I'm trying to work out from facial expressions and body language who is tense with whom. Good politicians make great poker players. I can't tell where the tension is coming from, just that it is there. What has happened? No one is giving anything away. This is Kevin's meeting, and it is clear that he will be calling the shots.

'I won't be calling the election tomorrow,' he tells me. 'We are not ready yet. I'm not happy with the campaign preparation and I want to be sure we are ready before we call it.' In private, I will disagree later. But I'm far too timid to disagree with Kevin to his face right now. I'm waiting for him to tell me that he's not supporting my Senate bid. I'm gearing up for a fight.

'I need you to fly down to Melbourne on the 6 a.m. flight tomorrow. I want you to go to campaign headquarters and I want you to do a full review of our campaign readiness. I want a completely independent analysis.'

'Of course.' I respond to this slightly crazy suggestion as though it is the most mundane of requests.

'Seat by seat,' he adds. 'I want to call the election next weekend. I intend to call it for the 7th of September. But I will only do it once I am satisfied that we are ready.' Seventh of September, remembering when the baby is due—late September, I think.

Kevin the wonk. The reality is that we are as ready as we will ever be. The campaign isn't about to change now. I will go down to Melbourne. I won't sleep for the next three nights; I'll be preparing binders of material. Seat-by-seat plans, outlining issues, funding and the like. I won't really change anything that was already happening, but I will process it and put it in the reports that Kevin likes. I'll give him the volume of material he needs.

He reads it all—because Kevin does that. He reads everything. He asks me questions and, that weekend, he calls the election.

'Oh and Sam,' he adds before I leave, 'I need you to move permanently to Melbourne. For the next few months. I need you in campaign headquarters. The boys here have convinced me not to clean out party headquarters, and I have agreed, but I want one of our people down there. Someone I trust.'

This is Kevin the ruler. I was one of 'his' people. As far as he was concerned, the others in campaign headquarters weren't. That was an unfair way to see the world, but there was plenty of tension at campaign headquarters—a by-product of the switchback from Julia to Kevin, and the scars from that left him trusting very few people.

The charmer, the wonk and the ruler. All in a few minutes.

I leave the house and take the forty-two steps back to the security gate, forgetting to count them this time, revelling in the relief that he's not trying to stop me going to the Senate at all. I'm not looking forward to breaking the news to Helen that I'm moving to Melbourne until the baby is born, but Helen understands that you don't say 'no' to any of the Kevins.

28

KAILA: THE ONE TO WATCH

There is something very eerie about the Sydney Town Hall when it is empty. Put a thousand people in it and the acoustics, and the energy, will bounce off its walls. But when it is empty it feels like a cathedral. The stage up front with a giant organ in the background, the lights, the wood panels, the red seats circling from above: these are signatures of *gravitas*. The Sydney Town Hall was built to be impressive, to exude power. And it does. When empty, every creak in the old building can be heard. There is an echo that flows from the outer waiting area into the hall. Before I can see her shadow, I hear the distinct small footsteps of Kaila Murnain entering the space. It is the sound of someone in a rush.

'So where the fuck is everyone?' I ask Kaila in an empty Town Hall at 8:00 p.m. on 12 February 2016. She looks tired. This throws me, because I rarely see her tired. Kaila is not the type of person to get exhausted. I've seen her work for forty-eight hours straight without a break. I've seen her spend the final weeks of a campaign working non-stop, feeding off nervous energy.

'I sent everyone home,' she finally tells me. The Sydney Town Hall has been set up for the NSW Labor Party Conference the next day. Four weeks earlier, Kaila Murnain took over as the General Secretary of the NSW Labor Party, a position that I once held. If this were the mafia, which it far too often feels like it is, tomorrow Kaila would be elected to the position of boss of the family.

'You sent them home?' I boggle. 'I would never have sent them home.'

'I know. We all hated that about you. You never let anyone leave. It was crazy. You had everyone running around in circles.'

There will be 880 people on the floor of the conference tomorrow. There will be cameras, journalists and a who's who of Australian Labor politics. But most importantly, there will be all the conference delegates from every branch and trade union that is affiliated with the Labor Party. This is their conference. I will know the names of all 880 people here tomorrow from a lifetime of working in the machine. Kaila will not only know their names; she will know the names of their children. She will know when their birthdays are and how they like their coffee. This is why she is the best at it. And she needs to be. There had never been a female General Secretary of the NSW Labor Party. This weekend will be the first time one will be elected. While the problems with female representation in public office are visible, in machine politics it is far worse and often swept under the carpet.

For Kaila to become party secretary she had to overcome more obstacles than any of her predecessors. Kaila is young (twenty-eight years of age), female and from rural New South Wales. None of these traits sit easily within an old and insular Labor Party machine. The internals of the Labor Party are governed more by its culture than by its rules. The rules exist, there are books of them, but to understand why young women have been held back for so long, you have to look at its culture. While there is no rule or cultural norm that is overtly sexist, when compounded with one another they have worked against any woman making it to the top. Take, for example, just the simple use of language. The words that are used to describe a successful general secretary bespeak very masculine qualities; a good General Secretary of the Labor Party is 'tough' and 'strong', and 'has balls'. It took nine years working in the party machine for Kaila to overcome these obstacles. This is a remarkably short time, considering that the party had never had a female assistant secretary, the 'number 2' spot, let alone a woman in the top job.

The first thing you notice about Kaila Murnain is that she is short. The second is that she is smiling. She is always smiling. It's a trait that can put people at ease and that, on far too many occasions, has resulted in her being underestimated. It also makes being angry at her very hard. 'Everyone does what she wants,' Prue Car, our mutual friend, reminds me. 'Not because they fear her, but because they love her.' The delegates love her. It's an affection that means that Kaila doesn't have to respond to problems by using the blunt force of 'crunching the numbers', a term used to describe the tactic of forcing an outcome by voting to crush opposition. For years, Kaila had been the fixer in the NSW Labor Party office, the person who was sent in to clean up the messes (on far too many occasions, mine). She ran the hardest campaigns, worked on the toughest jobs. Kaila was sent to do that not only because she got the outcomes, but because she had an innate ability to make those involved convinced that she was doing them a favour. She had to prove herself more than anyone else did. She had to have answers to questions, well meaning at times, as to why she didn't go off and have kids first—the intimation being that politics could wait.

There is a quote from Machiavelli that is never understood. He said that 'it is safer to be feared than loved', meaning by this that it is best to be both. Love is a powerful emotion. It drives people to irrational behaviour. If your supporters love you, they will walk to the ends of the world for you. As Graham Richardson used to say, 'Any fool can win a vote when they are right. Find me someone who can win a vote when they are wrong'. I remind him of all the wrong calls that I made. 'You're just lucky,' he smirks.

'Are you OK?' I ask Kaila, still taken aback by how tired she looks. She tells me that she is fine, which turns out to be true.

By morning, she will have slept and be back to her old self. But tonight she is tired, and showing a vulnerability that is normally very well concealed.

Tomorrow, Kaila will deliver the speech that we are here to rehearse. It will garner a standing ovation. The old women will tell her that they have been coming to conferences for over forty years and never thought that they would see a female party boss. The men will nod along, all telling stories about the time she visited their house as a young party official.

'I remember the first time I came here,' she reminisces. Kaila was a delegate to the conference from the rural New South Wales town of Narrabri when she was fifteen years old.

'I remember too. They made me watch how you voted.'

'Yeah, I realised that later. At the time, I thought it was strange how you kept hanging around, suggesting we go down and vote in the ballot together. Now I get it.' The Kaila from then and the present-day Kaila are two very different people. The Labor Party machine toughens people up. It makes you lose your innocence very quickly. It strikes me that she has now known me for almost longer than she hasn't.

'Are you sure it was thirteen years ago?' I ask.

'Yep. I was in school. That was when I knew I wanted to come to Sydney.'

A breeze runs through the hall, ruffling papers and highlighting just how empty the room is. 'Tom is on his way,' Kaila says. Tom Hollywood is her fiancé. Kaila is the only person who calls him 'Tom'. To everyone else, he is just 'Hollywood'. I tell her that I will wait with her.

Kaila practises her speech again. She doesn't need to. She knows it by heart by now. I know that there is no point telling her to stop. That's not how she works. She will keep practising it until she can't, until exhaustion catches her. It has to be perfect. It always has to be perfect.

Kaila doesn't know yet that in six months the NSW Branch of the Labor Party will have its best result in a generation, outperforming the rest of the country and delivering the lion's share of seat wins for Bill Shorten. This result will put Bill within an inch of the lodge, and Kaila will have delivered on the pledge in her speech we are rehearsing that she will bring a band of women into Federal Parliament. She doesn't know any of this—all she knows is that tomorrow is a big day and that tonight she is scared. There is only one thing that she can still control, and that is her speech, so she will focus on that. She practises it again.

'Kristina didn't want me to take the job at the NSW Labor Party nine years ago,' she reminds me after stopping for a drink. It's a moment of nostalgia that is so uncharacteristic, and I put it down either to nerves or to exhaustion. Kristina Keneally, then, was not yet premier and had strongly advised Kaila against making the move from being a government staffer to joining the NSW Labor Party machine.

'What was her reasoning?' I ask, recalling that it was contentious at the time but still unsure of the specifics.

'She thought I'd get used and spat out. That the place was a boys' club that would lock a young woman out. She was looking out for me.'

Kristina was right to a point. It was a boys' club. It did have a history of chewing up and spitting out young women. But perhaps she also underestimated Kaila's ability to overcome, and change, that encrusted culture.

The hall looks immaculate for the conference tomorrow. The seats have been put out, row after row. The stage is set. Lighting, sound, music—all ready to go. We anticipate the theatre of a conference that increasingly resembles a convention. Luke Foley, the Labor Party state leader, and Bill Shorten have both already been through and rehearsed their speeches.

Kaila will comfortably win the ballot that weekend. We both know this already. A month prior I could've told you the outcome of the vote down to a person. By the time that delegates have been selected, the ballot is sorted. That is the part that makes the difference. The cups of tea at houses, the time spent with delegates before the conference. The vote itself comes at the end of all that.

She will spend the day talking with the branch members from across New South Wales who trek to Sydney, year in and year out, to be part of the conference. And she'll remind them of the time that 'this' or 'that' happened, bringing smiles to faces. With as many of the 880 delegates as she possibly can, she will share moments, recall bygone times, look ahead, catch up.

Kaila knows that you have to be yourself. The delegates can smell a phoney a mile away. Her background wasn't the unions, or the university clubs or even Young Labor, though she did all of that at different times. She knows that Pat and Shorty Reville would have spent a whole day on a train to get here from Broken Hill, and that Shorty was the lead unionist from there back when Broken Hill was a union town. She knows the story of when he was nearly shot in a trade-union fight. She knows that Ary and Margie Vanzanten have come from Balranald, that they are friends with Fred and Glenys McInterney from the Hunter region, and that these delegates have been coming for over forty years to Labor Party conferences. For forty years, as Kaila well knows, they have been selecting Senators, party officials and members of Federal Parliament, and they love the Labor Party, warts and all.

Machine politics is a hard slog. Your life is consumed by the hours in car trips travelling across the state, the endless meetings, the stress that comes with constantly having to fix everyone else's problems, the years of labouring—innumerable acts of unseen sacrifice. It becomes hard to maintain friends and contacts outside a world that it so insular. To do well at the machine game, you have to love the nuts and bolts.

'Tomorrow will be a big day,' Kaila states after a pause in her speech. She is so unsure of her statement that it almost sounds like a question. But the statement isn't what she is really saying. Really, she is saying, 'There has never been a woman running the party before and I'm worried about how they will take it'.

I don't tell her that I worry the older men will struggle to accept this development. They might not mean to be sexist—they love her—but taking direction from a woman will be hard for them. I don't tell her that she will be held to a higher standard than I was or any other of her predecessors were, and that when she yells she will be called 'hysterical' rather than 'strong' (this adjective is reserved for blokes). Nor do I tell her that if she slips, some will use that as proof that it was never quite right for a woman to undertake this role. I keep it under my hat that her enemies will start rumours that she is planning to get pregnant and that such an occurrence will put the party into a bind, as if being a mother and running a political party are mutually exclusive. And I don't say to her that she will need to keep winning elections, whereas the men didn't. I don't tell her any of these things because she doesn't need to hear such stuff from me. She knows. This has been her life.

So I lie. I tell that they will treat her 'the same' as they did all the men who came before her. And we sit in an empty hall. In silence.

29

BILL SHORTEN: THE ONE WHO WILL BE KING

Everyone was tired. Everyone except Bill Shorten. 'How is he still going? He's like the fucking Energiser bunny.' Bill's press secretary, Ryan Liddell, himself past the point of exhaustion, responds: 'It's because he actually enjoys all of this'.

I knew that this was true, but for some reason the answer depressed me, probably because it highlighted my own inadequacy as a campaigner. Bill had a decade on me and the world on his shoulders, and here I was hardly able to stay awake on the bus.

This was the afternoon of the 2016 federal election, the fifty-sixth day of the longest campaign in recent history. And it was four hours until the close of polling.

We are arriving at our fourth location for the day. It's a school in Western Sydney in the marginal seat of Lindsay and en route to Richmond Army Base, where Bill will be boarding a plane to Melbourne. I just had to get Bill on that plane; then my role in the campaign would be over. By this stage, after having spent seven weeks travelling the country on a giant bus emblazoned with Bill Shorten's face, I am done.

By now, the whole campaign is running on fumes and instinct. I know before the bus pulls up exactly what will happen. I know

273

because it is the same thing that always happens. Bill's media team will soon call the 'advance' team. They are the people who go everywhere before a leader to make sure that it is all ready for the leader's arrival. The cameras will be in place. The bus will pull up. Bill will jump out of the bus to be greeted by the local candidate. They will kiss if she is female. They will high five if he is male.

The candidate will lead Bill to whatever the event is. Today, it will be a voting booth. Bill will shake the hands of those who are handing out Labor how-to-vote cards. He will ask them what their names are. Bill won't go into the booth because that is against the rules, but he will greet those who are lining up for a sausage or to vote. They will take their photo with him. Someone will demand that Bill eat a sausage. He will insist on paying. They won't take his money. It will get awkward. Bill will profess that he can't possibly eat another sausage. He will eat it. Social media will mock the way he eats it. Even though he enjoyed it, later he will tell us it was eaten under duress. We will roll our eyes. Apparently, the calories don't count if you were talked into it. The cameras will be rolling. The media team will try to do everything to get Bill back on the bus, back on schedule. Bill will resist. They will eventually get him back to the bus. Bill will leave, saying thank you again to the volunteers handing out how-to-vote cards. He will remember their names. The bus will leave and we will do all of this again when we reach the next location.

What makes today different, of course, is that it is the last day that we will be doing this.

'It just doesn't make sense. What do they know that we don't?' I ask Ryan. He is as perplexed as I am. The final batch of Labor polling has come through and it tells us that the election result will be on a knife-edge. Yet my phone has been running hot with journalists wanting to get the story of what happens next. 'What do you mean next?' I ask.

'After the election, when you guys lose. You do know you are going to lose. And lose decisively? What happens then?'

My father-in-law has been travelling with Bill for most of the past eight weeks. As a campaign veteran, he has seen it all. 'There is nothing more useless than a leader on election day. They mistake movement for action. The die is cast.' And so it was.

In the film *Primary Colours,* staffers try to show their hard-bitten professionalism by talking about what they'll do 'after it's all over'. But there's none of that on the bus, at the booths or at HQ. No one is thinking about tomorrow.

'Have you written drafts for the two speeches?' I ask Bill's speechwriter James Newton. James is not your speechwriter from central casting. He looks more like an AFL player than a book worm. He is tall, sporty and has an infectious laugh. Everyone likes him, which is rare in a political office. Throughout the campaign, he would have written a couple of hundred thousand words at a pace that is frightening for the rest of us. By 'two speeches' I meant both a victory and a concession speech for Bill to deliver that night. 'This isn't West Wing, Sam, we just write one speech once we know the result,' he responds, deadpan.

On the ground, it didn't feel like we were going to lose, and certainly not decisively. The mood felt good, really good. Nothing about the feeling at polling booths that day made the government's recent behaviour intelligible. For the past week, the government had all but stopped campaigning. 'They finish at one o'clock in the afternoon and just go back to their hotel rooms,' the journalists who were travelling with the prime minister would tell us. The government was running the low-risk strategy that works when you already have it in the bag. The media was telling us that we just couldn't possibly win.

But the published polls, and our private polls, were painting a different picture—that of a close election. And this concurred with the sense on the ground.

So we kept asking ourselves the same question: 'What do they know that we don't?' James framed it best on that final day. 'Either they are in a bubble or we are. We will know the answer in a few hours.'

Of course, at this stage we didn't yet know that the journos were the ones who were wrong, that Bill would come closer to winning than any first-term Labor leader since the 1950s. The prime minister, it turned out, was not able to front the cameras until the early hours of the next morning, and when he did make his address, it took the form of a tantrum and not a victory speech. Bill will have proven all of his doubters wrong. As yet, we don't know any of this. All we know is that the campaign has been long, and we are tired.

By now, Bill is back on the bus and, pumping with energy, he resumes the conversation that we were having before the event. He asks again which seats we all thought we were going to win, where the opportunities were, and what more could be done between now and 6:00 p.m.

He isn't nervous. He isn't stressed. In fact, he is more at ease than I have ever known him to be in the past fifteen years. It is making me edgy watching how calm he is. I want to snatch his mobile phone back from my 2-year-old daughter so that Bill can reply to the messages and return the phone calls coming in, but he happily waits for her to finish watching YouTube. How can he seem so composed when tomorrow morning he will either be our next prime minister or answering questions on whether he still has a future as opposition leader?

There is a calm to Bill now, a calm that hasn't always come naturally to him. It hides the years of hard work, dedication, fight and focus that have carried him to this point. Looking at Bill now, the untrained observer might think that Bill Shorten's path has been easy.

'Oh and they made me eat another sausage. Fat lot of good the run this morning did me. But what was I meant to do? Reject it in front of all those volunteers?' Bill pleads with a smile to his travelling team on the bus. Everyone rolls their eyes as we move on to the next location. And there, we do it all again.

Bill is constantly underestimated. When he became the secretary of a bordering-on-dysfunctional Victorian Branch of the Australian Worker's Union in the mid-1990s, it was meant to be the end of him. When, later, he became the national secretary, that was supposed to be only a temporary measure. Yet he was able to turn the union around. Bill was never meant to win a federal preselection, but he won it unopposed. His first portfolio as Parliamentary Secretary for Disabilities and Children's Services was predicted to be a place in which the Federal Caucus would bury him, but then he turned around and created the National Disability Insurance Scheme (NDIS).

Not many thought that he was going to win the ballot for the party leadership. All of this, of course, was before a royal commission that was meant to mark the end of him. And then there was the rise of the once-popular Malcolm Turnbull. Bill Shorten's imminent certain political death has been often remarked upon.

At every point, Bill has pulled through. Whenever I'm asked why or how, I tell them about the first time I met Bill.

I first crossed paths with Bill Shorten in a most unexpected way. I opened a handwritten letter sent to a return address that I had provided in the hope of soliciting donations for the Sydney University ALP Club. My first reaction was to wonder who on earth handwrites letters? This was 2001, and while it was perhaps before the rise of Facebook and Twitter, the handwritten letter was surely a thing of the past. My second reaction was more peevish. How come there isn't a cheque in the envelope? What a cheap bastard.

I probably should have bothered to read the letter first. Bill Shorten was, at this stage, the National Secretary of the Australian Workers Union, and I was an 18-year-old university student. In the power structures of the Australian Labor Party, Bill was a man with considerable influence and I was a complete nobody.

This made the letter particularly odd. It read:

Sam, thanks for the letter. I can't give you a donation from the Union but happy to kick in $250 of my own money. Swing past for a coffee when you are next in Melbourne to pick up a cheque.

Cheers
Bill Shorten

At the bottom of the letter was a phone number for his assistant. I had written to every national secretary of every trade union for a donation, and Bill was the only one to respond.

So I went to Melbourne. I had a coffee with him that was scheduled for fifteen minutes but went for an hour, and walked away having less of an understanding of Bill than I had beforehand.

We kept in touch. Sometimes when he was coming to Sydney I would get a call and pick him up from the airport, and we would go for a coffee or lunch.

Why, I wondered, was Bill being so nice to me? There was no way Bill knew who I was before I sent him that letter. I wasn't anybody to know. I hadn't done anything.

I didn't know back then that this was just what Bill did. He met people. Not for any direct purpose. He just realised that the type of person brash enough to write letters to national union secretaries seeking donations was someone who might be interesting—someone to know.

Back on the bus, someone (OK, it was me) fires up the karaoke machine. It's hard to land on a song that doesn't feel like it's tempting fate, one way or another. We skip 'We are the Champions' and settle on 'Bohemian Rhapsody'. Chloe Shorten and Rupert (who is thirteen and can actually sing) get everyone else involved, and the quality of performance suffers.

At the airport, we line up for a group photo in front of the bus. Bill and I share a big hug and I get teary. I blame the exhaustion, the grinding travel itinerary. I repeat my promise to drive the bus to the governor-general's house if we win. Everyone cheers again. That's how tired we are.

Bill bounds up the steps and into the plane. The polls will close soon; he still hasn't voted and he's not slowing down.

This is the Bill that people rarely see, or credit. But I'm astonished by his sheer dogged determination to work, by the unrelenting force of personality that keeps propelling him forward, regardless of the obstacle ahead. He takes no notice of the long queue of people telling him to bide his time.

This is how Bill has succeeded—by pushing through when others with thinner skin would have folded. Maybe that's part of the reason why Bill is so good with people. He knows that things have never really come easy for him, so he can empathise with others who battle through life.

We barrack for the underdog. Not because we like to see the tall poppy get cut down, but because we *identify* with the underdog.

For a lot of Australians, life is hard work. It's a slog. There are plenty of people out there who've been written off and under-estimated and told not to bother. Maybe Bill gets where they're coming from a lot better than someone who's always been the favourite.

When the votes were counted on 2 July and in the week that followed, it became clear that the Liberals, not us, were missing a piece of information. We knew Bill Shorten and they didn't.

Malcolm Turnbull made a big mistake in having an eight-week election campaign. As the campaign progressed, people got to know Bill and they started to like him. The Liberals didn't realise that. They treated him like a static figure. That is not Bill. Bill keeps moving. From the campaign bus I could see the change. People started to be friendlier. They started to see that Bill enjoyed the campaign. They got to know Bill Shorten. And they liked what they saw.

When the Liberals were going around telling people that Turnbull would win 'with the wind in his hair' and wrapping up their days with yum cha for lunch, they were making the same mistake that so many people had made about Bill in the past. They underestimated his abilities as a campaigner and they massively underestimated the issues on which he'd chosen to fight the election.

This was written all over Turnbull's face on election night. He wasn't just furious, he was mystified. He couldn't comprehend how it had come to this.

At 1:35 the next morning, I got a text message from Bill. 'Are you awake?' I was. I had just wrapped up five hours of television coverage with Channel 7 at 1:00 a.m. and then had gone for a drink. I was drunk—more from the exhaustion than from the two drinks that I'd just had with Jacqui Lambie, who was doing the television coverage with me.

'Do you think we can form government?' I didn't and I told him so. Not because I had any real insight. At these moments, we all share the same information. There were no new facts; there hadn't been for a few hours.

At 7:00 am I was ordering a greasy breakfast burger while Bill went for a run. He was getting ready for the next campaign. I was nursing a hangover.

'What advice would you give someone wanting to be involved in politics?', the 20-year-old barista asks.

'Turn up. Fight for the issues you are passionate about. Find mentors. Treat people right and make a few friends.'

What I should have added was 'Keep copious notes'. Who knows? He might write a book about it one day.

INDEX

Abbass (father's friend)   10
'Agro' (puppet)   58
Ahmad (grandfather)
   life in Iran   32–3, 35–8
   moves to Australia   39
   saves children from
     enlistment   40–1
Albanese, Anthony   118, 259, 263
Aly, Anne   108–9
Angell, Richard   6
Arendt, Hannah   17
Arthur, Sharnelle   127, 232
Attenborough, David   87
Audrey (Broken Hill
   resident)   205–6
Azadeh (Layla's daughter)   70

Badham, Van   140–1
Bagnall, Andy   6
Barron, Peter
   friends with Graham
     Richardson   251
   on Shorten campaign   274–5

Sam mentored by   121–2
   wedding speech   63–4
Bennett, Chloe   103
Berati, Reza   29–31
Berlia, Aditya   100–1
Bernard (victim of financial
   crime)   176–8, 180–3
Bhatt, Arvind   109
Biggar, Ann-Maree   58
Bolton, Brendan
   interviews whistleblower   184,
     186–7, 195
   on Pauline Hanson   171–2
Bowen, Chris
   at Rudd meeting   258, 263
   on negative gearing   167,
     219–20
Burke, Tony   232
Bush, George W.   106
Butler, Sue   3–6

Car, Prue   87–9, 104, 268
Carr, Bob   118, 252–3

Cavanagh, Brendan 112
Chalmers, Jim and Laura 96–7, 232
Chisholm, Anthony 232
Claassens, Alex 199
Clements, Jamie 117
Crews, Bill 241–8
Crosby, Sam 103–4, 139, 192
Cubbin, David 103

Dastyari, Azadeh (sister)
  arrested with mother in Iran 15–17
  becomes lawyer 23–4
  command of English 48
  conception of 75–6
  learns from TV shows 58–60
  on family's arrival in Australia 19
  on next generation 49–50
  on 'survivor's guilt' 12
Dastyari, Ella (mother)
  arrested in Iran 9, 16–18
  aspirations for her children 23–4
  departure from Iran 28
  fortune telling by 53–6
  memories of Iran 12–13
  move to South Penrith 56
  overseas travel by 62–3
  runs small business 50
  stories of her best friend 66–73
  stories of her father 32–3, 36–8, 41
Dastyari, Eloise (daughter)
  at Hannah's school nativity play 145, 148

holds garage sale 235
pets bought for 77
Santa photos 150, 153
Dastyari, Hannah (daughter)
  holds garage sale 231, 235
  Persian heritage 63
  pets bought for 77
  Santa photos 150, 153
  school nativity play 144–5, 148–50
Dastyari, Helen (wife)
  daughters' Santa photos 150–1
  friends with Graham Richardson 251
  honeymoon with 113
  meets mortgage broker 217–18
  on hate mail 135–43
  on Kevin Rudd 260–1
  on naming children 74
  pets acquired by 77–82
  Sam attends weddings with 99–100
  wedding to Sam 101–3, 245
Dastyari, Kamal (uncle) 42–3
Dastyari, Naser (father)
  as taxi driver 57
  aspirations for his children 23–4
  birth of 43
  buys first car 85–7
  leaves Iran 28
  memories of Iran 9–14, 18
  move to South Penrith 56
  overseas travel by 62–3
  pets named by 80
  runs small business 50

Dastyari, Sam
  arrives in Australia   20–2
  as NSW Labor General
    Secretary   112–13
  at daughter's school nativity
    play   144–50
  at Parkes Elvis festival   126–34
  changes name from
    Sahand   75–7
  education of   60–3
  experiences at weddings
    94–104
  experiences with cars   87–93
  hate mail to   135
  in Forbes   130
  in rented
    accommodation   213–15,
    218–19
  learns from TV shows   57–60
  leaves Sydney University Law
    School   62–3
  marries Helen Barron   101–3,
    245
  meets with Rudd   258–65
  memories of Iran   27–9
  on Aboriginal incarceration
    209–10, 226–7
  on banking   188–93
  on disempowerment   196–203
  on financial crime   176–83
  on focus groups   163–5
  on illicit drug use   221–7
  on One Nation   170–5
  on politics   159–67, 234–6
  on staying focused   123–5
  on whistleblowers   184–8, 190,
    195

  parents' experiences in Iran
    9–19
  pets acquired by   77–82
  religious views   246–7
  resigns over expenses claim
    232–3
  runs for Senate   167–8
  teenage picnic party   225–6
  US travel   105–8, 110–11
  visits Broken Hill   204–7,
    210–12
  visits refugee camp   24–7
Dastyari, Solomeh   136
Dunn, Jamie   58
Dutton, Peter   25, 27

Faramarz (father's friend)   10–11
Fifield, Mitch   171
Fitzgibbon, Joel   232
Foley, Luke   270
Fugaccia, Tony   61–2

Gaiman, Neil   25
Gillard, Julia   261–2
Grigorovitch, Luba   199

Hanson, Pauline
  attitude to Muslims   246
  rural support for   126–7
  Sam invites to share halal snack
    pack   5
  threat from   169–75
Hassan (father's friend)   10–16
Hawke, Bob   159, 167–8
Hawker, Bruce   263
Hayes, Gerard   199–200
Hobbes, Thomas   146

Hollywood, Tom   269
Holt, Peter   176, 178–82
Howard, John   38, 261
Hull, Eliza   206–7
Humphries, Rachel   206–7

Iran, Shah of   21

Jack (merchant sailor)   202
Jackson, Rose   103–4, 209
Jason (power station
     employee)   196

Keating, Paul   122, 137, 252
Keith, Ken   128
Kelly, Graeme   199–200
Keneally, Kristina   112–16, 118,
     270
Khomeini, Ayatollah   21, 69
Kleinschmidt, Kilian   24–7

Lambie, Jacqui   280
Layla (mother's friend)   66–73
Liddell, Ryan   273–4

Machiavelli, Niccolo   268
Macpherson, Col   153–4
Madigan, Dee   141–2
Makepeace, Troy   197
Mannering, Lucy   145–8
Mannering, Sybilla   145–6
Márquez, Gabriel García   43
McInterney, Fred and Glenys   271
McIntosh, Josh   213–15
Milligan, Jo   6
Milne, Alice   126, 131
Minns, Chris   117–18

Minou (grandmother)   35, 43–6,
     246
Mishy (dog)   80–1
Mookhey, Nitin 'Daniel'   94–6
Morey, Mark   199–200
Moriarty, Tara   199–200
Morris, Jeff   190–2
Murnain, Kaila   266–72

Naneh (great-grandmother) 34–5
Nanva, Bob
     at ALP conference   199
     buys house   215–19
     teaches Sam to drive   89–90
     wedding of   97–9
Nanva, Sally   97–9
Newton, James   275
Nguyen, Don   191

Obama, Barack   76
O'Neill, Peter   30

Pat (mother-in-law)   151
Peter (power station employee)
     196–7
Pissy (cat)   81–2
Putin, Vladimir   171–2

Rayner, Jen   121
Reagan, Ronald   108
Reville, Pat and Shorty   271
Richardson, Graham   249–56,
     268
Robertson, John   118
Rudd, Kevin   29–30, 112–13,
     257–65
Ruddock, Philip   38

Sahin, Oktay   3
Samira (cousin)   225
Secord, Walt   112
Shah of Iran   21
Sheldon, Tony   201
Shorten, Bill
   ALP seats gained under   270
   at ALP conference   199
   consults Peter Barron   122
   election campaign   247–8,
      273–80
   on negative gearing   166–7
Shorten, Chloe and Rupert   278
Silber, Mitchell   109
Sinclair, Cameron   25–7
Steel, Anne   132
Steve (neighbour)   228–32, 235–7

Tamsin (friend)   94
Theo (neighbour)   80
Thistlethwaite, Matt   113
Triggs, Gillian   62–3
Trump, Donald   171, 201
Tucker, Ron   193–4
Turnbull, Malcolm   166, 188,
   279

Vanzanten, Ary and Margie   271

Watts, Tim   232
Wednesday (dog)   217–18
Weinstein, Harvey   25
Whitlam, Gough   162, 166